Exploring Snowdonia Anglesey and Lleyn Peninsula

Compiled by Peter, Helen & J... Marsh

Snowdon from Capel Curig

Contents

General Key Map (inside front cover)
North Snowdonia Key Map............................ 2
North Snowdonia Tours 3
South Snowdonia Key Map 34
South Snowdonia Tours 35
Anglesey Key Map 66
Anglesey Tours 67
Lleyn Peninsula Key Map 98
Lleyn Peninsula Tours............................. 99
Other Places of Special Interest..................... 130
Tourist Information Centres....................... 139
A Few Welsh Place Names 140
Advice on Mountain Safety........................ 140
Index.. 141

NORTH SNOWDONIA KEY MAP

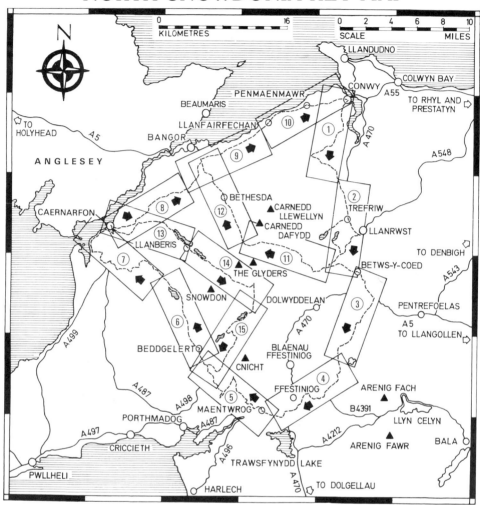

On the Ffestiniog Railway

EXPLORING NORTH SNOWDONIA

The Llanberis Pass

The main route covered by this section of the guide encircles most of the classic Snowdonia mountain country. Starting at Conwy with its fine castle and massive town walls, it heads southwards to Llanrwst and Betws-y-Coed before crossing bare upland country to Ffestiniog and Maentwrog. It now heads north-westwards beneath the western flanks of Snowdon itself to castle-dominated Caernarfon before returning north-eastwards to Conwy. Cross-routes head into the mountain heartlands of Snowdonia and there are splendid views to be had on every side. Colwyn Bay and Llandudno do not lie on our route through North Snowdonia but they are too important to leave out and are described on pages 132 and 135 respectively.
One small piece of advice before you set out on your journey — there are so many wonderful things to be seen — great mountains, deep valleys, shining lakes and rushing streams, open moorland and shady forest — that the eyes can easily become sated. So drive slowly, stop often, and give yourself time to absorb the spirit of this wild and romantic landscape.

Map 1 — Directions

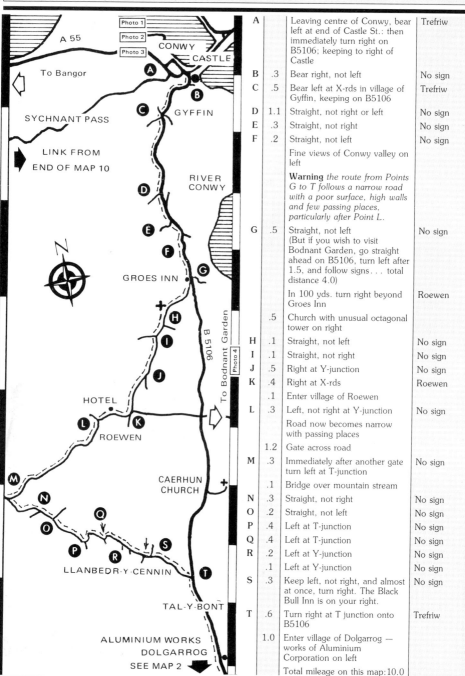

	kms Ref. Miles	Directions	Sign-posted
A		Leaving centre of Conwy, bear left at end of Castle St.; then immediately turn right on B5106; keeping to right of Castle	Trefriw
B	.3	Bear right, not left	No sign
C	.5	Bear left at X-rds in village of Gyffin, keeping on B5106	Trefriw
D	1.1	Straight, not right or left	No sign
E	.3	Straight, not right	No sign
F	.2	Straight, not left	No sign
		Fine views of Conwy valley on left	
		Warning the route from Points G to T follows a narrow road with a poor surface, high walls and few passing places, particularly after Point L.	
G	.5	Straight, not left (But if you wish to visit Bodnant Garden, go straight ahead on B5106, turn left after 1.5, and follow signs... total distance 4.0)	No sign
		In 100 yds. turn right beyond Groes Inn	Roewen
	.5	Church with unusual octagonal tower on right	
H	.1	Straight, not left	No sign
I	.1	Straight, not right	No sign
J	.5	Right at Y-junction	No sign
K	.4	Right at X-rds	Roewen
	.1	Enter village of Roewen	
L	.3	Left, not right at Y-junction	No sign
		Road now becomes narrow with passing places	
	1.2	Gate across road	
M	.3	Immediately after another gate turn left at T-junction	No sign
	.1	Bridge over mountain stream	
N	.3	Straight, not right	No sign
O	.2	Straight, not left	No sign
P	.4	Left at T-junction	No sign
Q	.4	Left at T-junction	No sign
R	.2	Left at Y-junction	No sign
	.1	Left at Y-junction	No sign
S	.3	Keep left, not right, and almost at once, turn right. The Black Bull Inn is on your right.	No sign
T	.6	Turn right at T junction onto B5106	Trefriw
	1.0	Enter village of Dolgarrog — works of Aluminium Corporation on left	
		Total mileage on this map: 10.0	

CROWN COPYRIGHT RESERVED

On Route

1. Telford's Suspension Bridge and Conwy Castle

Conwy

Despite traffic congestion, Conwy remains an attractive small town, given a medieval air by the dominating Castle and contemporary town walls. If you can, approach it first from the east, and as you cross the river by the modern road bridge, on your left stands Telford's famous suspension bridge, built in 1822 and now preserved by the National Trust, and beyond that, the tubular railway bridge built by Stephenson in 1846. At the time of writing a tunnel is being constructed to carry the A55 beneath the Conwy estuary, which will remove much traffic from the town.

Next, the Castle (CADW) — ☎ (0492) 592358, started by Edward I in 1283, as were Caernarfon and Harlech, and finished in 1289. The town itself is joined to the Castle by Edward's fortified town walls, which still almost encircle the town centre and which are more than a mile in length. The five gates, three original and two of later date, are still in use, and you can walk along much of the wall-top and enjoy fine views of Castle, town and river. Below the walls, with car access only through the Lower, or Water Gate (at the foot of High Street), is the River Quay, still used by fishing boats. On the Quay, and built against the town wall is what is claimed to be the 'smallest house in Great Britain'.

For 100 years before Edward built Conwy, the site was occupied by the Cistercian Abbey of Aberconwy; he moved the Abbey further up the river valley to
Continued on Page 23

2. Plas Mawr, Conwy

3. The 'Smallest House' in Britain, Conwy

Bodnant Garden (NT)

This is one of Britain's outstanding gardens and within its 80 acres there is a series of terraces looking across the Conwy Valley to the mountains of Snowdonia. There are fine collections of camellias, azaleas, rhododendrons and magnolias, and buildings within the garden include the delightful Pin Mill which is sited at the end of a formal canal. Teas and light refreshments — ☎ (0492) 650460.

Roewen

An attractive village of restored greystone and whitewashed cottages, a pleasant inn, and a stream hiding behind gardens full of flowers.

Llanbedr-y-Cennin

Noted for the 16th century Olde Black Bull Inn. On the hill above the village stands a pre-Roman hillfort (Pen-y-Gaer). The charmingly simple medieval church is surrounded by ancient yews and has a fine old wooden porch.

Caerhun Church

This is another tiny medieval church on the site of the Roman fort of Canovium. To find it, turn left at Point T on B5106; in 1 mile there is a signed lane on the right leading to the church.

Dolgarrog

Apart from the Aluminium Works, this village is noted mainly for a hydro-electric generating station fed from two reservoirs, Llyn Cowlyd, and Llyn Eigiau in the hills above. In 1925 16 lives were lost when the Eigiau dam burst.

4. Bodnant Garden

Map 2

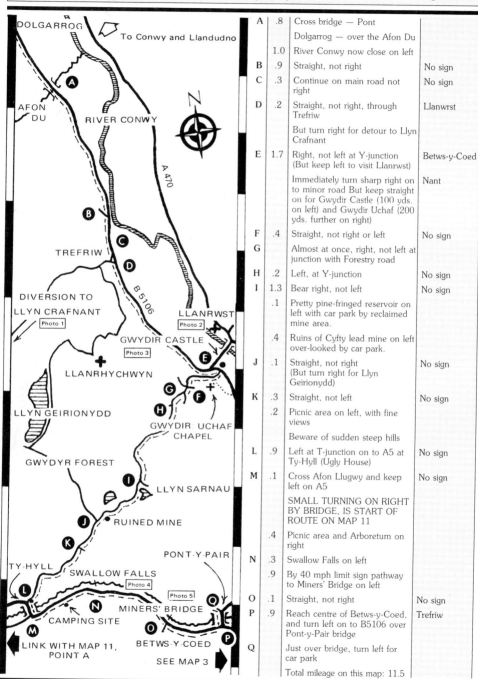

Ref	kms/Miles	Directions	Signposted
A	.8	Cross bridge — Pont Dolgarrog — over the Afon Du	
	1.0	River Conwy now close on left	
B	.9	Straight, not right	No sign
C	.3	Continue on main road not right	No sign
D	.2	Straight, not right, through Trefriw	Llanrwst
		But turn right for detour to Llyn Crafnant	
E	1.7	Right, not left at Y-junction (But keep left to visit Llanrwst)	Betws-y-Coed
		Immediately turn sharp right on to minor road But keep straight on for Gwydir Castle (100 yds. on left) and Gwydir Uchaf (200 yds. further on right)	Nant
F	.4	Straight, not right or left	No sign
G		Almost at once, right, not left at junction with Forestry road	
H	.2	Left, at Y-junction	No sign
I	1.3	Bear right, not left	No sign
	.1	Pretty pine-fringed reservoir on left with car park by reclaimed mine area.	
	.4	Ruins of Cyfty lead mine on left over-looked by car park.	
J	.1	Straight, not right (But turn right for Llyn Geirionydd)	No sign
K	.3	Straight, not left	No sign
	.2	Picnic area on left, with fine views	
		Beware of sudden steep hills	
L	.9	Left at T-junction on to A5 at Ty-Hyll (Ugly House)	No sign
M	.1	Cross Afon Llugwy and keep left on A5	No sign
		SMALL TURNING ON RIGHT BY BRIDGE, IS START OF ROUTE ON MAP 11	
	.4	Picnic area and Arboretum on right	
N	.3	Swallow Falls on left	
	.9	By 40 mph limit sign pathway to Miners' Bridge on left	
O	.1	Straight, not right	No sign
P	.9	Reach centre of Betws-y-Coed, and turn left on to B5106 over Pont-y-Pair bridge	Trefriw
Q		Just over bridge, turn left for car park	
		Total mileage on this map: 11.5	

CROWN COPYRIGHT RESERVED

On Route

Betws-y-Coed (*The Chapel in the Wood*)
This greystone village, popular for Victorian honeymoons and made famous by the artist, David Cox, stands on A5 at the-junction of two rivers, the Llugwy and the Conwy. There are three attractive bridges, Pont-y-Pair (*Bridge of the Cauldron*) over the Llugwy, Telford's cast-iron Waterloo bridge taking the A5 over the Conwy, and a suspension footbridge hidden behind the Old Church of St. Michael and All Angels (14th century). This sleeps peacefully behind the railway station, ignored by the holiday crowds.

Too easily accessible, Betws-y-Coed is often a little congested, but out-of-season is still one of the best touring, fishing and walking centres in Wales. Do not miss a visit to Y Stablau (The Stables), in the centre of the village. This is the Snowdonia National Park Information Centre — ☏ (0690) 2665/2426 and provides a general introduction to the National Park with an audio-visual theatre where slide shows can be seen during the main summer months. The R.S.P.B. have a major centre within the complex and there is also information on the Gwydir Forest, with details of six walks in the vicinity. Do not miss a visit to the 'Trains' — Railway Museum in the old goodsyard by the BR station — ☏ (0690) 2568 nor the Motor Museum— ☏ (0690) 2632 which is nearer the centre.

Dolwyddelan Castle and the Fairy Glen
You must find time to explore the Lledr valley at least as far as Dolwyddelan (*The Little Irishman's Meadow*) — the castle (CADW) with its well preserved square keep was built by the Welsh in the 12th century, and is the reputed birthplace of Llywelyn the Great (1170). Fork right from the A5 at Point E on to the A470; on left about ¾ mile from the-junction, near the meeting of the Lledr and the Conwy, is the Fairy Glen which is well worth a visit.

Conwy and Machno Falls
You can hardly miss the entrance to the Conwy Falls from the Restaurant car park on your right as you turn from the A5 on to the B4406 (Point F). For the Machno Falls turn right from the B4406 beside Penmachno Woollen Mill (Point G) (see below). Nearby is the so called 'Roman Bridge', really an old pack-horse bridge.

Penmachno Woollen Mill
Visitors may tour this mill to see the weavers at work and to view an audio-visual presentation of 'The Story of Wool', from lambing to finished cloth. There is a Mill Wool and Craft Shop — ☏ (0690) 2545.

Penmachno
A small greystone and slate quarrymen's village astride the swift flowing Afon Machno, here crossed by a rugged five-arched bridge.

Ty Mawr (NT) (Fork right at Point J)
Situated in a remote valley, this late-medieval farmhouse was the birthplace of Bishop William Morgan, who made the first complete translation of the Bible into Welsh. There is a 'Bishop Morgan Trail' starting from the car park and leading through attractive woodland — ☏ (0690) 3213.

1. The Afon Llugwy at Betws-y-Coed

2. Pont-y-Pair

3. St. Mary's Church, Betws-y-Coed

4. The Conwy Falls

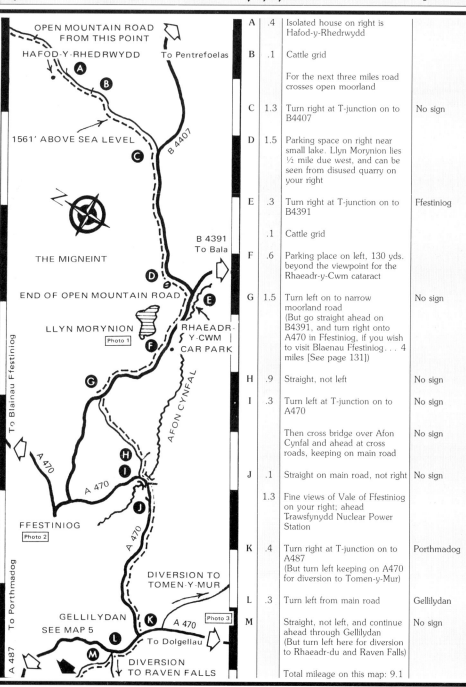

Map 4

Ref.	kms/Miles	Directions	Sign-posted
A	.4	Isolated house on right is Hafod-y-Rhedrwydd	
B	.1	Cattle grid	
		For the next three miles road crosses open moorland	
C	1.3	Turn right at T-junction on to B4407	No sign
D	1.5	Parking space on right near small lake. Llyn Morynion lies ½ mile due west, and can be seen from disused quarry on your right	
E	.3	Turn right at T-junction on to B4391	Ffestiniog
	.1	Cattle grid	
F	.6	Parking place on left, 130 yds. beyond the viewpoint for the Rhaeadr-y-Cwm cataract	
G	1.5	Turn left on to narrow moorland road (But go straight ahead on B4391, and turn right onto A470 in Ffestiniog, if you wish to visit Blaenau Ffestiniog... 4 miles [See page 131])	No sign
H	.9	Straight, not left	No sign
I	.3	Turn left at T-junction on to A470	No sign
		Then cross bridge over Afon Cynfal and ahead at cross roads, keeping on main road	No sign
J	.1	Straight on main road, not right	No sign
	1.3	Fine views of Vale of Ffestiniog on your right; ahead Trawsfynydd Nuclear Power Station	
K	.4	Turn right at T-junction on to A487 (But turn left keeping on A470 for diversion to Tomen-y-Mur)	Porthmadog
L	.3	Turn left from main road	Gellilydan
M		Straight, not left, and continue ahead through Gellilydan (But turn left here for diversion to Rhaeadr-du and Raven Falls)	No sign
		Total mileage on this map: 9.1	

CROWN COPYRIGHT RESERVED

On Route

Llyn Conwy
The source of the River Conwy, this remote lake, set high in the treeless expanse of the Migneint, can be reached by turning left on B4407 at Point C; then in 1.4 miles follow track by old farmhouse on left (no cars).

The Migneint
This literally is *The Swampy Place*, a broad moorland region, mainly 1,500 feet or more above sea level, and the source of many streams. With its wide expanse of heather and marshy grasses, it is the home of snipe, grouse and curlew, and is overlooked from the east and south-east by the twin peaks of Arenig Fach and Arenig Fawr (See Page 45). This is a wild, largely trackless area, and should only be tackled by those used to walking in remote places.

Llyn Morynion
There are at least two legends providing the reason for its name, *The Lake of the Maidens*, and they both tell of a group of maidens in distress who chose drowning in the lake as the only alternative to a life of dishonour. It provides a pleasant excuse for a walk and can be reached from Point D.

Blaenau Ffestiniog (See Page 131)

Rhaeadr-y-Cwm
To see this spectacular cataract on the Afon Cynfal, park at Point F and walk to the viewpoint 130 yards back. The road is narrow and busy, so be careful, particularly with children. The Cynfal Falls (Rhaeadr-y-Cynfal), 3 miles downstream, can be reached from Ffestiniog.

Tomen-y-Mur
This is the site of an important Roman station and fort built in the 1st century A.D. at the junction of two Roman roads, the most important of which was the Sarn Helen, which ran from Conwy in the north, right down to Carmarthen, a total distance of 120 miles. The mound still standing there is medieval, supposed to have been constructed by William Rufus in 1095. To find it take the A470 from Point K eastwards towards Dolgellau, in ¼ mile turn left, and in 1½ miles, just beyond a wood, the mound can be seen on a small hill to the right.

Trawsfynydd Nuclear Power Station
(See also pages 43 and 63)
This intrusion of the nuclear age within the boundaries of the National Park takes its cooling water from Llyn Trawsfynydd. The buildings were designed by Sir Basil Spence and the site was carefully landscaped in the forlorn hope that it could be made to harmonise with its surroundings. There is a car park with information and a nature trail nearby. Pre-booked parties may visit this station all the year (no children under 14). (*Write to C.E.G.B., Trawsfynydd, Blaenau Ffestiniog, Gwynedd LL41 4DT.*)

Rhaeadr-du and Raven Falls (See also page 43)
To reach these falls in a deep, and unusually dark (Du means black) ravine, turn left at Point M as you enter the village at Gellilydan. After 1½ miles along a gated road, follow the signed footpath on your left.

1. Llyn Morynion

2. Cottage near Ffestiniog

3. Llyn Trawsfynydd

Map 5

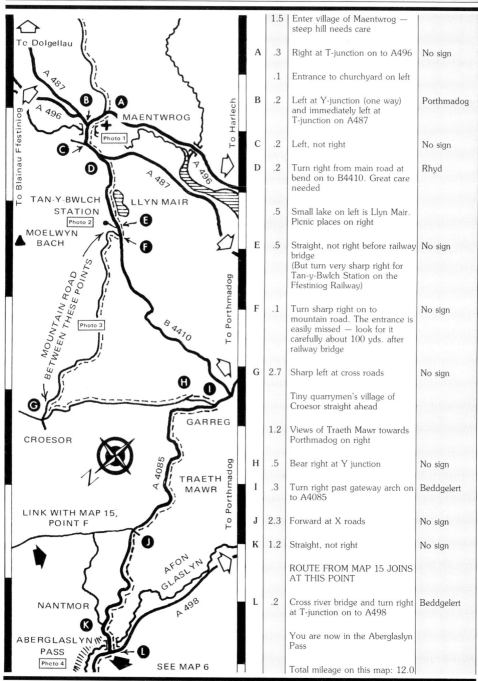

Ref Miles	Directions	Sign-posted
1.5	Enter village of Maentwrog — steep hill needs care	
A .3	Right at T-junction on to A496	No sign
.1	Entrance to churchyard on left	
B .2	Left at Y-junction (one way) and immediately left at T-junction on A487	Porthmadog
C .2	Left, not right	No sign
D .2	Turn right from main road at bend on to B4410. Great care needed	Rhyd
.5	Small lake on left is Llyn Mair. Picnic places on right	
E .5	Straight, not right before railway bridge (But turn very sharp right for Tan-y-Bwlch Station on the Ffestiniog Railway)	No sign
F .1	Turn sharp right on to mountain road. The entrance is easily missed — look for it carefully about 100 yds. after railway bridge	No sign
G 2.7	Sharp left at cross roads	No sign
	Tiny quarrymen's village of Croesor straight ahead	
1.2	Views of Traeth Mawr towards Porthmadog on right	
H .5	Bear right at Y junction	No sign
I .3	Turn right past gateway arch on to A4085	Beddgelert
J 2.3	Forward at X roads	No sign
K 1.2	Straight, not right	No sign
	ROUTE FROM MAP 15 JOINS AT THIS POINT	
L .2	Cross river bridge and turn right at T-junction on to A498	Beddgelert
	You are now in the Aberglaslyn Pass	
	Total mileage on this map: 12.0	

CROWN COPYRIGHT RESERVED

On Route

Maentwrog *(See also page 43)*
In a setting reminiscent of Switzerland this pleasant village takes its name from the large stone in the churchyard said to have been thrown from the hills above by the giant Twrog. For further details, see page 43.

1. Maentwrog

Ffestiniog Railway

Originally built in 1836 to connect the Ffestiniog slate quarries with the harbour at Porthmadog, it fell into disuse in 1939, but was revived in 1954. From sea level at Porthmadog the line crosses the Glaslyn estuary, with splendid views of the Snowdonia Range and of Harlech and the coast. It then climbs up on a ledge on the hillside giving some of the finest views obtainable from a carriage window anywhere in Britain. The full 13½ mile journey to Blaenau Ffestiniog takes about 65 minutes each way, and many of the services are hauled by unique steam engines. There are gift shops at Porthmadog, Tan-y-Bwlch and Blaenau Ffestiniog, a self-service restaurant at Porthmadog and station buffets at Tan-y-Bwlch and Blaenau Ffestiniog — ☎ (0766) 512340.

2. At Tan-y-Bwlch Station

Tan-y-Bwlch to Croesor

The narrow mountain road from Point F near Tan-y-Bwlch station to Croesor needs care as it is steep in places and there are several gates to be opened and shut (this is essential to prevent sheep straying) but the wild scenery makes it all worth while. On your right the rugged slopes lead up to the peaks of Moelwyn Bach (2,334 ft.) and Moelwyn Mawr (2,527 ft.); and to your left the wide expanse of the Traeth Mawr with Porthmadog and the sea beyond. To the right at Point G lies Cwm Croesor, dominated by the rocky face of Cnicht (2,265 ft.).

Traeth Mawr

Until 1815 a navigable arm of the sea reached to the Aberglaslyn Pass. William Madocks, M.P., who built the Regency village of Tremadog, created the artificial barrier at Porthmadog known as the Cob; this led to the reclamation of all the land between Porthmadog and the Pass, known as the Traeth Mawr *(The Big Sand)*.

3. Cnicht from our mountain road

Aberglaslyn Pass

Aberglaslyn means 'Mouth of the River of the Blue Lake' a reference to the time when the sea reached the foot of the pass. It is one of the showplaces of Wales, and horribly crowded in summer — beware of badly parked cars obstructing the narrow road. The 700 ft. high pine-clad cliffs enclose river, road and remnants of the old Welsh Highland Railway (see Porthmadog, page 139). The ancient bridge (Point L) — if you can find anywhere to park — makes a good viewpoint.

4. The Aberglaslyn Pass

Map 6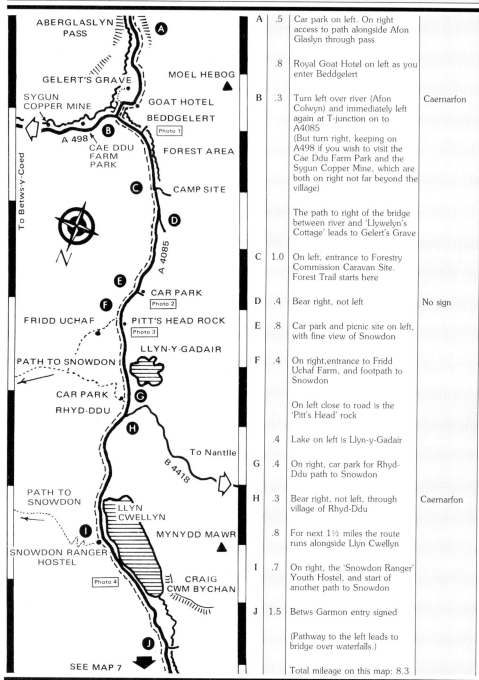

Ref.	kms	Miles	Directions	Sign-posted
A		.5	Car park on left. On right access to path alongside Afon Glaslyn through pass	
		.8	Royal Goat Hotel on left as you enter Beddgelert	
B		.3	Turn left over river (Afon Colwyn) and immediately left again at T-junction on to A4085 (But turn right, keeping on A498 if you wish to visit the Cae Ddu Farm Park and the Sygun Copper Mine, which are both on right not far beyond the village)	Caernarfon
			The path to right of the bridge between river and 'Llywelyn's Cottage' leads to Gelert's Grave	
C		1.0	On left, entrance to Forestry Commission Caravan Site. Forest Trail starts here	
D		.4	Bear right, not left	No sign
E		.8	Car park and picnic site on left, with fine view of Snowdon	
F		.4	On right, entrance to Fridd Uchaf Farm, and footpath to Snowdon	
			On left close to road is the 'Pitt's Head' rock	
		.4	Lake on left is Llyn-y-Gadair	
G		.4	On right, car park for Rhyd-Ddu path to Snowdon	
H		.3	Bear right, not left, through village of Rhyd-Ddu	Caernarfon
		.8	For next 1½ miles the route runs alongside Llyn Cwellyn	
I		.7	On right, the 'Snowdon Ranger' Youth Hostel, and start of another path to Snowdon	
J		1.5	Betws Garmon entry signed	
			(Pathway to the left leads to bridge over waterfalls.)	
			Total mileage on this map: 8.3	

CROWN COPYRIGHT RESERVED

On Route

Beddgelert (*Gelert's Grave*)

Although more likely to be derived from St. Kelert, who was associated with an early Celtic monastery on the site of the present church, the name of this village has been made famous by the apocryphal legend of Llywelyn's faithful hound slain by its master, when it had in fact saved his child from a wolf. The story was probably the commercial inspiration of one David Pritchard, first landlord of the Goat Hotel, who erected the cairn in the meadow near the river which is said to be the faithful animal's grave.

The National Trust have an Information Centre at Llywelyn's Cottage in the centre of the village — ☎ (0766) 86293. Just to the north-east of the village, on the right of the A498, will be found the Cae Ddu Farm Park — ☎ (0766) 86345 and, a short distance beyond, the interesting Sygun Copper Mine — ☎ (0766) 86595.

The Peak overlooking Beddgelert on the west is the 2,566 ft. Moel Hebog (*Hill of the Hawk*). It can be climbed by a track starting on the north side of the Royal Goat Hotel.

Beddgelert Forest Park

First designated as a 'Forest Park' in 1937, this extensive area, largely to the left of our road beyond Beddgelert, is now well covered with firs and larches. There is a good camp site, car parks, and a number of forest walks.

Snowdon (See also page 31 and 33)

The whole of the route on Map 6 from Beddgelert onwards is dominated to the east by the Snowdon massif. Fairly easy footpaths to the summit start from Points F, G and I, the one at Rhyd-Ddu being the most convenient, as there is a good car park. Full directions for these, and other climbs within the scope of any reasonably fit person can be found in W. A. Poucher's 'Welsh Peaks' (Constable). But before you start, be sure to read page 140, and take the advice on clothes and footwear; don't walk alone, or in bad weather, and allow plenty of time. For reference to the Snowdon Ranger Path, see below, for the P.Y.G. Track and the Miners' Path, see page 31, and for the Watkin Path, see page 33.

Peaks to be seen to the west of the route include Moel Lefn (*The Smooth Hill*—2,094 ft.) behind the Camp Site at Point C; Mynydd Drws-y-Coed, (*Mountain of the Doorway to the Woods*—2,329 ft.) behind Llyn-y-Gadair; and Mynydd Mawr (2,290 ft.) behind Llyn Cwellyn.

Pitts Head

This is a large glacial boulder on the left of our road beyond Point F. When seen from a certain angle it is said to resemble the profile of William Pitt.

The Snowdon Ranger

The Youth Hostel of that name, at Point I, is the start of one of the routes up Snowdon (see above). This is almost certainly the oldest route up Snowdon, being named after John Morton, the first mountain guide in the area, and the landlord of the then Snowdon Ranger Inn.

1. Llywelyn's Cottage, Beddgelert

2. Snowdon from Point E

3. The 'Pitt's Head' Rock

4. Llyn Cwellyn and Craig Cwm Bychan

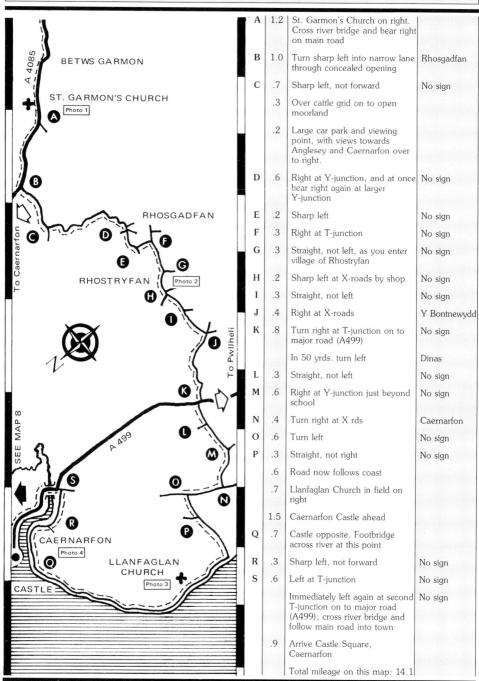

Map 7

	kms Ref Miles	Directions	Signposted
A	1.2	St. Garmon's Church on right. Cross river bridge and bear right on main road	
B	1.0	Turn sharp left into narrow lane through concealed opening	Rhosgadfan
C	.7	Sharp left, not forward	No sign
	.3	Over cattle grid on to open moorland	
	.2	Large car park and viewing point, with views towards Anglesey and Caernarfon over to right.	
D	.6	Right at Y-junction, and at once bear right again at larger Y-junction	No sign
E	.2	Sharp left	No sign
F	.3	Right at T-junction	No sign
G	.3	Straight, not left, as you enter village of Rhostryfan	No sign
H	.2	Sharp left at X-roads by shop	No sign
I	.3	Straight, not left	No sign
J	.4	Right at X-roads	Y Bontnewydd
K	.8	Turn right at T-junction on to major road (A499)	No sign
		In 50 yrds. turn left	Dinas
L	.3	Straight, not left	No sign
M	.6	Right at Y-junction just beyond school	No sign
N	.4	Turn right at X rds	Caernarfon
O	.6	Turn left	No sign
P	.3	Straight, not right	No sign
	.6	Road now follows coast	
	.7	Llanfaglan Church in field on right	
	1.5	Caernarfon Castle ahead	
Q	.7	Castle opposite. Footbridge across river at this point	
R	.3	Sharp left, not forward	No sign
S	.6	Left at T-junction	No sign
		Immediately left again at second T-junction on to major road (A499); cross river bridge and follow main road into town	No sign
	.9	Arrive Castle Square, Caernarfon	
		Total mileage on this map: 14.1	

CROWN COPYRIGHT RESERVED

On Route

Betws Garmon
This village straggles for more than a mile along the main Beddgelert-Caernarfon road, to beyond St. Garmon's Church, a simple and well-proportioned building dating from 1841. At the end of the village the road crosses the Afon Gwyrfai by a graceful three-arched 18th century bridge, built by local man, Harry Parry, claimed by friends to be 'the modern Inigo'.

Llanfaglan Church (See also page 119)
Now disused except for an occasional burial, this tiny ancient building stands alone in a field on your right as you follow the shore of the Menai Strait. The lintel inside the door was once a Roman tombstone and there are other re-used Roman stones in the walls — evidence of the Roman occupation of this key area opposite the southern shores of Anglesey. There is a car park and picnic site not far to the south of the church, overlooking deep-set Foryd Bay and this should provide good opportunities for bird-watching especially in wintertime.

Caernarfon
The unobstructed view of Edward I's finest castle across the River Seiont comes as a happy surprise at the end of a rather dull route. Old maps show a toll bridge at this point, but it has been replaced by a footbridge, and if you wish to reach the castle by road, you must drive a mile inland before crossing the river to return to the town on the opposite bank.

The Castle (CADW) — ☎ (0286) 77617, started by Edward I in 1283, and finished by the first Prince of Wales in 1327, stands on the site of an 11th century Norman motte and bailey. Castle and medieval town, enclosed within walls, of which much remain intact, were protected by two rivers, the Seiont and the Cadnant.

Twice unsuccessfully besieged by Owain Glyndwr, fought over during the Civil Wars, captured by Parliamentary forces in 1646, and condemned to demolition in 1660; in spite of all this, the Castle's outer walls still stand unharmed and magnificent. Inside, another story; much of the interior has vanished, replaced by neatly trimmed lawns, but still to be seen is the room where Edward II may have been born — though the Castle was probably not finished in time — and Queen Eleanor's gate where he was shown to the people of Wales as their Prince, although he was not installed as Prince of Wales until 1301 when 17. Whatever the truth, more recent Princes have been proclaimed here with all due pageantry. The Queen's Tower now houses the Regimental Museum of the Welsh Fusiliers and is well worth visiting.

The medieval town walls (CADW) enclose only a small part of the modern town. Nowadays the centre is often congested, but parking is usually possible on the Slate Quay beneath the Castle walls. If you succeed, climb the steep slope past the statue of David Lloyd George, into Castle Square, which still has several good Georgian frontages. In the town are some fine 19th century buildings — the County Hall

Continued on Page 19

1. St. Garmon's Church

2. Moel Eilio from Rhostryfan Road

3. Llanfaglan Church

4. Caernarfon Castle and Slate Quay

Map 8

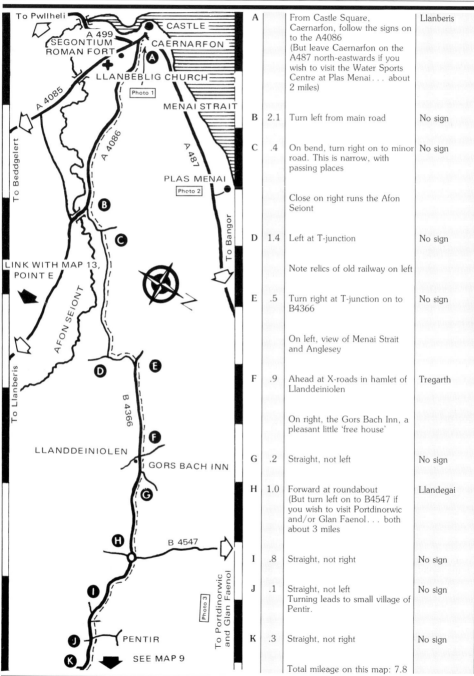

Ref.	kms / Miles	Directions	Sign-posted
A		From Castle Square, Caernarfon, follow the signs on to the A4086 (But leave Caernarfon on the A487 north-eastwards if you wish to visit the Water Sports Centre at Plas Menai... about 2 miles)	Llanberis
B	2.1	Turn left from main road	No sign
C	.4	On bend, turn right on to minor road. This is narrow, with passing places	No sign
		Close on right runs the Afon Seiont	
D	1.4	Left at T-junction	No sign
		Note relics of old railway on left	
E	.5	Turn right at T-junction on to B4366	No sign
		On left, view of Menai Strait and Anglesey	
F	.9	Ahead at X-roads in hamlet of Llanddeiniolen	Tregarth
		On right, the Gors Bach Inn, a pleasant little 'free house'	
G	.2	Straight, not left	No sign
H	1.0	Forward at roundabout (But turn left on to B4547 if you wish to visit Portdinorwic and/or Glan Faenol... both about 3 miles)	Llandegai
I	.8	Straight, not right	No sign
J	.1	Straight, not left Turning leads to small village of Pentir.	No sign
K	.3	Straight, not right	No sign
		Total mileage on this map: 7.8	

CROWN COPYRIGHT RESERVED

On Route

Caernarfon *Continued from Page 17*
close to the Castle entrance on its north side, a covered market in Palace Street, and the Conservative Club in Market Street.

Apart from the walls themselves, little earlier remains. However, there are a few 17th and 18th century houses, also the Black Boy Inn in Northgate Street, and the 14th century town and garrison Church of St. Mary built into the north-east corner of the walls.

In a terrace opposite the castle is Oriel Pendeitch, an exhibition and art gallery together with a Tourist Information Centre — ☎ (0286) 672232. See also the steam-dredger *Seiont II*, the main exhibit of a Maritime Museum based at the Doc Victoria, and if you have time, visit the fine Arfon Leisure Centre, which offers a wide range of recreational activities, and which lies to the north-east of the town, on the B4366.

1. Caernarfon Castle

Plas Menai

This fine watersports centre is situated about two miles north-east of Caernarfon, and was built by the Sports Council for Wales. The majority of its craft are sailboats, some for experts, but most are suitable for first time sailors, including dinghies, surfboards and keelboats. There are day, weekend and five-day courses for residents and non-residents, and day visitors should check in before 9 am except for swimming sessions. It has a heated indoor pool, bars, restaurant and luxurious accommodation for residents. [☎ (0248) 670964 *for full details and advance bookings.*]

Portdinorwic (Felinheli) (Turn left at Point H)

This ancient port on the Menai Strait was traditionally founded by the Norsemen, who used it as a base for their raids upon the neighbouring coasts in the 8th and 9th centuries. Its row of old greystone houses was once the home of fishermen, but in the 19th century it was developed by the Assheton-Smiths of nearby Vaynol Hall as a port through which slate could be shipped from their vast quarries at nearby Llanberis, to which it was connected by a railway specially built in 1824-5 (part of which has survived as the Llanberis Lake Railway – see Llanberis, page 29).

2. Sailing off Plas Menai

In the summer season it is now a popular sailing centre, with sailing courses and yacht hire, and during the quieter months ocean-going yachts are to be found here undergoing refits, or simply moored up for the winter. There are fine views across the Menai Strait to the old ferry point of Moel-y-don and tall-spired Llanedwen church close by (see page 71), and walks up into the hill country behind the town.

Glan Faenol (NT) (Turn left at Point H)

Situated about a mile north-east of Portdinorwic, this is a 1½ mile parkland walk, with fine views out over the Menai Strait towards Plas Newydd (see page 69), and back towards the mountains of Snowdonia.

3. At Port Dinorwic

Map 9

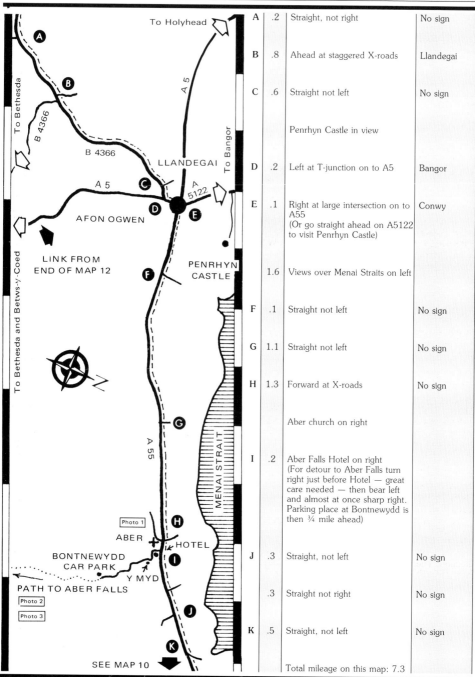

Ref	kms/Miles	Directions	Sign-posted
A	.2	Straight, not right	No sign
B	.8	Ahead at staggered X-roads	Llandegai
C	.6	Straight not left	No sign
		Penrhyn Castle in view	
D	.2	Left at T-junction on to A5	Bangor
E	.1	Right at large intersection on to A55 (Or go straight ahead on A5122 to visit Penrhyn Castle)	Conwy
	1.6	Views over Menai Straits on left	
F	.1	Straight not left	No sign
G	1.1	Straight not left	No sign
H	1.3	Forward at X-roads	No sign
		Aber church on right	
I	.2	Aber Falls Hotel on right (For detour to Aber Falls turn right just before Hotel — great care needed — then bear left and almost at once sharp right. Parking place at Bontnewydd is then ¾ mile ahead)	
J	.3	Straight, not left	No sign
	.3	Straight not right	No sign
K	.5	Straight, not left	No sign
		Total mileage on this map: 7.3	

CROWN COPYRIGHT RESERVED

On Route

Bangor

A 3-mile detour from Point E, along the A5122 will take you the small city and 'university town' of Bangor. If you are prepared to brave the traffic, the cathedral is worth a visit; it stands on the site of a structure destroyed by Owain Glyndwr in 1402, and rebuilt between 1496 and 1532. The present building was completely restored by Sir Gilbert Scott in 1866–70.

The town itself began with the founding of a monastery in the 6th century A.D., but there was probably a settlement here in pre-Roman times. More recently, its position commanding the approach to Anglesey led to Bangor becoming the centre of much fighting during the Civil Wars, and the outcome of the Second Civil War in 1647 was finally settled between here and Beaumaris. Bangor is justifiably proud of its University. Its buildings are some of the best in North Wales and it has a fine academic record.

Bangor has its own theatre, the Theatr Gwynedd, where there is also a Tourist Information Centre — ☏ (0248) 352786. There is also a Museum of Welsh Antiquities and an Art Gallery.

At Lower Bangor a pier more than 500 yards long stretches two-thirds of the distance across the Menai Strait — the long walk will be fully repaid by impressive views. Nearby stands Porth Penrhyn, established for shipping slates from the great Bethesda quarries.

Penrhyn Castle (NT) (See illustration on page 27)

Situated in a fine park between the mountains and the sea, this 19th century castle, with its nine towers, barbican gateway and massive keep, is an outstanding example of neo-Norman architecture.

Continued on Page 27

Aber

(Short for 'ABERGWYNGREGYN' — *River Mouth of the White Shells.*)

The mound of Norman origin near the village, known as Y Myd, is the site of a palace of Llywelyn the Great. To the north lies the wide expanse of the Lavan Sands (*Traeth Lafan*), the site of the legend of the drowned palace of Llys Helig — alas, long proved untrue, as the stones uncovered at low tide have been shown to be natural in origin.

Aber Falls

These beautiful waterfalls can only be reached on foot from the car park at Bontnewydd. Although less than 2 miles' walk, the path is rough in places, and wet after rain — allow at least an hour in each direction. There are two falls; the first is the Rhaeadr Fawr (*Big Fall*), also known as the 'Mare's Tail', where the Afon Goch falls 120 ft. over a cliff. The Rhaeadr Bach (*Little Fall*), not quite so high but equally beautiful, can only be reached when the river is low by scrambling over the rocks at the foot of Rhaeadr Fawr, and following the wall along the slope on your right. The walks to and from the falls have now been 'consolidated' into the Coedydd Aber Trail, which is well described in a leaflet usually available from a modest sum at an honesty box at the car park.

1. Aber Church

2. On the path to Aber Falls

3. Rhaeadr Fawr—The Mare's Tail

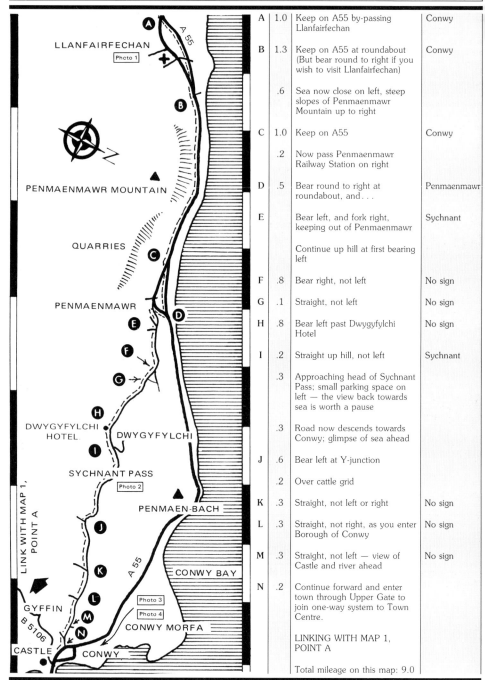

Map 10

Ref	kms/Miles	Directions	Signposted
A	1.0	Keep on A55 by-passing Llanfairfechan	Conwy
B	1.3	Keep on A55 at roundabout (But bear round to right if you wish to visit Llanfairfechan)	Conwy
	.6	Sea now close on left, steep slopes of Penmaenmawr Mountain up to right	
C	1.0	Keep on A55	Conwy
	.2	Now pass Penmaenmawr Railway Station on right	
D	.5	Bear round to right at roundabout, and...	Penmaenmawr
E		Bear left, and fork right, keeping out of Penmaenmawr	Sychnant
		Continue up hill at first bearing left	
F	.8	Bear right, not left	No sign
G	.1	Straight, not left	No sign
H	.8	Bear left past Dwygyfylchi Hotel	No sign
I	.2	Straight up hill, not left	Sychnant
	.3	Approaching head of Sychnant Pass; small parking space on left — the view back towards sea is worth a pause	
	.3	Road now descends towards Conwy; glimpse of sea ahead	
J	.6	Bear left at Y-junction	
	.2	Over cattle grid	
K	.3	Straight, not left or right	No sign
L	.3	Straight, not right, as you enter Borough of Conwy	No sign
M	.3	Straight, not left — view of Castle and river ahead	No sign
N	.2	Continue forward and enter town through Upper Gate to join one-way system to Town Centre. LINKING WITH MAP 1, POINT A Total mileage on this map: 9.0	

CROWN COPYRIGHT RESERVED

On Route

Llanfairfechan

Now by-passed by the busy A55, this is a quiet grey seaside resort with a mid-Victorian seafront and a good sandy beach, overshadowed to the east by the steep slopes of Penmaenmawr Mountain (1,550 ft.). There are few buildings of any note apart from the two churches. Near the old main road is Christ Church (English Services), built in 1855; it has a fine spire and good organ. The Little Church of St. Mary, standing above the village, is an older foundation, and has services in Welsh. The hill immediately to the south is Carreg Fawr (1,167 ft.).

1. Christ Church, Llanfairfechan

Penmaenmawr

This small holiday town shelters beneath Penmaen Mawr, the 'big stone headland' from which it takes its name, and looks across the water to north-eastern Anglesey with Puffin Island at its tip. Now by-passed by the busy A55, it has a traffic-free promenade from which sailing and water-skiing can be watched and a long sandy beach backed by shingle. This is squeezed between the sea and the mountains, much scarred here by great quarries, stone from which is still shipped from its little quay in considerable quantities.

The stone from some of these slopes was also much favoured by New Stone Age man, and many stone axes, picks and adzes, mostly abandoned and incomplete specimens, have been found above the town near Graiglwyd. Perhaps more significantly, geological analysis has revealed that implements of this period, discovered in many places throughout Wales and even in Derbyshire and Wiltshire, were made on this hillside 'axe factory'. On the mountain above will be found the Druid's Circle, one of the best-known of Wales' stone circles or henges, and which is almost certainly of Bronze Age origin. Both axe factory and stone circle are included in an interesting History Trail, based on the town. If neither axes nor circles are your forte, despair not, for the views alone make the considerable climb worthwhile.

Dwygyfylchi (*The Place of the Twin Semi-Circles*)

The village, with its tongue-twisting name, forms a pleasant suburb of Penmaenmawr in the valley below the Sychnant Pass. On your right at the foot of the Pass, between two hotels, the Fairy Glen, and the Dwygyfylchi, is a roadway leading to the Fairy Glen itself. This was named thus by the romantically inclined Victorians, and describes an attractive valley leading up to bracken-covered moorlands.

2. Sychnant Pass

Conwy *Continued from Page 5*

Maenan, and the existing abbey church became the Parish Church of St. Mary. Only parts of the walls and some buttresses remain of the original building. Much of the present church is 14th century, and there are some interesting features, including a fine 15th century screen and a Tudor font.

Near the top of the High Street stands *Plas Mawr*, a rambling Elizabethan house, built in 1585 by Robert Wynne of Gwydir; it is now the headquarters of the Royal Cambrian Academy of Art, and is open to the public. On the corner of High Street and Castle

Continued on Page 132

3. Aberconwy House

4. St. Mary's Church, Conwy

Map 11

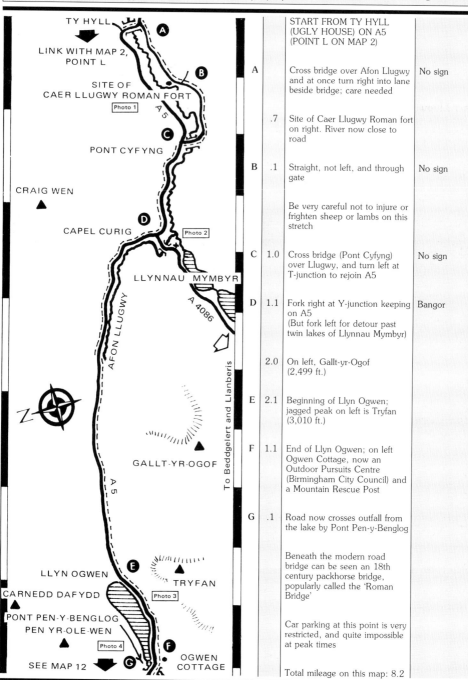

Ref	kms / Miles	Directions	Sign-posted
		START FROM TY HYLL (UGLY HOUSE) ON A5 (POINT L ON MAP 2)	
A		Cross bridge over Afon Llugwy and at once turn right into lane beside bridge; care needed	No sign
	.7	Site of Caer Llugwy Roman fort on right. River now close to road	
B	.1	Straight, not left, and through gate	No sign
		Be very careful not to injure or frighten sheep or lambs on this stretch	
C	1.0	Cross bridge (Pont Cyfyng) over Llugwy, and turn left at T-junction to rejoin A5	No sign
D	1.1	Fork right at Y-junction keeping on A5 (But fork left for detour past twin lakes of Llynnau Mymbyr)	Bangor
	2.0	On left, Gallt-yr-Ogof (2,499 ft.)	
E	2.1	Beginning of Llyn Ogwen; jagged peak on left is Tryfan (3,010 ft.)	
F	1.1	End of Llyn Ogwen; on left Ogwen Cottage, now an Outdoor Pursuits Centre (Birmingham City Council) and a Mountain Rescue Post	
G	.1	Road now crosses outfall from the lake by Pont Pen-y-Benglog	
		Beneath the modern road bridge can be seen an 18th century packhorse bridge, popularly called the 'Roman Bridge'	
		Car parking at this point is very restricted, and quite impossible at peak times	
		Total mileage on this map: 8.2	

CROWN COPYRIGHT RESERVED

On Route

Ty Hyll (*The Ugly House*) (See page 7)
The rough building dates from the middle ages (late 15th century) when by law any freeman could attempt to gain freehold rights on common land by building a fireplace and chimney and having smoke rising from it between dawn and dusk.

Caer Llugwy

This Roman fort stood on the road from Caerhun (*Canovium*) in the Conwy valley to Tomen-y-Mur (See Maps 4 and 19). It was partially excavated in 1920–22 but nothing of interest can be seen now. Most of the finds are in the Welsh Museum of Antiquities at Bangor.

1. Afon Llugwy near Caer Llugwy

Capel Curig

Standing at the junction of the A4086 and the A5, this famous fishing and climbing centre takes its name from St Curig, who was once Bishop of Dolbadarn. It is ringed by mountains, with the great peak of Moel Siabod to the immediate south, the foothills of the Carneddau range to the north, and to the west, Tryfan, the Glyders and Snowdon itself. It is one of the oldest and also probably the smallest of the North Wales resorts, but it straddles the A5 for nearly 2 miles and has a number of craft shops and some good hotel accommodation. The Victorian church is not of great interest to visitors, and neither is the 'old church', which although dating from the 13th century, was restored in 1839.

A detour along A4086 (turn left at Point D) past the twin lakes of Llynnau Mymbyr brings you a magnificent distant view of Snowdon, particularly striking against a setting sun in stormy weather.

2. Capel Curig—The Old Chapel

Capel Curig to Llyn Ogwen

The route to Llyn Ogwen reveals some of the most dramatic mountain scenery in Wales, apart from Snowdon itself. Much of it however cannot be seen from the road, and we must repeat our warning not to attempt any climbing alone, or without proper footwear and clothing. The Nature Conservancy provide a 2-mile Nature Trail and this is excellently described in their booklet, *Cwm Idwal Nature Trail*.

Peaks visible to the south (left) of the road are, first Gallt yr Ogof (2,499 ft.), then, opposite the beginning of Llyn Ogwen, the spectacular Tryfan (*Threefold Peak*), 3,010 ft. high, and behind Tryfan, the Glyders rising to more than 3,250 ft. Well known features such as Llyn Idwal and the 'Devil's Kitchen' can only be seen by climbing away from the road.

To the north of the road stand Pen Llithrig-y-Wrach (*Slippery Headland of the Witch*—2,621 ft.), Pen-yr-Helgi-du (2732 ft.), Craig Llugwy (3,184 ft.) and Carnedd Dafydd (*Cairn of Prince David*—3,426 ft.).

In bad weather when the mists come down, Llyn Ogwen is a wild and eerie place, a fit setting for the legend that it was here Sir Bedivere, last of Arthur's Knights, cast Excalibur into the water. His bones are said to be buried on Tryfan.

3. Llyn Ogwen

4. The 'Roman Bridge', Pont Pen-y-Benglog

Map 12

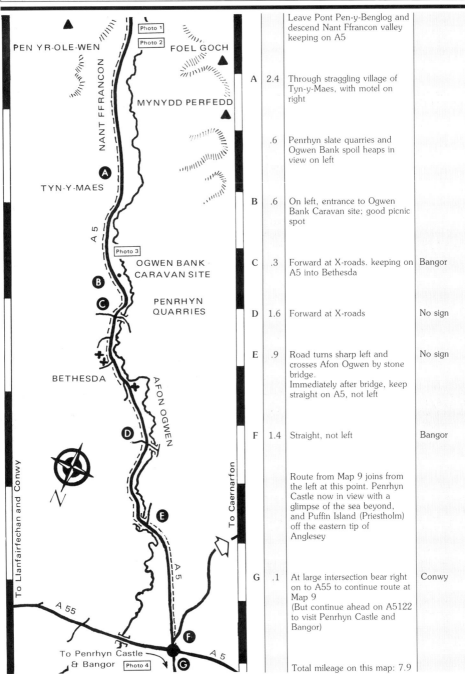

Ref	kms/Miles	Directions	Sign-posted
		Leave Pont Pen-y-Benglog and descend Nant Ffrancon valley keeping on A5	
A	2.4	Through straggling village of Tyn-y-Maes, with motel on right	
	.6	Penrhyn slate quarries and Ogwen Bank spoil heaps in view on left	
B	.6	On left, entrance to Ogwen Bank Caravan site; good picnic spot	
C	.3	Forward at X-roads, keeping on A5 into Bethesda	Bangor
D	1.6	Forward at X-roads	No sign
E	.9	Road turns sharp left and crosses Afon Ogwen by stone bridge. Immediately after bridge, keep straight on A5, not left	No sign
F	1.4	Straight, not left	Bangor
		Route from Map 9 joins from the left at this point. Penrhyn Castle now in view with a glimpse of the sea beyond, and Puffin Island (Priestholm) off the eastern tip of Anglesey	
G	.1	At large intersection bear right on to A55 to continue route at Map 9 (But continue ahead on A5122 to visit Penrhyn Castle and Bangor)	Conwy
		Total mileage on this map: 7.9	

CROWN COPYRIGHT RESERVED

On Route

Nant Ffrancon

The Afon Ogwen escapes from Llyn Ogwen at Pont Pen-y-Benglog and leaps into this dramatic glaciated valley in a series of waterfalls. The A5 road keeps to the east side, overshadowed by the rugged slopes and crags of Pen yr Ole Wen (*The Summit of the Bright Sunlight*) and Carnedd Dafydd. To the west, the overshadowing peaks include Y Garn, Foel Goch and Carnedd Filiast. At the foot of the valley is the minute hamlet of Ty'n-y-maes, where George Borrow drank 'tolerably good wine', after his walk down from Llyn Ogwen in the company of a friendly but teetotal carpenter. Thomas Pennant, writing in his *Tour in Wales* in 1778, described this road as 'the most dreadful horse path in Wales', and he had seen a few Welsh horse paths in his time!

Bethesda

This busy quarrying town at one time housed more than 2,000 workers from the Penrhyn slate quarries, but these now operate on a very much reduced scale. The quarries existed in the time of Elizabeth I, but were not systematically worked until the period when Richard Pennant of Liverpool married the Penrhyn heiress and himself became Baron Penrhyn in 1783. To cater for the workers' souls, several grandiose chapels were built, notably 'Jerusalem' and 'Siloam', and 'Bethesda' in the High Street, after which the town was named. The town is hemmed in on the west by enormous spoil heaps and the quarries themselves are reckoned to be the deepest in the world, with a series of 60-foot-high terraces and a total depth of over 1,000 feet. These quarries, which produce a variety of coloured slate in blue, green and red, are open to groups of visitors from April to September by arrangement and under a guide. There is a caravan and camping site at Ogwen Bank, off the A5 just to the south of the town.

Penrhyn Castle *Continued from Page 21*

This was a style which greatly appealed to the new, romantically inclined industrial magnates of the 19th century, and Penrhyn is the result of the ambitions of the Pennants, a family whose wealth came from the great slate quarries of Snowdonia only a few miles away. A late 18th century Gothic mansion, built by Samuel Wyatt, had to be swept away to make room for the castle, and this new building is said to have cost at least half a million pounds, a great deal of money in those days.

A visit here is well worthwhile, and the castle's interior is enriched with much carved wood and stone, and with slate from the family quarries. The furniture is on a monumental scale befitting its impressive surroundings, and there is also a museum of industrial locomotives, an exhibition of dolls, and a natural history display. There are many walks in the surrounding parkland and gardens, and views of the mountains of Snowdonia and the Menai Strait from some of the paths are outstandingly beautiful. Shop and tea room — ☎ (0248) 353084.

1. The head of the Nant Ffrancon Pass

2. Nant Ffrancon from Pont Pen-y-Benglog

3. Picnic site at Ogwen Bank

4. Penrhyn Castle

Miles	Map 13	kms Ref. Miles	Directions	Sign-posted
			Leave Castle Square, Caernarfon on A4086	Porthmadog
		A .1	At roundabout take A487	Porthmadog
		.2	At larger roundabout take A4085	Beddgelert
		.2	On left, site of Roman fort of Segontium	
		.1	Llanbeblig Church on left	
		B 1.0	Left at roundabout in village of Caeathro	Pontrug
		.3	Straight not left	No sign
		C 1.2	Turn right at T junction on to A4086	Llanrug
			Within 100 yds., turn right at T-junction on to A4086	No sign
		D 1.0	Straight, not right	No sign
		E .3	Forward over X-roads in village of Llanrug	No sign
		F .6	Forward at X-roads	No sign
		.6	Straight not right	Llanberis
		G .3	Straight, not right	Llanberis
		H .3	Straight not left	Llanberis
			Llanberis Pass in view ahead	
		.1	Llyn Padarn close to road on left for next 1½ miles	
		1.5	Turn right off By-pass into Llanberis	Llanberis
		I .5	Keep on through Llanberis St. Padarn's Church on right	
			Total mileage on this map: 8.1	

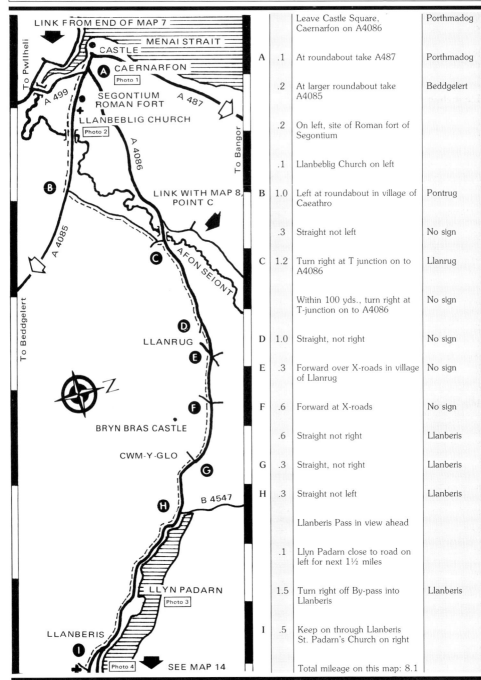

CROWN COPYRIGHT RESERVED

On Route

Caernarfon (See Page 17 and 19)

Segontium
Sir Mortimer Wheeler excavated this rectangular Roman fort in 1920. Most of the wall plan is clearly defined, but lacks the labelling which would make it more interesting. The museum is small, but contains some fascinating local discoveries.

Llanbeblig Church
Most of this church is 14th century, and is dedicated to St. Peblig, who may have been Publicius, son of Emperor Maximus and Empress Helen, and uncle of Constantine the Great. The tower has unusual stepped battlements; the interior is dark, but the Vaynol chapel contains a fine altar tomb. The churchyard is overgrown and full of leaning slate gravestones.

Llanrug
This is a typical quarrymen's village, with a restored and stuccoed church under a 15th century roof.

Bryn Bras Castle
This mansion was built as a castle in about 1830 in extravagant neo-Norman style, around an earlier structure. It is romantically sited against a background of high mountains above Llanrug, and lies in a splendid 30 acre garden, with rhododendrons, roses and hydrangeas, a walled knot garden, woodland walks, pools and waterfalls. There is also a 'mountain walk' with fine views of Snowdonia and Anglesey. Part of the very much 'lived-in' interior is open to view, and this includes hall, galleried staircase, drawing room, morning room and library. Refreshments are available in the Garden Tearoom and on the lawns, and there is also a picnic area — ☎ (0286) 870210.

Llanberis
Standing at the south-eastern end of Llyn Padarn, and not far from the north-western end of Llyn Peris, the village of Llanberis is in the very heart of Snowdonia, and is perhaps best known as the terminus of the Snowdon Mountain Railway. There is however much more to see and do here, and in view of the possible congestion it is best to park either at the northern end of the village, or perhaps preferably at the large park by the Welsh Slate Museum, near the Gilfach Ddu terminus of the Llanberis Lake Railway. This narrow gauge railway, built to carry slate, has been converted to take passengers along the shore of Llyn Padarn, a two mile run to Pen-y-llyn, with a stop at Cei Llydan, where there are lake-side and tree-shaded picnic sites. It is possible to leave the train here and join another one later in the day. This railway line runs through much of the Padarn Country Park, the central feature of which is the Llyn Padarn Walk which circles the entire lake. Shortly after leaving Gilfach Ddu it passes a viewing platform andd beyond this will be found the Quarry Hospital Visitor Centre, which was once the hospital for employees of the Dinorwic Quarry Company and which contains much of its original equipment as well as special displays on

Continued on Pages 134 and 135

1. Segontium Roman Fort

2. Llanbeblig Church, Caernarfon

3. Llanberis Lake Railway

4. Llyn Padarn from Dolbadarn Castle

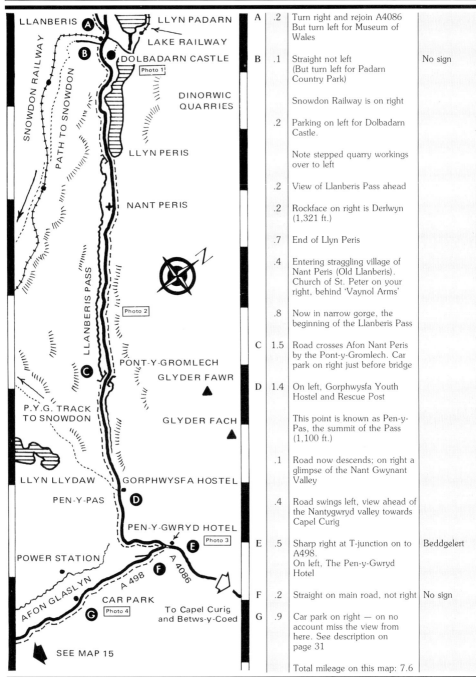

Miles	Map 14	kms Ref. Miles	Directions	Sign-posted
		A .2	Turn right and rejoin A4086 But turn left for Museum of Wales	
		B .1	Straight not left (But turn left for Padarn Country Park)	No sign
			Snowdon Railway is on right	
		.2	Parking on left for Dolbadarn Castle.	
			Note stepped quarry workings over to left	
		.2	View of Llanberis Pass ahead	
		.2	Rockface on right is Derlwyn (1,321 ft.)	
		.7	End of Llyn Peris	
		.4	Entering straggling village of Nant Peris (Old Llanberis). Church of St. Peter on your right, behind 'Vaynol Arms'	
		.8	Now in narrow gorge, the beginning of the Llanberis Pass	
		C 1.5	Road crosses Afon Nant Peris by the Pont-y-Gromlech. Car park on right just before bridge	
		D 1.4	On left, Gorphwysfa Youth Hostel and Rescue Post	
			This point is known as Pen-y-Pas, the summit of the Pass (1,100 ft.)	
		.1	Road now descends; on right a glimpse of the Nant Gwynant Valley	
		.4	Road swings left, view ahead of the Nantygwryd valley towards Capel Curig	
		E .5	Sharp right at T-junction on to A498. On left, The Pen-y-Gwryd Hotel	Beddgelert
		F .2	Straight on main road, not right	No sign
		G .9	Car park on right — on no account miss the view from here. See description on page 31	
			Total mileage on this map: 7.6	

CROWN COPYRIGHT RESERVED

On Route

Dolbadarn Castle (CADW)

The remains of this castle, with its 40ft high tower, stand on a rocky hillock, with fine views of Llyn Padarn, and of Llyn Peris, with the Llanberis Pass beyond. It was built by Llywelyn the Great in the early years of the 13th century, and must have dominated this southern entry to the pass most effectively. The tower, which once had a conical roof, is traditionally the place where Owain Goch (Red Owen) was held prisoner for no less than 20 years by his far from friendly brother, the last Prince Llywelyn.

1. Dolbadarn Castle

Nant Peris *(Old Llanberis)*

This village stands at the foot of Llanberis Pass, overhung on one side by the north ridge of Snowdon, and on the other by the slopes of Elidir Fawr and Y Garn. The minute medieval church of St Peris is a typically simple building of stone and slate. It was heavily restored in 1848 and unfortunately even the early 16th century rood screen did not escape the attention of the 'improvers'. There is a useful bus service that picks up walkers and climbers from the free car park near the church, to take them to other starting points for the ascent of Snowdon — the 'Snowdon Sherpa'.

2. Llanberis Pass

Snowdon (See also pages 15 and 33)

The group of peaks which form the Snowdon massif, known collectively as Eryri *(Abode of Eagles)* form the southern backdrop of this route. Three of them exceed 3,000 feet — the highest of all Y Wyddfa *(Tumulus or Grave Mound*—3,560 ft.), next Crib-y-Ddysgl *(Crest of the Dish*—3,493 ft.) and Crib Goch *(Red Crest*—3,023 ft.); nearly as lofty is Y Lliwedd *(Saw-like Edge*—2,947 ft.). Hidden among the peaks are several lakes, the largest Llyn Llydaw, a reservoir which feeds the power station in the Nant Gwynant valley.

Two of the best known routes to the summit of Y Wyddfa start from Pen-y-Pas — the P.Y.G. track and the Miners' track. These are fairly easy for fit people in good weather, but our advice still applies — before setting out, study a good guide such as Poucher's Welsh Peaks, don't climb alone, and wear the right clothes and boots. If parking is a problem, why not head down to Nant Peris and make use of the Snowdon Sherpa' bus service (see above).

3. Pen-y-Gwryd Hotel

The Llanberis Pass

While the flanks of Snowdon line the whole of the southern side of the Pass, the seemingly impassable rock faces and steep boulder-strewn buttresses on the northern side belong to three major peaks — Y Garn (3,104 ft.), and the Glyders *(Fawr*—3,279 ft., and *Fach*—3,262 ft.). These are the haunts of the dedicated rock climbers, who can usually be seen roped together on the sheer cliffs above the car park

Continued on Page 33

Pen-y-Gwryd (See Page 33)

4. Snowdon from viewpoint on A498

Map 15

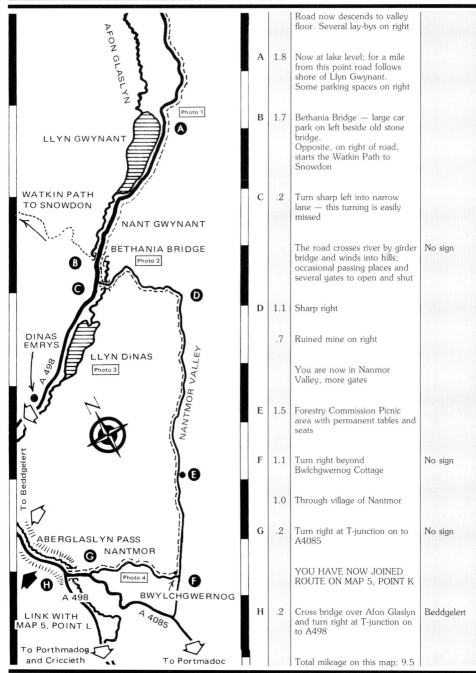

Ref.	Miles	Directions	Sign-posted
		Road now descends to valley floor. Several lay-bys on right	
A	1.8	Now at lake level; for a mile from this point road follows shore of Llyn Gwynant. Some parking spaces on right	
B	1.7	Bethania Bridge — large car park on left beside old stone bridge. Opposite, on right of road, starts the Watkin Path to Snowdon	
C	.2	Turn sharp left into narrow lane — this turning is easily missed	
		The road crosses river by girder bridge and winds into hills; occasional passing places and several gates to open and shut	No sign
D	1.1	Sharp right	
	.7	Ruined mine on right	
		You are now in Nanmor Valley, more gates	
E	1.5	Forestry Commission Picnic area with permanent tables and seats	
F	1.1	Turn right beyond Bwlchgwernog Cottage	No sign
	1.0	Through village of Nantmor	
G	.2	Turn right at T-junction on to A4085	No sign
		YOU HAVE NOW JOINED ROUTE ON MAP 5, POINT K	
H	.2	Cross bridge over Afon Glaslyn and turn right at T-junction on to A498	Beddgelert
		Total mileage on this map: 9.5	

CROWN COPYRIGHT RESERVED

On Route

The Llanberis Pass *Continued from Page 31*
at Pont-y-Gromlech and similar places where spectators can watch through field-glasses. At the summit, Pen-y-Pas (1,100 ft.) stands the Gorphwysfa Hostel and Mountain Rescue Post, once an Inn; the car park is usually full from early morning.

Pen-y-Gwryd (*Head of Cai's Fathomwide Pass*)

Legend has it that Cai was one of Arthur's Knights, and big enough to block the pass with his outstretched arms. The Hotel, at the foot of the Glyders, has been the base for Everest climbers in training.

Nant Gwynant Valley

From the car park at Point G on Map 14, you can enjoy the finest views in Wales. High in front, and slightly to your left, the summit of Snowdon, Y Wyddfa; the other peak to its right is Crib Goch. Below them, but just hidden lies Llyn Llydaw; from it you can see the pipeline down the hillside feeding the power station on the Afon Glaslyn in the valley below.

Then look to your left down the incomparable Nant Gwynant Valley, with Llyn Gwynant (*Lake of the Sparkling Stream*) reflecting the wooded hills — there is nothing more beautiful in the whole of Wales. Beyond rises the peak of Moel Hebog to the west of Beddgelert.

The grassy banks of the lake beside the main road (Map 15, Point A) are rightly favoured as a picnic spot, and the few parking spaces are therefore often full; but stop if you can to explore the hillside on the left of the road to be rewarded by wonderful views of the lake and the Snowdon range.

The Watkin Path

This pathway to Snowdon was constructed by Sir Edward Watkin, a railway engineer and early protagonist of the Channel Tunnel who spent his retirement nearby. It starts close by the Bethania bridge, and in about 1½ miles passes the Gladstone Rock, where a tablet records the opening of the path by W.E. Gladstone on September 13th, 1892, when the statesman was 84.

Llyn Dinas

A half-mile detour along A498 from Point C brings you to this lake, nearly as lovely as Llyn Gwynant. Beyond the lake, about halfway to Beddgelert and to the right of the road, stands Dinas Emrys, a crag associated in legend with Vortigern and the site of a hill fort from Iron Age times.

Nantmor Valley and Cae Dafydd

The mountain road which leaves A498 at Point C takes you into the beautiful and secluded valley of the Nantmor. There are several ideal picnic spots, including one provided by the Forestry Commission, from which there is a pleasant forest walk.

1. Llyn Gwynant

2. Bethania Bridge

3. Llyn Dinas

4. Near Nantmor

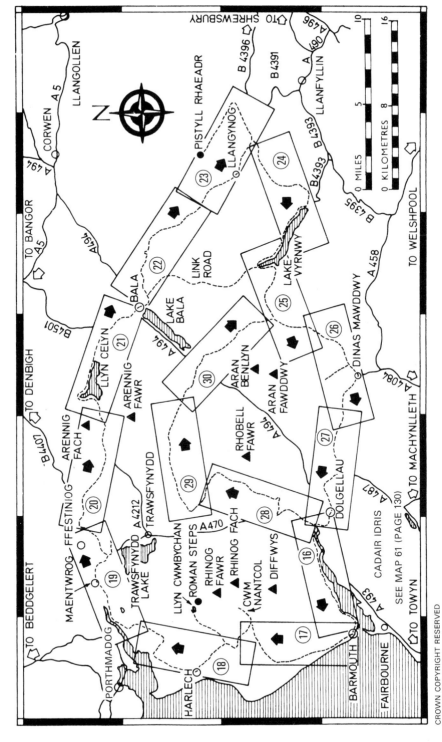

EXPLORING SOUTH SNOWDONIA

Harlech Castle

Starting from Dolgellau, westwards to Barmouth and then north along the coast to Harlech, most of the route covered by this section lies within the Snowdonia National Park, but we have also included parts of the Berwyn Mountains and Lake Vyrnwy. Beyond this lovely lake our main route heads westwards over high country returning to Dolgellau. A cross route explores the attractive Coed-y-Brenin Forest before heading over further wild mountain country to Bala. There is also a pleasant area of National Park country to the south and south-west of Dolgellau, including the mountain massif of Cadair Idris. This is not covered by our routes, but full reference to the places here will be found on pages 130–139.

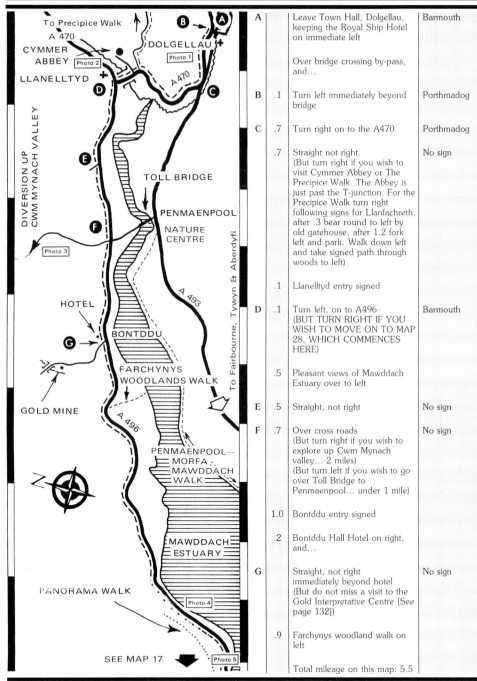

Map 16	kms/Ref/Miles	Directions	Sign-posted
A		Leave Town Hall, Dolgellau, keeping the Royal Ship Hotel on immediate left	Barmouth
		Over bridge crossing by-pass, and...	
B	.1	Turn left immediately beyond bridge	Porthmadog
C	.7	Turn right on to the A470	Porthmadog
	.7	Straight not right. (But turn right if you wish to visit Cymmer Abbey or The Precipice Walk. The Abbey is just past the T-junction. For the Precipice Walk turn right following signs for Llanfachreth, after .3 bear round to left by old gatehouse, after 1.2 fork left and park. Walk down left and take signed path through woods to left)	No sign
	.1	Llanelltyd entry signed	
D	.1	Turn left, on to A496 (BUT TURN RIGHT IF YOU WISH TO MOVE ON TO MAP 28, WHICH COMMENCES HERE)	Barmouth
	.5	Pleasant views of Mawddach Estuary over to left	
E	.5	Straight, not right	No sign
F	.7	Over cross roads (But turn right if you wish to explore up Cwm Mynach valley... 2 miles) (But turn left if you wish to go over Toll Bridge to Penmaenpool... under 1 mile)	No sign
	1.0	Bontddu entry signed	
	.2	Bontddu Hall Hotel on right, and...	
G		Straight, not right immediately beyond hotel (But do not miss a visit to the Gold Interpretative Centre [See page 132])	No sign
	.9	Farchynys woodland walk on left	
		Total mileage on this map: 5.5	

On Route

Dolgellau (See Page 59)

The Precipice Walk Nature Trail
(See Route Directions.)

This well known walk of about three miles encircling the high ridge of Foel Cynwch and Foel Faner (*Foel*: a bare hill) is all within the Nannau Estate. Picnicking and camping are not allowed, but the walk itself is accessible by courtesy of the owner. By following the signs and the red waymarks you will pass through woodlands, around the precipice itself, with magnificent views out over the Mawddach valley, to the Rhinogs and the Snowdon range far beyond, returning behind the ridge and along the shores of Llyn Cynwch. As the sign at the entrance states, "*Much of the precipice section is believed to have been formed by sheep traversing the side of the mountain. Accordingly in places it is very narrow and precipitous. It is not suitable as a walk for the aged, infirm, children or any persons who suffer from fear of heights or dizziness.*" However all those who are fortunate enough not to fall into any of the above categories should certainly take this splendid walk.

Cymmer Abbey (CADW)

Founded in the 12th century by Cistercians from the abbey of Cymhir in remote country near Rhayader, Cymmer Abbey stands close to the banks of the Mawddach river. Unfortunately there is a camp site close by, but the lovely lancet windows at the east end of the abbey church still give an impression of serenity and strength.

Llanelltyd Bridge
(For Llanelltyd village see page 61.)

A pleasant old stone bridge near the head of the lovely Mawddach estuary. The poet Ruskin reckoned the view from near here to be one of the finest in Europe.

Cwm Mynach (*The Monks Valley*)

By turning right at Point F it is possible to drive almost two miles up this quiet valley, which was the scene of hectic gold mining activity in the mid-19th century and again in the early 1900s. However if you do decide to drive rather than walk, avoid holiday times as the road is steep and narrow, and there are no adequate parking facilities at the end of the public road. From the end of the road there is a track (for walkers only) to Llyn Mynach, from whence one can walk up westwards to the summit ridge of Diphwys (2,462 ft.), and then north to the lakes of Llyn Hywel and Llyn-y-Bi, beneath the great rock face of Rhinog Fach. Before tackling any of the hill walks mentioned in this guide, ensure that you are adequately equipped, and that you have a copy of the appropriate Ordnance Survey Landranger Map (Sheet 124).

Penmaenpool (See Page 45)

Bontddu (See Page 132)

Farchynys Woodlands Walks (See Page 45)

1. Dolgellau Church   2. Cymmer Abbey

3. Cwm Mynach

4. Mawddach Estuary

5. Prospect from Barmouth

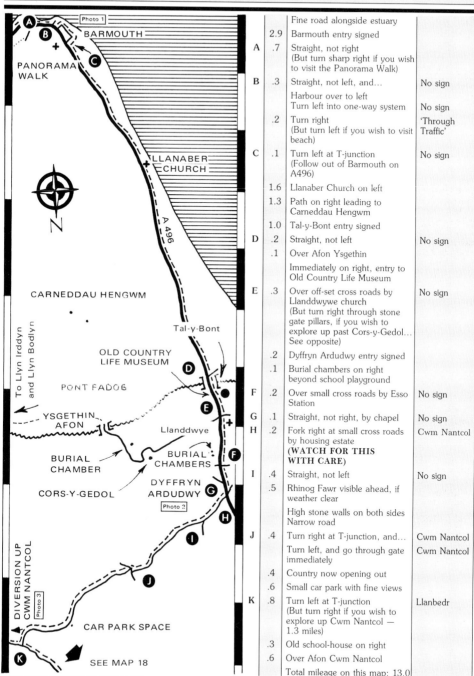

Map 17

kms Ref. Miles	Directions	Sign-posted
	Fine road alongside estuary	
2.9	Barmouth entry signed	
A .7	Straight, not right (But turn sharp right if you wish to visit the Panorama Walk)	
B .3	Straight, not left, and...	No sign
	Harbour over to left Turn left into one-way system	No sign
.2	Turn right (But turn left if you wish to visit beach)	'Through Traffic'
C .1	Turn left at T-junction (Follow out of Barmouth on A496)	No sign
1.6	Llanaber Church on left	
1.3	Path on right leading to Carneddau Hengwm	
1.0	Tal-y-Bont entry signed	
D .2	Straight, not left	No sign
.1	Over Afon Ysgethin	
	Immediately on right, entry to Old Country Life Museum	
E .3	Over off-set cross roads by Llanddwywe church (But turn right through stone gate pillars, if you wish to explore up past Cors-y-Gedol... See opposite)	No sign
.2	Dyffryn Ardudwy entry signed	
.1	Burial chambers on right beyond school playground	
F .2	Over small cross roads by Esso Station	No sign
G .1	Straight, not right, by chapel	No sign
H .2	Fork right at small cross roads by housing estate **(WATCH FOR THIS WITH CARE)**	Cwm Nantcol
I .4	Straight, not left	No sign
.5	Rhinog Fawr visible ahead, if weather clear	
	High stone walls on both sides Narrow road	
J .4	Turn right at T-junction, and...	Cwm Nantcol
	Turn left, and go through gate immediately	Cwm Nantcol
.4	Country now opening out	
.6	Small car park with fine views	
K .8	Turn left at T-junction (But turn right if you wish to explore up Cwm Nantcol — 1.3 miles)	Llanbedr
.3	Old school-house on right	
.6	Over Afon Cwm Nantcol	
	Total mileage on this map: 13.0	

CROWN COPYRIGHT RESERVED

On Route

Panorama Walk, Barmouth
(Turn sharp right at Point A. Drive up steep road with hair-pin bend. Sign to 'Walk' on right, after .7 mile. Watch for sign with care.)

The splendid views of the Mawddach estuary with Cader Idris across the water, and the distant Arans beyond the head of the estuary, are well worth the slight effort involved.

Barmouth
Small harbour town beneath steep hillsides, whose popularity as a holiday resort bloomed rapidly with the coming of the railway in the 19th century. It has an impressive red sandstone church (1889) perched above most of the town, although its mother church was Llanaber (see below). It has a long sandy beach, bright holiday shops and hotels, and an attractive little harbour overlooked by a small round building, put up in the 1820s to accommodate drunken sailors and gold miners from the Bontddu area, who must have turned the town into a miniature Dawson City when the local 'goldrush' was at its height.

Dinas Oleu, an area of cliffland just above the town, was the first property acquired by the National Trust, being given by Mrs. F. Talbot in 1895, the year that the Trust was founded.

1. Barmouth Harbour

Llanaber Church
Pleasant little building standing above the shoreline in a churchyard crammed with monumental gravestones. Building started here in about 1200, was completed within fifty years, and has been altered very little since (the restoration of 1858 being unusually sympathetic). We particularly liked the old stone flagged floor, the stout arcading, the chancel higher than the nave, with its beautifully lit roof, and the tall lancet windows. At high tide, if one stands quietly in the church, the sound of waves on the shore below comes clearly through... all in great contrast to the busy holiday caravan sites nearby.

2. Burial Chamber, Dyffryn Ardudwy

Carneddau Hengwm
An extensive group of Bronze Age stone circles and burial chambers about a mile to the east of our road beyond Llanaber. This is not specifically signed and we suggest that you check locally before setting off on foot from the road.

Tal-y-Bont
Attractive hamlet with an old bridge over a stream, and not far away, the Old Country Life Museum. Walk up into the hills to Llyn Irddyn and Llyn Bodlyn (about three and five miles).

Llanddwywe Church
Smaller than Llanaber church and much later in date, being mostly in the Perpendicular style. It has an attractive interior, especially the family chapel of the Vaughans of Cors-y-Gedol.

Cors-y-Gedol (See Page 45)

Dyffryn Ardudwy (See Page 49)

Cwm Nantcol (See Page 53)

3. The Rhinogs from Cwm Nanctol

Map 18

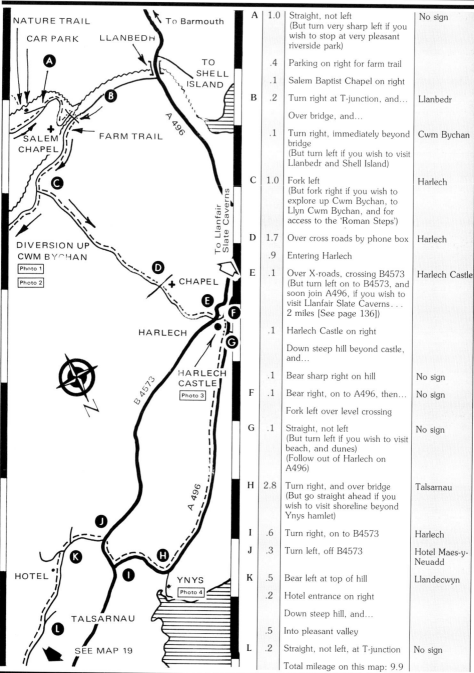

Ref	kms / Miles	Directions	Sign-posted
A	1.0	Straight, not left (But turn very sharp left if you wish to stop at very pleasant riverside park)	No sign
	.4	Parking on right for farm trail	
	.1	Salem Baptist Chapel on right	
B	.2	Turn right at T-junction, and...	Llanbedr
		Over bridge, and...	
	.1	Turn right, immediately beyond bridge (But turn left if you wish to visit Llanbedr and Shell Island)	Cwm Bychan
C	1.0	Fork left (But fork right if you wish to explore up Cwm Bychan, to Llyn Cwm Bychan, and for access to the 'Roman Steps')	Harlech
D	1.7	Over cross roads by phone box	Harlech
	.9	Entering Harlech	
E	.1	Over X-roads, crossing B4573 (But turn left on to B4573, and soon join A496, if you wish to visit Llanfair Slate Caverns... 2 miles [See page 136])	Harlech Castle
	.1	Harlech Castle on right	
		Down steep hill beyond castle, and...	
	.1	Bear sharp right on hill	No sign
F	.1	Bear right, on to A496, then...	No sign
		Fork left over level crossing	
G	.1	Straight, not left (But turn left if you wish to visit beach, and dunes) (Follow out of Harlech on A496)	No sign
H	2.8	Turn right, and over bridge (But go straight ahead if you wish to visit shoreline beyond Ynys hamlet)	Talsarnau
I	.6	Turn right, on to B4573	Harlech
J	.3	Turn left, off B4573	Hotel Maes-y-Neuadd
K	.5	Bear left at top of hill	Llandecwyn
	.2	Hotel entrance on right	
		Down steep hill, and...	
	.5	Into pleasant valley	
L	.2	Straight, not left, at T-junction	No sign
		Total mileage on this map: 9.9	

CROWN COPYRIGHT RESERVED

On Route

Cwm Nantcol Nature Trail
This starts from the attractive riverside car park and picnic area at Point A and explains on plaques the scenery of the Nantcol gorge and waterfalls.

Salem Chapel
This building has a delightfully unspoilt 18th century interior complete with pulpit and sloping box pews. There is a reproduction of S.C. Vosper's sharply observed painting 'Salem' hung here, for this was the chapel that provided both his setting and his congregation.

Cefn-Isa Farm Trail
This two mile long trail starts at Salem Chapel and illustrates the story of Welsh hill farming.

Llanbedr and Shell Island
These two places are off our route, but can be reached quite easily from Point B. Llanbedr is, with some justice, claimed to be the tidiest village in Wales, and despite the busy A496, has considerable charm.

Mochras Peninsula or Shell 'Island' lies beyond Llanbedr, and is a pleasant seaside place, with sands, rock pools and dunes, and also splendid views northwards across Tremadog Bay. To the south of Llanbedr will be found the Maes Artro Tourist Village, which provides a wide variety of leisure facilities including a sea life aquarium, a recreated old Welsh street, a model village and a Wild West fort. There are also studio workshops, a craft shop, a coffee shop and a licenced restaurant — ☎ (0341) 23467.

Cwm Bychan, Llyn Bychan and the Roman Steps
(Fork right at Point C. Total diversion length 3.5 miles each way.)

This diversion takes us up the beautiful Cwm Bychan, with its rock strewn stream, running through woodlands of oak, beech and ash, with bracken never far away. Eventually it emerges into more open country, just before climbing gently up beside the shore of Llyn Bychan. This is a deservedly popular place, and peak visiting times should be avoided.

To climb the Roman Steps (certainly not Roman, but probably a medieval pack trail) park your car at the far end of the lake, turn right, cross a bridge, and follow a path through the wood beyond. The best stretch of steps is some distance onwards on the far side of a stone wall. It is possible to walk beyond the steps and to link back to Bwlch Drws (see Cwm Nantcol, Page 53).

Llanfair Slate Caverns (See Page 136)

Harlech
Built on the slopes of a hillside overlooking Tremadog Bay, Harlech, once the county town of the old County of Meirioneth, now centres largely upon its splendid 13th century castle (CADW). Built by Edward I in about 1290, as one of a chain of coastal
Continued on Page 55

Ynys (See Page 63)

1. Llyn Cwm Bychan

2. The Roman Steps

3. Harlech Castle

4. Ynys Shoreline

Map 19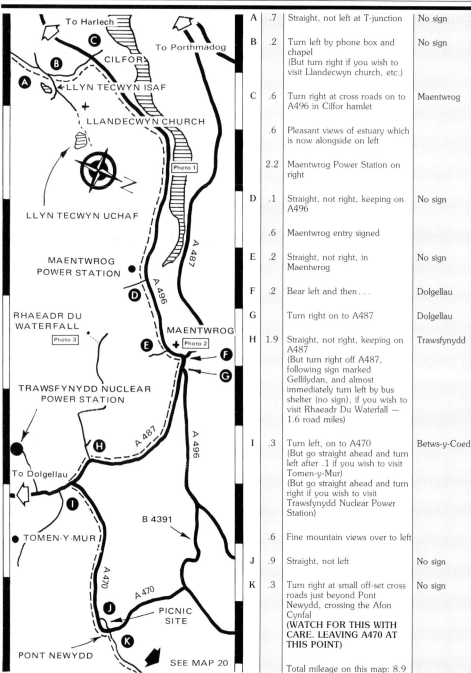

Ref.	kms / Miles	Directions	Sign-posted
A	.7	Straight, not left at T-junction	No sign
B	.2	Turn left by phone box and chapel (But turn right if you wish to visit Llandecwyn church, etc.)	No sign
C	.6	Turn right at cross roads on to A496 in Cilfor hamlet	Maentwrog
	.6	Pleasant views of estuary which is now alongside on left	
	2.2	Maentwrog Power Station on right	
D	.1	Straight, not right, keeping on A496	No sign
	.6	Maentwrog entry signed	
E	.2	Straight, not right, in Maentwrog	No sign
F	.2	Bear left and then...	Dolgellau
G		Turn right on to A487	Dolgellau
H	1.9	Straight, not right, keeping on A487 (But turn right off A487, following sign marked Gellilydan, and almost immediately turn left by bus shelter (no sign), if you wish to visit Rhaeadr Du Waterfall — 1.6 road miles)	Trawsfynydd
I	.3	Turn left, on to A470 (But go straight ahead and turn left after .1 if you wish to visit Tomen-y-Mur) (But go straight ahead and turn right if you wish to visit Trawsfynydd Nuclear Power Station)	Betws-y-Coed
	.6	Fine mountain views over to left	
J	.9	Straight, not left	No sign
K	.3	Turn right at small off-set cross roads just beyond Pont Newydd, crossing the Afon Cynfal **(WATCH FOR THIS WITH CARE. LEAVING A470 AT THIS POINT)**	No sign
		Total mileage on this map: 8.9	

CROWN COPYRIGHT RESERVED

On Route

Diversion to Llandecwyn
(Turn right at Point B)
First we pass the little reed bordered Llyn Tecwyn Isaf, where there are several opportunities to park beside the open road at the lake's edge. Then fork left (.3 beyond Point B) and climb steeply up from the lake until you reach Llandecwyn church. This is not in itself very interesting, but the views out over Tremadog Bay are very fine (including Harlech, Portmeirion and Snowdon). Beyond the church there is a track for walkers to Llyn Tecwyn Uchaf, and on over the mountains towards Maentwrog, following the course of the old coach road between Harlech and Ffestiniog.

1. Estuary road beyond Cilfor

Maentwrog Power Station
A hydro-electric power station, fed by massive pipes from Trawsfynydd Lake, which was artificially created for this purpose in the 1920s. Note the two pipes descending the hillside and the foamy outfall into the stream below the turbine house.

Maentwrog
Set in the beautiful vale of Ffestiniog, this village was built by slate magnate William Oakley in the early 19th century, and there is a lingering 'Romantic' flavour about the terraces of slate cottages beneath wooded hillsides. The church, with its little slate covered spire was entirely rebuilt by the Victorians, and has a severe, but immaculate interior. However the yew shaded churchyard contains a large stone ... Maen Twrog ... the stone of Twrog, from which the village takes its name. Legend has it that a giant by the name of Twrog, (and what a splendid name for a giant) threw it down at the church from the hills above, about the year 610.

Rhaeadr Du *(The Black Waterfall)*
For details of this 1.6 mile diversion by car from Point H, see route directions. Drive beyond the large black hydro-electric supply pipes and follow path down left, across small field and down through woods. Follow noise of the waterfall, which will be sighted between the trees, falling into a dark pool. This appears to be a remote, unspoilt place, and it is hard to believe that the Nuclear Power Station is only two miles away. (See also page 11.)

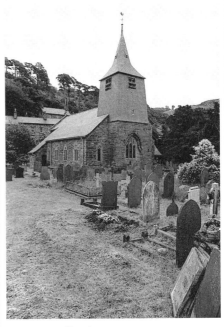
2. Maentwrog Church

Trawsfynydd Nuclear Power Station
(Go straight ahead at Point I, and then turn right.)
This impressive power station is sited on the shores of Trawsfynydd Lake, and uses no less than thirty-five million gallons of its water every hour for cooling purposes. With this amount of warm water re-circulating in the lake it is not surprising that the fishing here is excellent. (See also page 11.)

Tomen-y-Mur (See Page 11.)

3. Rhaeadr Du

Map 20

Miles	kms Ref. Miles	Directions	Sign-posted
	.8	Fine view of the dome shaped Manod Mawr ahead	
A	.3	Bear right, on to B4391	No sign
	.9	Car park on right, with good views over to right	
		Good views back right, to the Afon Cynfal valley with woods on far side. Also view beyond of Rhaeadr-y-Cwm Waterfall (See opposite)	
	.5	Over cattle-grid	
		Road now unfenced	
B	.1	Straight, not left by petrol station	Bala
		Now passing through fine open country	
	1.1	Over bridge crossing Nant-y-Groes	
	.4	Young forest on left	
	1.2	Young forest now on right	
	.8	Arennig Fach now visible ahead left	
	.8	Over bridge crossing small stream	
	.1	Over cattle-grid	
		Arennig Fawr now visible ahead	
	.4	Power cables cross road here	
C	.2	Turn left, on to A4212	Bala
		Total mileage on this map: 7.6	

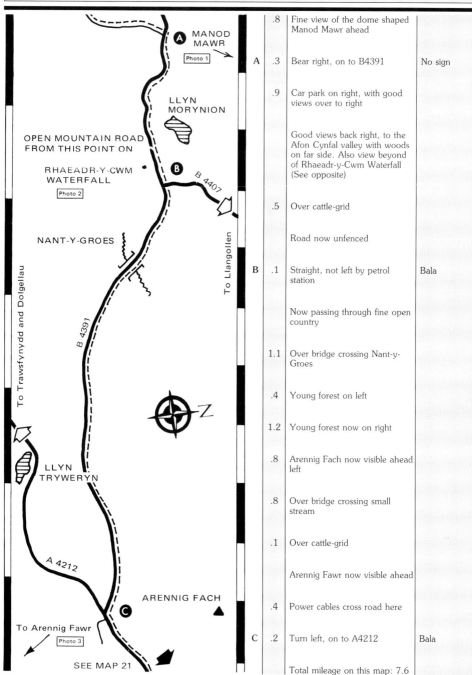

CROWN COPYRIGHT RESERVED

On Route

Manod Mawr *(The Big Mountain)*
   Large dome shaped mountain (2,166 ft.) visible ahead of us after Map 19, Point K.

Rhaeadr-y-Cwm
   These falls on the Afon Cynfal are visible from the 'viewpoint' 130 yards beyond the car park (beyond Point A). The walk along the narrow busy road between car park and viewpoint is rather dangerous and children should be supervised. However don't miss this if possible.

The Arenigs
   Our long stretch of mountain road on Map 20, although reasonably busy in summer, has a wildness about it, quite unlike anything that we have encountered since leaving Dolgellau. Its earlier stages are relatively featureless, although the foresters have been busy in recent years, with vast new plantations now becoming established on both sides of the road. About three miles beyond the filling station at Point B, two peaks come into view... Arenig Fach (2,264 ft.) over to our left, and Arenig Fawr (2,800 ft.) ahead and to the right. Arenig Fawr is the more dramatic of the two, and is topped by a small cairn, with a plaque in memory of the crew of eight United States airmen, who died when their Flying Fortress bomber crashed into the mountain in 1943.
   Do not attempt to climb Arenig Fawr (or any of the other Welsh mountains) without expert advice. May we suggest that, as a start, you purchase Ordnance Survey's Landranger Map 124 and a copy of W.A. Poucher's excellent book, *The Welsh Peaks* (Published by Constable).

Penmaenpool (See Pages 36 and 37)
   The toll-bridge over the Mawddach estuary (Open 7 a.m. until 10.30 p.m.) is overlooked by the little white painted George III Hotel.
   There is an interesting Nature Information Centre here, which is situated close to the start of the Penmaenpool — Morfa Mawddach Walk, a six-mile 'nature trail' along the course of the old railway line which used to run along the southern shore of the lovely Mawddach Estuary.

Farchynys Woodlands Walk
(See Pages 36 and 37)
   Pleasant walk down left, through oak woods to a picnic site on the Mawddach estuary... about ¾ mile.

Cors-y-Gedol (See Pages 38 and 39)
   Turn right at Point E, and follow up to the right of Cors-y-Gedol, the house of the ancient Vaughan family. Our road runs through a farmyard, and then turns, over open moorland, where there is a Neolithic burial chamber on the right (1.3 miles from main route). It is possible to drive just beyond, over Pont Fadog, which would make a good starting point for walking to Llyn Irddyn and Llyn Bodlyn, in the hills to the west.

1. Manod Mawr

2. Rhaeadr-y-Cwm

3. Arennig Fawr from our road

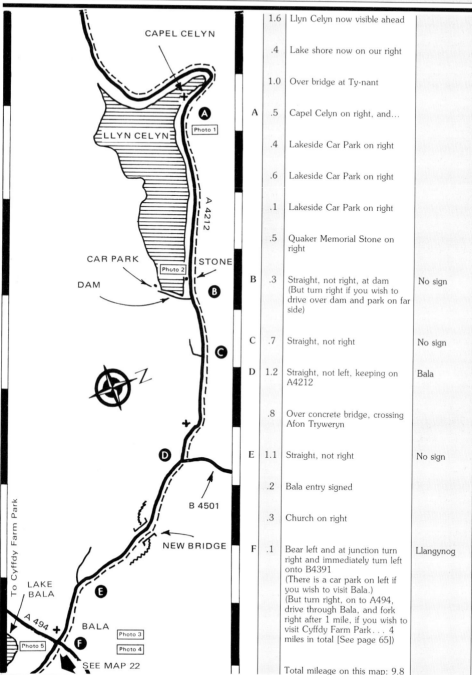

On Route

Llyn Celyn

This is a 'holding reservoir' built by Liverpool Corporation on the River Tryweryn in the 1960s to control the flow of water in the River Dee, which is joined by the Tryweryn just below Lake Bala. The design of the dam, with its sloping grass covered front and discreet outlet 'valve', is evidence of the care taken by architect Sir Frederick Gibberd to blend these works into the surrounding countryside. Whenever the works of man are imposed upon our wild places there will inevitably be criticism from one source or another, but Llyn Celyn appears to us to meet most of them.

1. Llyn Celyn

Capel Celyn

Satisfying little granite building on the shores of Llyn Celyn, replacing the chapel that lies buried beneath its waters. It contains a simple slate memorial listing the people whose remains were removed to the new graveyard behind it. An inscription reads... "The Architect had in mind a memorial resembling a ship coming in from over the waters, the curve of the north end resembling its bow". Do not miss a quiet visit here.

Quaker Memorial Stone

A large rough hewn boulder close to the Llyn Celyn dam, with a plaque reading... "Under these waters and near this stone stood Hafod Fadog, a farmstead where in the 17th and 18th centuries, Quakers met for worship. On the hillside above was a space encircled by a low stone wall where larger meetings were held and beyond the house was a small burial ground. From this valley came many of the early Quakers, who emigrated to Pennsylvania, driven from their homes by persecution to seek freedom in the New World".

2. Quaker Memorial, Llyn Celyn

Llyn Celyn Dam

Grass covered dam with a public road crossing over to a good car park on the far side. There are pleasant views eastwards down the valley from the dam road.

Bala

Busy little market town and tourist centre situated at the north-eastern end of Llyn Tegid (Bala Lake). It is well placed for those wishing to explore the eastern parts of Snowdonia, the Berwyn Mountains and Lake Vyrnwy. Most of its activity is concentrated on the long High Street (Stryd Fawr), which stretches from the bridge over the Afon Tryweryn almost to the shores of the lake, and which follows the exact course of the Roman road that ran from Chester to the nearby fort at Caer Gai and on to the coast near Dolgellau. There is a proud statue of Thomas Ellis, M.P., 'Chief Liberal Whip in 1894', a Georgian Town Hall almost opposite, and a whole series of bright and cheerful shops, restaurants and hotels.

In quieter Tegid Street will be found Capel Tegid, outside which stands the statue of Thomas Charles, the founder of the Welsh Sunday School Movement, and the British and Foreign Bible Society. It was to here that Mary Jones made her famous twenty-eight

Continued on Page 64

3. Town Hall, Bala

4. Thomas Ellis, Bala

5. Lake Bala, North West Shore

47

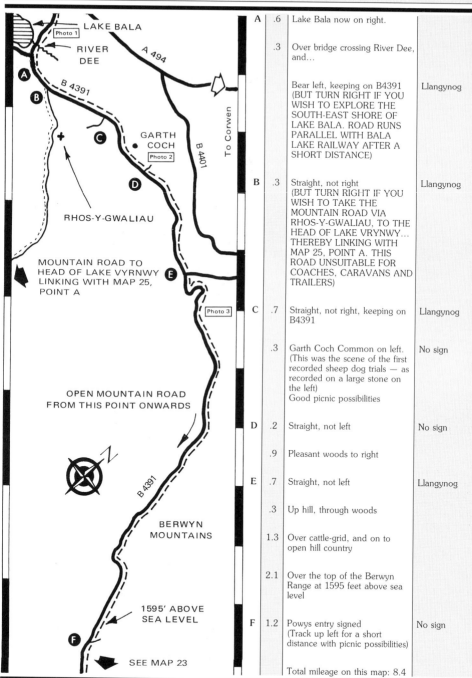

Map 22

Ref.	kms/Miles	Directions	Sign-posted
A	.6	Lake Bala now on right.	
	.3	Over bridge crossing River Dee, and...	
		Bear left, keeping on B4391 (BUT TURN RIGHT IF YOU WISH TO EXPLORE THE SOUTH-EAST SHORE OF LAKE BALA. ROAD RUNS PARALLEL WITH BALA LAKE RAILWAY AFTER A SHORT DISTANCE)	Llangynog
B	.3	Straight, not right (BUT TURN RIGHT IF YOU WISH TO TAKE THE MOUNTAIN ROAD VIA RHOS-Y-GWALIAU, TO THE HEAD OF LAKE VRYNWY... THEREBY LINKING WITH MAP 25, POINT A. THIS ROAD UNSUITABLE FOR COACHES, CARAVANS AND TRAILERS)	Llangynog
C	.7	Straight, not right, keeping on B4391	Llangynog
	.3	Garth Coch Common on left. (This was the scene of the first recorded sheep dog trials — as recorded on a large stone on the left) Good picnic possibilities	No sign
D	.2	Straight, not left	No sign
	.9	Pleasant woods to right	
E	.7	Straight, not left	Llangynog
	.3	Up hill, through woods	
	1.3	Over cattle-grid, and on to open hill country	
	2.1	Over the top of the Berwyn Range at 1595 feet above sea level	
F	1.2	Powys entry signed (Track up left for a short distance with picnic possibilities)	No sign
		Total mileage on this map: 8.4	

CROWN COPYRIGHT RESERVED

On Route

Lake Bala *(Llyn Tegid)*
As almost every guide book states, this is the largest area of natural water in Wales, being about four and a half miles long and about two thirds of a mile wide. The lake is a relatively quiet place, much favoured by anglers and sailing dinghy enthusiasts, with no power boating allowed. It is almost unique in being one of only two places in Britain where the Gwyniad, an alpine species of fish, is to be found. This is rarely caught, but the fishing on the lake is excellent generally.

There are roads down both sides of the lake, and either of these could be used to link on to Map 30 at Llanuwchllyn, or beyond it to link on to Map 16 at Dolgellau. (For Bala Lake Railway, see page 65.)

River Dee *(Afon Dyfrdwy)*
Rises beneath Dduallt, about five miles southwest of Lake Bala, flows into the lake at its southern end, and out again, at its northern end near the town of Bala.

Mountain Road Division to Lake Vyrnwy
By turning right at Point B, it is possible to follow an attractive, and sometime adventurous road through Rhos-y-Gwaliau, up wooded Cwm Hirnant, and over to the head of Lake Vyrnwy, thus linking with Map 25, Point A (about nine miles in all).

Garth Coch *(The Red Hill)*
(See Route Directions).
A pleasant area of common land bounded on the west side by a small stream flowing northwards to the Dee. It is possible to drive on to this turf and bracken covered area for picnics. Watch with care for the turn, as it can easily be missed.

The Berwyn Mountains
A wonderful mountain area extending north westwards from the shores of Lake Vyrnwy to Corwen and Llangollen in the Dee valley. They are crossed by only one road, the B4391, that we are using. The Berwyns are softer in outline than the mountains further to the west, being older and more weathered. The highest mountains of the range, Moel Sych (2,713 ft.) and Cadair Berwyn (2,712 ft.) lie about four miles to the north-east of our road (where it crosses its highest point... See Route Directions). Although they do not make a dramatic prospect, the views in this direction are broad and open, and with their covering of turf, bracken and heather, the Berwyns invite exploration on foot. Walking is in fact relatively easy, but ensure that you have the Ordnance Survey's Landranger Map 125, a compass and proper equipment generally if you plan to go far from the road... the weather can soon change, on all but the kindest of summer days.

Dyffryn Ardudwy (See Pages 38 and 39)
Do not miss the two Neolithic burial chambers behind the school (See Route Directions, Page 38). These are better specimens that that behind Cors-y-Gedol, but the setting is less elemental.

1. Lake Bala, North end

2. Garth Coch Common

3. Our road beyond Point E

4. Above Craig Wen (see page 51)

Map 23

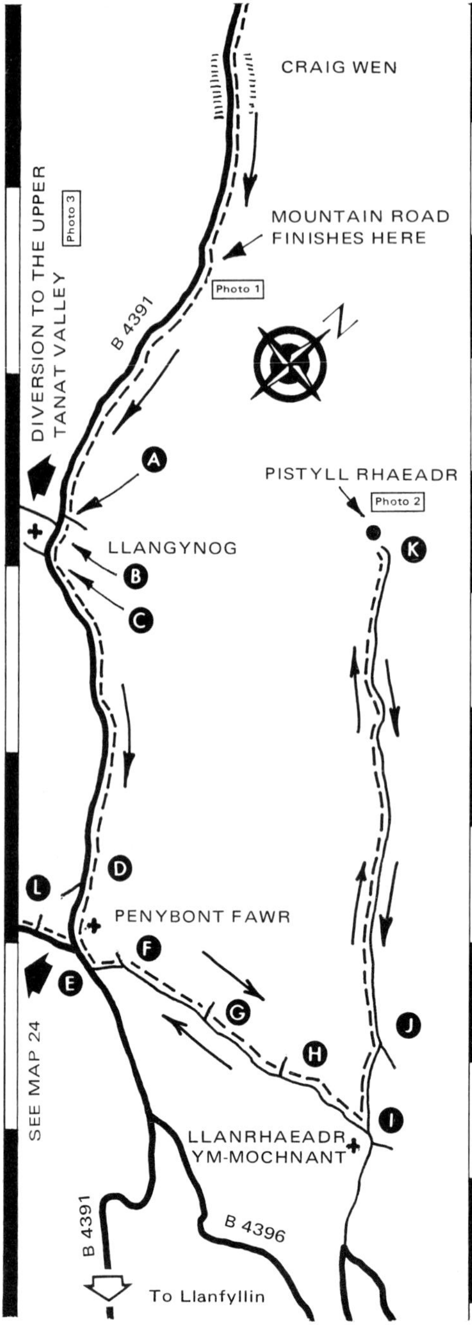

Ref.	Miles	Directions	Sign-posted
		Splendid views down this valley with our road passing across the steep, sloping crags of Craig Wen.	
	1.3	Over cattle-grid leaving the open hill country of the Berwyns	
	.9	Still descending hill	
	.6	Llangynog entry signed	
A	.6	Bear right by petrol station	Llanfyllin
B	.1	Fork left, just beyond Tanat Valley Hotel (But fork right and go straight, not right by Llangynog church if you wish to drive up the Upper Tanat Valley to Pennant Melangell church)	Llanfyllin
C	.1	Bear left by chapel, beyond bridge, keeping on B4391	No sign
D	1.8	Straight, not right	No sign
	.1	Penybont Fawr entry signed	
	.1	Church on left	
E	.1	Turn right at T-junction on to B4396	Lake Vyrnwy
		BUT GO AHEAD AND TURN LEFT BY THE RAILWAY INN, IF YOU WISH TO DIVERT TO PISTYLL RHAEADR VIA LLANRHAEADR-YM-MOCHNANT. ROUTE DETAILS ARE AS FOLLOWS:	
F	.2	Bear right at T-junction beyond bridge	No sign
G	1.0	Straight, not left at Y-junction	No sign
H	.6	Straight, not left at T-junction	No sign
	.4	Llanrhaeadr-ym-Mochnant entry signed	
	.2	Over stream, and...	
I	—	Turn left at T-junction in town	'Waterfall'
J	1.1	Straight, not right	'Waterfall'
K	2.5	Arrive at falls car park	
		NOW TURNABOUT AND RETRACE YOUR JOURNEY AS FAR AS PENYBONT FAWR, TAKING THE LAKE VYRNWY (B4396) ROAD OUT OF THE VILLAGE AT POINT E AS INDICATED ABOVE... YOU ARE NOW BACK ON THE MAIN ROUTE...	
L	.3	Straight, not right, at T-junction	No sign
		Total mileage on this map (including the 12 miles diversion to Pistyll Rhaeadr): 18.0	

CROWN COPYRIGHT RESERVED

On Route

Cwm Rhiwarth

Our road drops down from the Berwyns to Llangynog on the north-east side of this deep valley, with splendid rock faces (*craigs*) on the opposite side. For a short time the road passes over a rock face itself... the Craig Wen... and this provides a dramatic piece of driving. Nervous passengers will be grateful to us for planning a descent on the inside of this precipice road, rather than an ascent on the outside.

Llangynog

Small village situated at the point where Cwm Rhiwarth runs into the Tanat valley. There are a few shops, a hotel, and a white painted inn dated 1751. It is dominated by the spoils of old lead mines, for at one time ore was hauled from here down the railway to Pool Quay on the Severn below Welshpool, for shipment by barge to the Black Country. Today the mines are closed, the little railway gone, and Llangynog is left to sleep in the sun, dependent on sheep, summer visitors and a few enthusiastic fishermen.

Cwm Pennant – The Upper Tanat Valley

(For this diversion, turn right at Point B, and immediately go straight, not right by Llangynog church.)

This diversion of 2.1 miles each way takes us almost to the head of the lush Tanat valley, to the little Norman church of Pennant Melangell. If you wish to visit the church, turn down left after 1.4 to collect the key from Mr. Jones at Tan-y-Foel Farm. The church is in a lovely setting with high hills on both sides of the valley. It is a neat little building, with a pleasant, wooden slatted, belfry (a reminder of the Border Country this) upon its squat tower, and a simple porch marked 'Edward Madock and David Thomas 1737'. The interior contains a pleasant 15th century rood screen and two effigies, one of whom is supposed to be of St. Melangell herself.

Penybont Fawr

An unremarkable village in the Tanat valley with a few shops (including one that provides fish and chips) and the Railway Inn... a lingering reminder of the days when trains used to pass this way up the Tanat Valley Railway to its terminus at Llangynog.

Pistyll Rhaeadr

(For details of this six miles each way diversion, see Route Directions opposite.)

This diversion to one of the 'Seven Wonders of Wales' should not be missed, for here at the head of a long narrow valley, the Afon Disgynfa falls over a sheer cliff about 230 feet, and the total height of the falls is over 300 feet. The rock face at the end of the valley, over which the stream falls is framed with trees, and being lucky enough to come here on a quiet sunny day in early spring, we were delighted with the whole sparkling scene.

1. Above Llangynog

2. Pistyll Rhaeadr

3. Pennant Melangell Church

Map 24

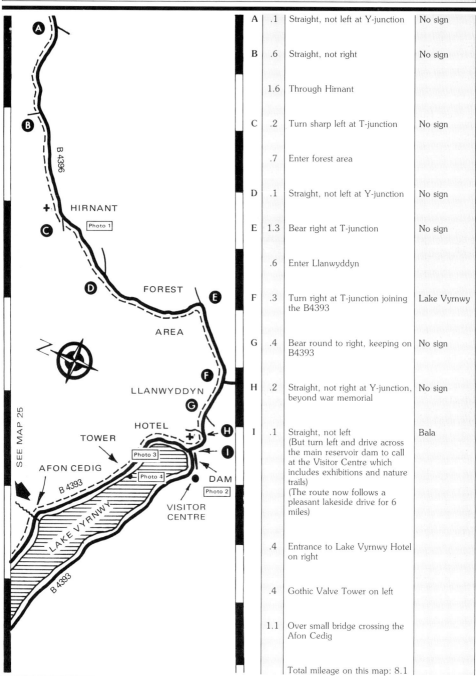

Ref	kms/Miles	Directions	Sign-posted
A	.1	Straight, not left at Y-junction	No sign
B	.6	Straight, not right	No sign
	1.6	Through Hirnant	
C	.2	Turn sharp left at T-junction	No sign
	.7	Enter forest area	
D	.1	Straight, not left at Y-junction	No sign
E	1.3	Bear right at T-junction	No sign
	.6	Enter Llanwyddyn	
F	.3	Turn right at T-junction joining the B4393	Lake Vyrnwy
G	.4	Bear round to right, keeping on B4393	No sign
H	.2	Straight, not right at Y-junction, beyond war memorial	No sign
I	.1	Straight, not left (But turn left and drive across the main reservoir dam to call at the Visitor Centre which includes exhibitions and nature trails) (The route now follows a pleasant lakeside drive for 6 miles)	Bala
	.4	Entrance to Lake Vyrnwy Hotel on right	
	.4	Gothic Valve Tower on left	
	1.1	Over small bridge crossing the Afon Cedig	
		Total mileage on this map: 8.1	

CROWN COPYRIGHT RESERVED

On Route

Hirnant
Attractive hamlet in Cwm Hirnant, with church and chapel, small post office stores, and a pleasant farm house.

Llanwyddyn Forest Area
We were unfortunate to pass this way twice when major clearing operations were in progress, and the roads and hillsides looked more like a battlefield than a forest. However this area should usually provide a fitting introduction to Lake Vyrnwy. Llanwyddyn itself is a Forestry Commission 'model village' and not of much interest to visitors. Check your petrol before passing the filling station at Point F... it will be some time before you pass another.

Lake Vyrnwy
This is the main source of water for Liverpool Corporation, and was formed by the building of a dam in the late 19th century... an age when man was still proud of his ability to impose his will upon the wild places, and leave his mark for all time. The massive stone dam and 'Gothic' valve tower rising like Chateau Chillon from the waters of the lake, provide an interesting contrast with the more modest approach used by the same Corporation some seventy years later at Llyn Celyn (See Page 47). We think that both solutions have their own merits, and will comment no further. Do not miss a visit to the interesting Vyrnwy Visitor Centre, with its exhibitions, maps, leaflets and nature trails — ☎ (0691) 73278.

The woodlands planted soon after the lake was formed, have now matured, and the road around it, with trees and rhododendrons often providing a frame for our views across the water, is a warm and domesticated section of our route... in marked contrast to the wilder mountain section ahead. We saw a red squirrel here... the first that we had seen from our car for several years.

Cwm Nantcol (See Pages 38 and 39)
(Try to visit at non-peak times)
Our road beyond Point H, Map 17 is narrow and enclosed on both sides by stone walls and careful driving is most essential. However the view of the Rhinogs that eventually reveals itself is well worth any trouble taken. Be sure to follow this road up the cwm to its conclusion by turning right at Point K. Maes-y-Garnedd (*The Field of Stones*) Farm, at the end of our road, was the birthplace of John Jones, a brother-in-law of Oliver Cromwell, and one of the regicide judges.

This is a wonderfully tranquil place (we visited it in March) and it is possible to walk from here over the Bwlch Drws (*The Pass of the Doors*), between Rhinog Fach and Rhinog Fawr, to the A470 road about six miles to the east. By bearing to the left after about three miles beyond Maes-y-Garnedd, it is possible to link back (on foot) to the Roman Steps (See Page 41), but make sure that you have the additional guidance of the Ordnance Survey's Landranger Map 124 before attempting either of these walks.

1. *Beyond Hirnant*

2. *The Vyrnwy Dam*

3. *Lake Vyrnwy*

4. *Valve Tower, Lake Vyrnwy*

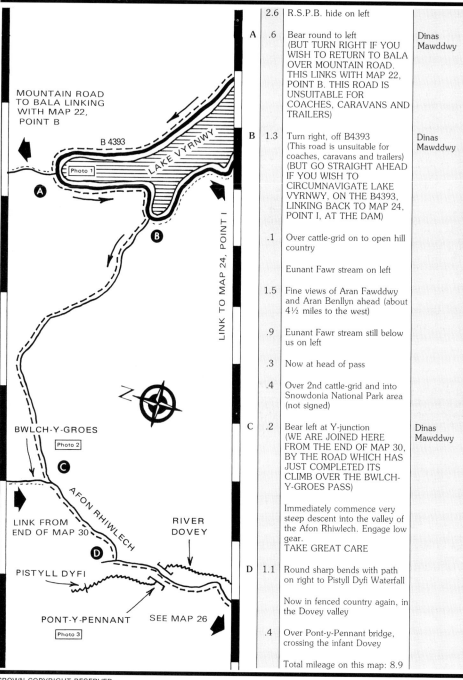

On Route

Mountain Road Diversion to Bala

By turning right at Point A, it is possible to follow an attractive and sometimes adventurous road over the hills, down Cwm Hirnant, through Rhos-y-Gwaliau, turning left and left again, on to B4391, and following in to Bala... thus making a self contained circular route.

Mountain Road towards Bwlch-y-Groes
(Pass of the Cross)

This leaves Lake Vyrnwy by way of the Eunant valley, and climbs, sometimes steeply, up to the moors of Waun-y-Gadfa, and, after 3.4 miles, reaches a road junction (Point C). Our main circle route goes to the left, but if you turn right and drive for only .3, you will arrive at a car parking space on the left. This marks the head of Bwlch-y-Groes, which at 1,790 feet above sea level is the highest pass crossed by a road in Wales. There are splendid views northwards down Cwm Cynllwyd towards the Arenigs, and westwards to Aran Fawddwy and Aran Benllyn. And now back to the main route....

Afon Rhiwlech Valley

The descent from Point C (just below Bwlch-y-Groes) is very steep, and we would advise all drivers to keep in low gear for about a mile. The Afon Rhiwlech is not very special, but the sweeping black rocks and scree of Craig-y-Pant beyond it brings real drama to this steep road down into the Dovey valley.

Blaen Pennant Waterfalls and The Dovey Valley

The Dovey (or *Dyfi* as we should call it) rises in a beautiful little tarn, Creiglyn Dyfi, beneath the rocky cliffs of Aran Fawddwy (not visible from our road). Our first sight of the Dovey could be at the long series of waterfalls beyond Blaen Pennant Farm (Point D) which we assume to be called the Pistyll Dyfi, and which is overlooked by the rocks of Ogof Ddu (*The Black Cave*).

From this point onwards we shall follow the Dovey down its valley as far as Dinas Mawddwy. The valley bottom is principally devoted to farming, and the road is walled in or hedged in, but there are rhododendrons in many of the hedges, and on some of the mountain slopes above.

Harlech *Continued from Page 41*

fortresses to contain the Welsh, it was of considerable importance until the 16th century. It also had a brief hour of glory in the 17th century, being the last Royalist stronghold in Britain to surrender to Parliament (1647). Its superb over-all design remains absolutely clear today, with its four great towers at the corners of the curtain walls... all sited magnificently above the coastline... a perfect example of the real beauty that lies in strength of purpose. Do not miss a visit here, for the views out over Tremadog Bay to the Snowdon range and the long line of the Lleyn Peninsula, will never be quite forgotten, once you have looked out from the tall battlements of Harlech — ☏ (0766) 780552.

1. Lake Vyrnwy

2. Bwlch-y-Groes

3. Shearing Time near Pont-y-Pennant

Map 26

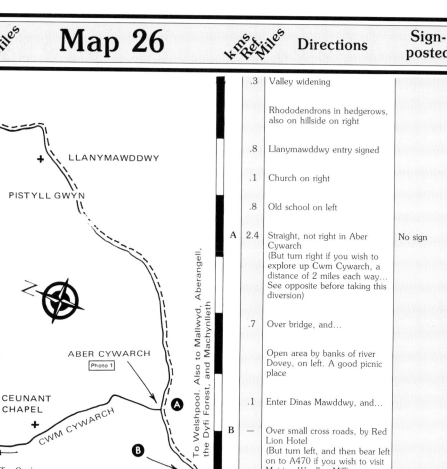

WATERFALL

SEE MAP 27

CROWN COPYRIGHT RESERVED

Ref.	kms / Miles	Directions	Sign-posted
	.3	Valley widening	
		Rhododendrons in hedgerows, also on hillside on right	
	.8	Llanymawddwy entry signed	
	.1	Church on right	
	.8	Old school on left	
A	2.4	Straight, not right in Aber Cywarch (But turn right if you wish to explore up Cwm Cywarch, a distance of 2 miles each way... See opposite before taking this diversion)	No sign
	.7	Over bridge, and...	
		Open area by banks of river Dovey, on left. A good picnic place	
	.1	Enter Dinas Mawddwy, and...	
B	—	Over small cross roads, by Red Lion Hotel (But turn left, and then bear left on to A470 if you wish to visit Meirion Woollen Mill) (Also turn left here if you wish to visit Mallwyd, Aberangell and the Dyfi Forest, or Machynlleth... [See pages 130–139])	
C	.2	Bear right, on to A470	Dolgellau
D	.6	Straight, not left, keeping on A470	No sign
		Fine open road with extensive valley views	
E	.4	Straight, not right, keeping on A470	No sign
		Dramatic waterfall, visible ahead right, coming right down mountainside in various stages	
		Total mileage on this map: 6.1	

On Route

Llanymawddwy

An unusually pretty village sheltering in the upper Dovey valley with colourful cottage gardens, and a small church. This is approached beneath a neat lychgate, and contains within, a medieval octagonal font with scalloped edges (giving it the appearance of an inverted acorn). Ask in the village for the best directions for Pistyll Gwyn (*The White Waterfall*), which lies about a mile and a half to the west of our road. We confess that we have not visited this, but understand that it is well worth the walk.

1. Cottages at Aber Cywarch

Aber Cywarch

Pleasant hamlet close to the point where the Afon Cywarch flows into the Dovey, with two pretty terraces of cottages overlooking our road at Point A.

Diversion up Cwm Cywarch

(For experienced hill walkers or climbers.)

This road diversion of two miles each way takes us within sight of the towering rock face of Craig Cywarch. This is itself a favourite with rock climbers, but the car parking space near the end of the road is also the best access point for those who wish to tackle the Aran group via the Hengwm valley. (May we again recommend W. A. Poucher's *The Welsh Peaks* for this expedition.)

Dinas Mawddwy

... at present little more than a collection of filthy huts. But though a dirty squalid place, I found it anything but silent and deserted. Fierce-looking red-haired banditti of old, were staggering about, and sounds of drunken revelry echoed from the huts...

Things seemed to have settled down since George Borrow visited Dinas Mawddwy in 1854, when, as he observed, the place seems to have been dominated by miners and quarrymen.

Although Dinas never seems to have fully recovered economically from the closure of its lead mines and slate quarries, it now has at least one fascinating industry in addition to the inevitable forestry. This is the Meirion Woollen Mill, which is now based at the old railway yard, and which produces a variety of Welsh woollen cloths. This is open to visitors, together with a well stocked showroom and a cafe (in the old station). (Turn left at Point B, follow out on A470, and turn right by the Buckley Arms.)

2. Dinas Mawddwy

While visiting the mill do not miss the short walk from the car park to see the historic Pont Minllyn. This is a beautiful little twin-arched bridge built by Rev. Dr. John Davies, a famous Welsh scholar who was rector of neighbouring Mallwyd from 1604 to 1644. A study of Landranger Sheet 124 will also reveal good walking possibilities in the Dinas Mawddwy area, including a pleasant circular walk passing close to Pen-y-graig and Hendref, both to the east of the village, beyond the Dyfi, and another walk to the west of the village, up into afforested mountainside country.

3. At the Meirion Mill

Map 27

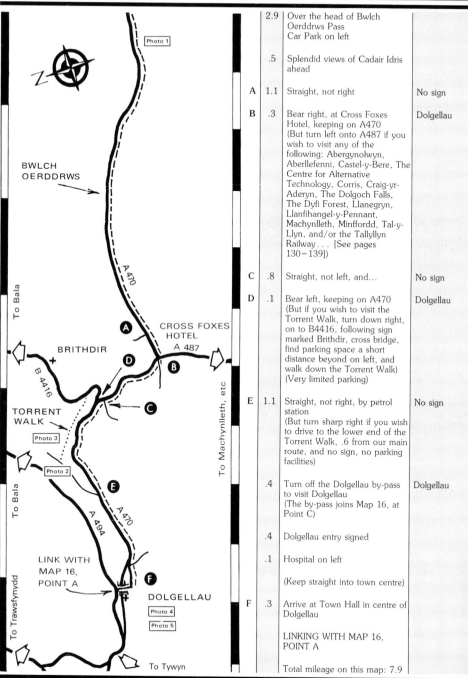

	kms Ref. Miles	Directions	Sign-posted
	2.9	Over the head of Bwlch Oerddrws Pass Car Park on left	
	.5	Splendid views of Cadair Idris ahead	
A	1.1	Straight, not right	No sign
B	.3	Bear right, at Cross Foxes Hotel, keeping on A470 (But turn left onto A487 if you wish to visit any of the following: Abergynolwyn, Aberllefenni, Castel-y-Bere, The Centre for Alternative Technology, Corris, Craig-yr-Aderyn, The Dolgoch Falls, The Dyfi Forest, Llanegryn, Llanfihangel-y-Pennant, Machynlleth, Minffordd, Tal-y-Llyn, and/or the Tallyllyn Railway... [See pages 130–139])	Dolgellau
C	.8	Straight, not left, and...	No sign
D	.1	Bear left, keeping on A470 (But if you wish to visit the Torrent Walk, turn down right, on to B4416, following sign marked Brithdir, cross bridge, find parking space a short distance beyond on left, and walk down the Torrent Walk) (Very limited parking)	Dolgellau
E	1.1	Straight, not right, by petrol station (But turn sharp right if you wish to drive to the lower end of the Torrent Walk, .6 from our main route, and no sign, no parking facilities)	No sign
	.4	Turn off the Dolgellau by-pass to visit Dolgellau (The by-pass joins Map 16, at Point C)	Dolgellau
	.4	Dolgellau entry signed	
	.1	Hospital on left	
		(Keep straight into town centre)	
F	.3	Arrive at Town Hall in centre of Dolgellau	
		LINKING WITH MAP 16, POINT A	
		Total mileage on this map: 7.9	

CROWN COPYRIGHT RESERVED

On Route

Bwlch Oerddrws (*The Pass of the Cold Door*)
This very appropriately named pass is crossed by the busy A470, and is not our favourite stretch of route. The road is fenced, and there is one small car park at the head of the pass (1065 ft.). However once the descent westwards is well under way, splendid views of Cader Idris (*The Chair of Idris*) develop and the countryside opens out considerably.

The Torrent Walk

(Access to this 'Walk' may be made via Points D or E... See Route Directions.)
This famous footpath is within the bounds of the Caernywch Estate, but is open to the public by permission of the owners. The 'Walk', under a mile in length, follows the south western side of the Clywedog stream, which is boulder strewn and tree shaded for the entire length of the walk. Here, on a sunny day in summer, are tree shaded pools, with shafts of sunlight upon a seemingly endless series of falls. However when we last visited here on a July afternoon after heavy rain, the force of the torrent was deafening, and spray hung in the air beneath dripping trees.

Car parking space is very limited at the top access point (beyond Point D), but non-existent at the bottom access (beyond Point E).

Dolgellau (See Page 36 and opposite)

Beautifully sited below the northern slopes of Cadair Idris, in the broad, wooded valley of the Afon Wnion, a short distance above its confluence with the Mawddach, Dolgellau is a natural route centre and a great favourite with visitors. Until the creation of the new enlarged county of Gwynedd, it was the administrative capital of the now absorbed county of Meirionnydd (Merioneth). It is still a busy market town, with a cattle and sheep market each Friday, and has a pleasantly vital air every day of the week. Built of lightish grey granite and slate, its buildings have a quiet dignity, especially in the area around its market square, where most of them are early 19th century in origin. Shops, inns, public buildings and hotels — all have a welcoming look, and road traffic through the centre, now happily much reduced by a bypass, is slowed to a modest pace when faced with the delightful irregularity of its street plan.

These narrow lanes, with their character shops and restaurants are well worth exploring, and not far to the north of the square will be found a fine seven-arched bridge over the Afon Wnion, with a Tourist Information Centre at its town end — ☎ (0341) 422888). Near the main car park in the town centre will be found Bryn Melyn Studio, where craftsmen may be seen at their work and where a wide variety of craft produce may be purchased.

The Parish Church has a medieval tower, a broad 18th century nave, and an apsidal chancel built in the 19th century. The interior is very pleasing, with an attractively lit dome-shaped ceiling to the chancel, unusually beautiful Victorian stained glass, and the effigy of a knight below one of the windows — Meurig Ap Ynyr Fychan of Nannau (see page 37), who died in 1350.

1. Bwlch Oerddrws

2. Torrent Walk – Bridge over Afon Clywedog

3. Afon Clywedog – Torrent Walk

4. Window in Dolgellau Church

5. The Royal Ship Hotel, Dolgellau

Map 28

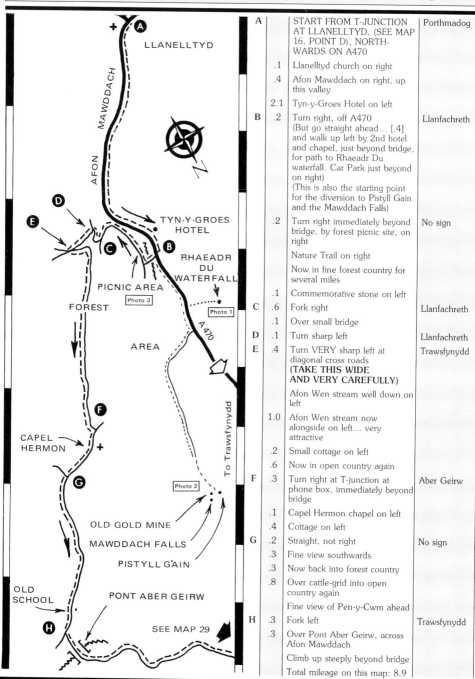

	Miles	Directions	Sign-posted
A		START FROM T-JUNCTION AT LLANELLTYD, (SEE MAP 16, POINT D), NORTHWARDS ON A470	Porthmadog
	.1	Llanelltyd church on right	
	.4	Afon Mawddach on right, up this valley	
	2.1	Tyn-y-Groes Hotel on left	
B	.2	Turn right, off A470 (But go straight ahead... [.4] and walk up left by 2nd hotel and chapel, just beyond bridge, for path to Rhaeadr Du waterfall. Car Park just beyond on right) (This is also the starting point for the diversion to Pistyll Gain and the Mawddach Falls)	Llanfachreth
	.2	Turn right immediately beyond bridge, by forest picnic site, on right	No sign
		Nature Trail on right	
		Now in fine forest country for several miles	
	.1	Commemorative stone on left	
C	.6	Fork right	Llanfachreth
	.1	Over small bridge	
D	.1	Turn sharp left	Llanfachreth
E	.4	Turn VERY sharp left at diagonal cross roads **(TAKE THIS WIDE AND VERY CAREFULLY)**	Trawsfynydd
		Afon Wen stream well down on left	
	1.0	Afon Wen stream now alongside on left... very attractive	
	.2	Small cottage on left	
	.6	Now in open country again	
F	.3	Turn right at T-junction at phone box, immediately beyond bridge	Aber Geirw
	.1	Capel Hermon chapel on left	
	.4	Cottage on left	
G	.2	Straight, not right	No sign
	.3	Fine view southwards	
	.3	Now back into forest country	
	.8	Over cattle-grid into open country again	
		Fine view of Pen-y-Cwm ahead	
H	.3	Fork left	Trawsfynydd
	.3	Over Pont Aber Geirw, across Afon Mawddach	
		Climb up steeply beyond bridge	
		Total mileage on this map: 8.9	

CROWN COPYRIGHT RESERVED

On Route

Llanelltyd (See Page 37 for Llanelltyd Bridge)
Neat village much disturbed by busy road traffic. However it has an exceptionally pleasant little, long low church, in a churchyard with old yew trees, looking out over the Mawddach valley. It has a series of early 19th century round headed windows, an attractive old north door within a small porch, and inside, a Jacobean pulpit, an interesting monument to Sir Robert Howell Vaughan, and the story of a chalice, which once belonged to Cymmer Abbey (See Page 37), and which was found on a nearby mountainside.

Rhaeadr Du *(The Black, or Dark, Waterfall)*
A Diversion
Go straight ahead at Point B, park on the right after .4, and walk back a few yards, leave the road by the side of a small chapel, walk up steep road through oak and beech wood, and then branch off along signed path, following noise of water.

Pistyll Gain and The Mawddach Falls
A Diversion
Go straight ahead at Point B, for .8, fork right, off A470 at de-restriction sign at end of Ganyllwyd, over small bridge, and immediately straight, not left. After .2 pass saw mill. After 1.2 park car at end of track. (Access for cars not allowed beyond this point.) Walk past bungalow, and take path off to right after about half a mile. Follow path to falls.

The two falls are fairly close to each other, Pistyll Gain is on the left, as we arrive, and is the tallest, and the Mawddach Falls are over to the right, and are greater in volume, and more impressive. Between the two falls, just above the confluence of the two streams, is a tongue of land with the extensive remains of gold workings (only discontinued in 1939), but the charm of this area lies in the falls and the heavily wooded valley in which they lie, a place of oak, beech, and pine, with the aroma of thyme heavy in the still summer air. Let us hope that this enchanted place does not once again fall victim to our desperate need for mineral wealth, for next time, there would be no modest mine entrances and waste spoils, but great swathes of open cast workings.

Coed-y-Brenin *(The King's Forest)*
This is a magnificent forest area, stretching some six miles north from Llanelltyd, and our route through the forest is well over three miles in length. There is a Forest Trail starting from the Picnic Site at Tyn-y-Groes (See Route Directions), and another at Dolgefeiliau on A470, about two and a half miles north of Tyn-y-Groes. At both points descriptive leaflets are available. There are of course a multitude of walks possible in the forest area, but following one of these trails will provide a most interesting introduction to the trees, the wildlife, the geology, and the scenery of Coed-y-Brenin.

Capel Hermon (See Page 63)

1. At Rhaeadr Du

2. The Mawddach Falls

3. Afon Mawddach and Coed-y-Brenin

4. Beyond Capel Hermon

Map 29

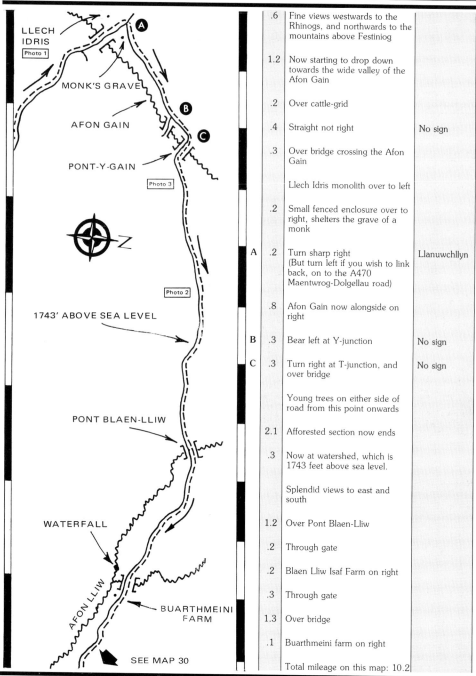

kms Ref Miles	Directions	Sign-posted
.6	Fine views westwards to the Rhinogs, and northwards to the mountains above Festiniog	
1.2	Now starting to drop down towards the wide valley of the Afon Gain	
.2	Over cattle-grid	
.4	Straight not right	No sign
.3	Over bridge crossing the Afon Gain	
	Llech Idris monolith over to left	
.2	Small fenced enclosure over to right, shelters the grave of a monk	
A .2	Turn sharp right (But turn left if you wish to link back, on to the A470 Maentwrog-Dolgellau road)	Llanuwchllyn
.8	Afon Gain now alongside on right	
B .3	Bear left at Y-junction	No sign
C .3	Turn right at T-junction, and over bridge	No sign
	Young trees on either side of road from this point onwards	
2.1	Afforested section now ends	
.3	Now at watershed, which is 1743 feet above sea level.	
	Splendid views to east and south	
1.2	Over Pont Blaen-Lliw	
.2	Through gate	
.2	Blaen Lliw Isaf Farm on right	
.3	Through gate	
1.3	Over bridge	
.1	Buarthmeini farm on right	
	Total mileage on this map: 10.2	

CROWN COPYRIGHT RESERVED

On Route

Capel Hermon (See Pages 60 and 61)
Small chapel beyond Point F, delightfully situated in the very heart of the Coed-y-Brenin Forest.

Llech Idris (*The Slate of Idris*)
A large upstanding monolith, possibly prehistoric, overlooking our low bridge across the Afon Gain, from a point a few hundred yards to the west.

1. Llech Idris

Monk's Grave
A stone slab surrounded by rusting iron railings a short distance over to our right, beyond the Afon Gain bridge. This is apparently inscribed in Latin 'HERE LIES PORIUS, A PLAIN MAN', but we could find no trace of this humble epitaph.

Our Route Over The Watershed
The country lying to the east of our bridge over the Afon Gain used to be an army firing range, but it now provides us with a splendidly remote piece of mountain route over seven miles in length. First we follow the Gain valley, and then up into young conifer plantations... make the most of the fine views back west, most of them will be lost when the trees grow up a few more feet.
Shortly after leaving the afforested section we reach the watershed between the rivers flowing west to Tremadog Bay and those feeding the Dee which flows north east to Liverpool Bay. The road here is at 1,743 feet above sea level, which is only 47 feet lower than Bwlch-y-Groes, but here we are almost on the top of wide open country, and not within the close confines of a pass. There are now fine views eastwards to the Berwyns, and south-eastwards to the Arans.

Rhaeadr Buarth Meini
This waterfall is over to the right of our road, just before Buarth Meini Farm, but it is on private property, and visits do not appear to be encouraged.

2. Afon Gain Country

Ynys (See Pages 40 and 41)
Quite hamlet beside the Traeth Bach 'estuary', with wide views northwards to the mountains of central Snowdonia, and the white lighthouse of Portmerion just across the water... a romantic place, especially in winter-time, when the saltings shelter oyster catchers, curlews, shelduck and teal; and low sunshine lights up the icy mudflats.

3. Bridge beyond Point C

Map 30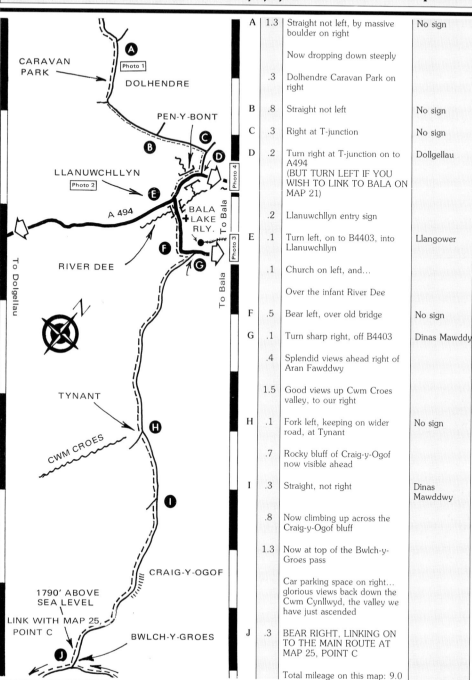

Ref	kms/Miles	Directions	Sign-posted
A	1.3	Straight not left, by massive boulder on right	No sign
		Now dropping down steeply	
	.3	Dolhendre Caravan Park on right	
B	.8	Straight not left	No sign
C	.3	Right at T-junction	No sign
D	.2	Turn right at T-junction on to A494 (BUT TURN LEFT IF YOU WISH TO LINK TO BALA ON MAP 21)	Dollgellau
	.2	Llanuwchllyn entry sign	
E	.1	Turn left, on to B4403, into Llanuwchllyn	Llangower
	.1	Church on left, and...	
		Over the infant River Dee	
F	.5	Bear left, over old bridge	No sign
G	.1	Turn sharp right, off B4403	Dinas Mawddy
	.4	Splendid views ahead right of Aran Fawddwy	
	1.5	Good views up Cwm Croes valley, to our right	
H	.1	Fork left, keeping on wider road, at Tynant	No sign
	.7	Rocky bluff of Craig-y-Ogof now visible ahead	
I	.3	Straight, not right	Dinas Mawddwy
	.8	Now climbing up across the Craig-y-Ogof bluff	
	1.3	Now at top of the Bwlch-y-Groes pass	
		Car parking space on right... glorious views back down the Cwm Cynllwyd, the valley we have just ascended	
J	.3	BEAR RIGHT, LINKING ON TO THE MAIN ROUTE AT MAP 25, POINT C	
		Total mileage on this map: 9.0	

CROWN COPYRIGHT RESERVED

On Route

Penybont
An old stone bridge across the Lliw, a short distance above its confluence with the Dee. It is visible from our road just before Point D.

Llanuwchllyn
We liked the statue of Sir O. M. Edwards, as a youth, at Point E. He was one of the great advocates for the teaching of Welsh in schools, and is buried in the Methodist cemetery in the village. The Old School House and the decorated, cast iron village pump in front of it, are just beyond, and both add a touch of character to an otherwise rather unexciting village.

Bala Lake Railway
This runs along the south-eastern shore of Bala Lake for 4½ miles, from Bala Station to Llanuwchllyn, following the course of an old main railway line. From Easter to mid-October steam and diesel locomotives which once worked in the slate quarries of North Wales now haul passenger coaches, some open, some closed, so that visitors can enjoy the views of mountains and lake in all weathers. Bala Station is within walking distance of the High Street, and at Llanuwchllyn there is a free car park and light refreshments ☏ (0678) 4666 *for further details.*

Cwm Cynllwyd
A pleasant wide valley running up south-eastwards to Bwlch-y-Groes (See Page 55). Our road follows along the eastern slope and looks down, at times almost vertically, on small farmsteads and across to the peak of Aran Benllyn. We pass the hamlet of Ty Nant. *(The House of the Dingle),* where George Borrow stopped to talk to 'a smiling young woman', and felt himself to be 'now indeed in Wales amongst the real Welsh'. Beyond Ty Nant, and near the head of the pass the road crosses the Craig-y-Ogof *(The Crag of the Cave),* and is poised dramatically over the highest of the valley farms below. And so to Bwlch-y-Groes itself... a fitting place to end our exploration of this enchanted country... amongst the mountains of Borrow's 'real Wales'.

Bala *Continued from Page 47*
mile walk from Llanfihangel-y-Pennant to collect her bible from Charles (see also page 136). The Tomen y Bala lies on the north side of the town, behind the Old Grammar School, and is almost certainly the remains of a Norman castle earthwork. The Victorian Parish Church, Eglwys Crist (Christ Church) is not of great architectural interest to visitors. Throughout the summer there is a most helpful Visitor Centre run by the Snowdonia National Park in the High Street — ☏ (0678) 520367.

Cyffdy Farm Park lies some four miles to the south-west of the town (see Route Directions, Point F) and has a number of rare breeds and paddock animals, together with opportunities for fishing and riding, a collection of old farm machinery, a Pets' Corner and children's playground, and demonstrations of hand milking — ☏ (0678) 4271.

1. Stream at Dolhendre

2. Llanuwchllyn

3. The Bala Lake Railway   (Photo by P. Ward)

4. Bala Lake (see also pages 47 and 49)

ANGLESEY KEY MAP

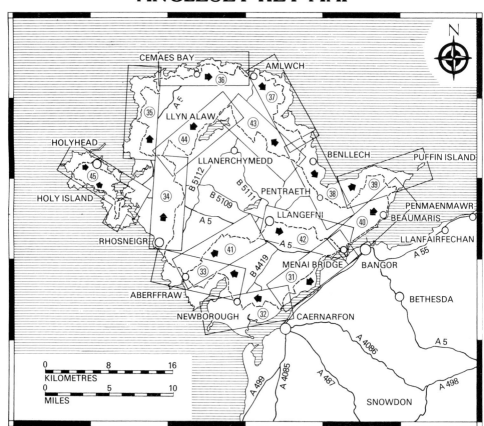

CROWN COPYRIGHT RESERVED

Beaumaris Castle

EXPLORING ANGLESEY

The Menai Suspension Bridge

Anglesey's most striking feature is without doubt its long and splendid coastline and our main circle route follows this for almost its entire length — a distance of nearly 90 miles. Here will be found bird-haunted cliffs and islands, a succession of beautiful sandy bays, many of which are deeply indented between dramatic rocky headlands. There is also a diversion which encircles Holy Island, its rocky shores being a special delight for bird-watchers. Our cross routes penentrate Anglesey's quiet and largely unspoilt interior, and this gentle landscape also has many secrets, including two reservoirs, many small medieval churches and a series of fascinating prehistoric monuments.

Map 31

Miles	kms Ref Miles	Directions	Sign-posted

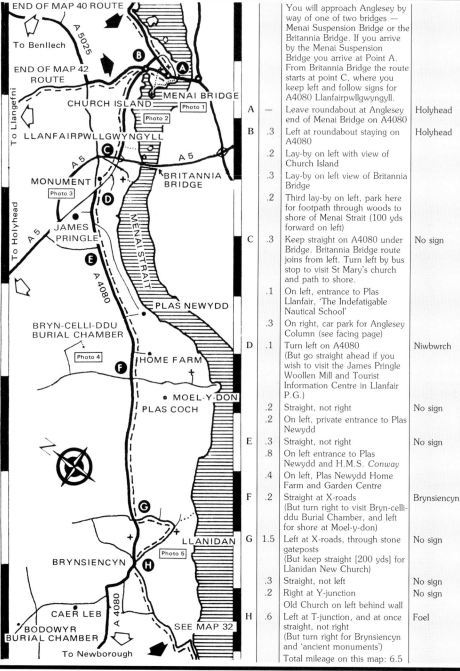

You will approach Anglesey by way of one of two bridges — Menai Suspension Bridge or the Britannia Bridge. If you arrive by the Menai Suspension Bridge you arrive at Point A. From Britannia Bridge the route starts at point C, where you keep left and follow signs for A4080 Llanfairpwllgwyngyll.

		Directions	Sign-posted
A	—	Leave roundabout at Anglesey end of Menai Bridge on A4080	Holyhead
B	.3	Left at roundabout staying on A4080	Holyhead
	.2	Lay-by on left with view of Church Island	
	.3	Lay-by on left view of Britannia Bridge	
	.2	Third lay-by on left, park here for footpath through woods to shore of Menai Strait (100 yds forward on left)	
C	.3	Keep straight on A4080 under Bridge. Britannia Bridge route joins from left. Turn left by bus stop to visit St Mary's church and path to shore.	No sign
	.1	On left, entrance to Plas Llanfair, 'The Indefatigable Nautical School'	
	.3	On right, car park for Anglesey Column (see facing page)	
D	.1	Turn left on A4080 (But go straight ahead if you wish to visit the James Pringle Woollen Mill and Tourist Information Centre in Llanfair P.G.)	Niwbwrch
	.2	Straight, not right	No sign
	.2	On left, private entrance to Plas Newydd	
E	.3	Straight, not right	No sign
	.8	On left entrance to Plas Newydd and H.M.S. *Conway*	
	.4	On left, Plas Newydd Home Farm and Garden Centre	
F	.2	Straight at X-roads (But turn right to visit Bryn-celli-ddu Burial Chamber, and left for shore at Moel-y-don)	Brynsiencyn
G	1.5	Left at X-roads, through stone gateposts (But keep straight [200 yds] for Llanidan New Church)	No sign
	.3	Straight, not left	No sign
	.2	Right at Y-junction	No sign
		Old Church on left behind wall	
H	.6	Left at T-junction, and at once straight, not right (But turn right for Brynsiencyn and 'ancient monuments')	Foel
		Total mileage on this map: 6.5	

CROWN COPYRIGHT RESERVED

On Route

Menai Suspension Bridge
This famous bridge was designed by Thomas Telford and opened in 1826. It is 1,000 feet long, with a central span of 579 feet; the roadway is 100 feet above high water, the minimum height which the Admiralty demanded to avoid interference with shipping.

Menai Bridge Town (See Page 91)

Llanfairpwllgwyngyll
This is the correct name of the village, but with an early eye to tourism a local tradesman expanded it to 'Llanfairpwllgwyngyllgogerychwyrndrobwllllantysiliogogogoch', meaning 'St. Mary's Church in the hollow of the white hazel near to the rapid whirlpool of Llandysilio of the red cave'. For practical purposes the name is shortened to Llanfairpwll, or even Llanfair P.G. Signs making use of the full title may be seen over a newsagents, a garage, and at the railway station. The latter is now operated by James Pringle, who have a large woollen shop here, together with a restaurant and Tourist Information Centre — ☏ (0248) 713177.

The Parish Church, rebuilt in 1853, lies between A5 and the Strait. An Obelisk in the churchyard commemorates those who died during the building of the Britannia Bridge. From the church a footpath leads down to the shore, where there is a 19th century monument to Nelson.

Britannia Bridge
This bridge was built by Robert Stephenson in 1850 to carry the main railway line to Holyhead, and consisted of two rectangular tubes, 1500 feet long. After a disastrous fire in 1970 a second tier was built to carry extra road traffic. With the more recent construction linking the bridge to the A5, this has become the main entrance by road to the Isle of Anglesey.

Plas Newydd (NT)
This fine early 19th century house, home of the Marquess of Anglesey, now belongs to the National Trust. It stands in beautiful parkland on the shore of the Strait, and the contents include family portraits by Lawrence, Hoppner and Winterhalter, and a 58ft mural painted by Rex Whistler in 1937.

Continued on Page 138

The Marquess of Anglesey's Column
Public admiration for the first Marquess, who was second in command to Wellington at Waterloo, when he lost a leg, was expressed in the building of a 100ft high monument on the rocky hillock of Craig-y-dinas. The bronze statue was added after his death in 1845 at the age of 86. A spiral staircase of 115 steps leads to the observation platform, from which there is a panoramic view of the Island and the Strait, with a background of Snowdonia. When traffic on A5 is heavy, visitors are warned not to attempt the right turn from our route into the car park, but to approach it from the opposite direction.

Bryn-celli-ddu Burial Chamber, Moel-y-don, Llanidan and Brynsiencyn (See Page 71)

1. The Menai Suspension Bridge

2. Britannia Bridge from Church Island

3. The Anglesey Column *4. Bryn-celli-ddu Burial Chamber*

5. Llanidan Old Church

Map 32

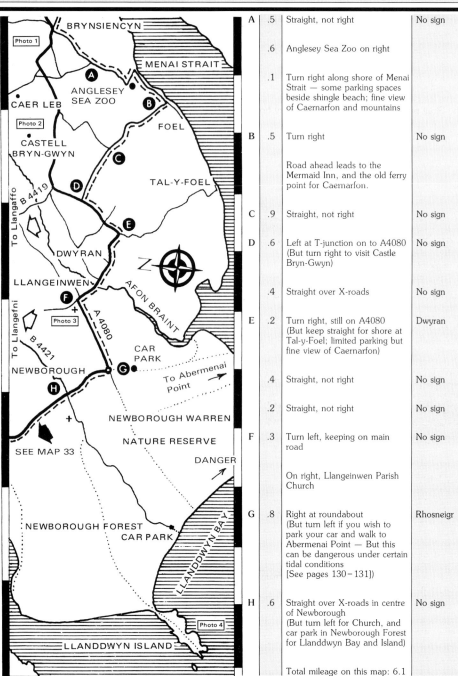

Ref.	kms/Miles	Directions	Sign-posted
A	.5	Straight, not right	No sign
	.6	Anglesey Sea Zoo on right	
	.1	Turn right along shore of Menai Strait — some parking spaces beside shingle beach; fine view of Caernarfon and mountains	
B	.5	Turn right	No sign
		Road ahead leads to the Mermaid Inn, and the old ferry point for Caernarfon.	
C	.9	Straight, not right	No sign
D	.6	Left at T-junction on to A4080 (But turn right to visit Castle Bryn-Gwyn)	No sign
	.4	Straight over X-roads	No sign
E	.2	Turn right, still on A4080 (But keep straight for shore at Tal-y-Foel; limited parking but fine view of Caernarfon)	Dwyran
	.4	Straight, not right	No sign
	.2	Straight, not right	No sign
F	.3	Turn left, keeping on main road	No sign
		On right, Llangeinwen Parish Church	
G	.8	Right at roundabout (But turn left if you wish to park your car and walk to Abermenai Point — But this can be dangerous under certain tidal conditions [See pages 130–131])	Rhosneigr
H	.6	Straight over X-roads in centre of Newborough (But turn left for Church, and car park in Newborough Forest for Llanddwyn Bay and Island)	No sign
		Total mileage on this map: 6.1	

CROWN COPYRIGHT RESERVED

On Route

Bryn-celli-ddu Burial Chamber (See Map 31)
This well preserved Neolithic chamber, still covered by a mound of earth, stands within four concentric stone circles, the remains of an earlier religious site. A 20ft passage leads to the inner chamber, in which there is an 8ft upright stone.

Moel-y-don (See Map 31)
The left turn from Point F on Map 31 to the shore of the Strait passes Plas Coch, a 16th century house now used as a holiday centre, and Llanedwen Church, rebuilt in 1856 with a very tall spire. The landing stage at Moel-y-don, a peaceful spot with a fine view of the Strait, was once used by a busy ferry to Port Dinorwic. In the 13th century this place saw a disastrous defeat of the English when 300 of Edward 's followers were slain by the Welsh.

Llanidan (See Map 31)
The secluded ruin of the 'old Church' dates mainly from the 14th century, but the original one was founded in A.D. 616 by St. Nidan. The New Church was built on the main road in 1844, using materials from the old one.

Brysiencyn (See Map 31)
This unusually compact village was the scene of bitter fighting in A.D. 61 when the Romans crossed the Strait to defeat the Druids. Here will be found the Anglesey Sea Zoo, based at an oyster hatchery, with many examples of sealife in a series of large tanks, from sharks to shrimps, and all under cover. There is a craft shop, a tea-room and seafood snacks are available — ☎ (0248) 430411. Near the village are several 'ancient monuments'. Leave Brynsiencyn on A4080 and take the first turning right; in ¼ mile you will find Caer Leb on your left. This is an enclosure of banks and ditches, probably occupied during the third century A.D. Carry on past Caer Leb and over cross roads; in ¾ mile you come to Bodowyr Burial Chamber in a field on the right. This has a massive capstone on three uprights, with other stones nearby. About ¼ mile north of A4080, down a farm road half way between Brynsiencyn and Point D (Map 32) is a Neolithic site known as Castell Bryn-Gwyn.

Llangeinwen
At one time this large parish was linked to Caernarfon by a regular ferry from the Mermaid Inn at Foel. The inn flourishes but the ferry has been closed for many years. The 12th century church was restored in 1812, and the squat pinnacled tower and a south chapel were added in 1839.

Newborough
Many of the villagers once made their living by rabbit catching amd making ropes and mats from the marram grass on Newborough Warren, one of the largest expanses of sand dunes in the country. The Parish Church stands high and windswept against a background of mountains; early 14th century, unusually long and narrow. Beyond the church a bumpy track runs for two miles through Newborough Forest to a car park close to the beach at Llanddwyn Bay. (Information, toilets, picnic facilities and Nature Trail.)

Continued on Page 75

1. Llanidan New Church

2. Bodowyr Burial Chamber

3. Llangeinwen Church

4. Llanddwyn Island

Map 33

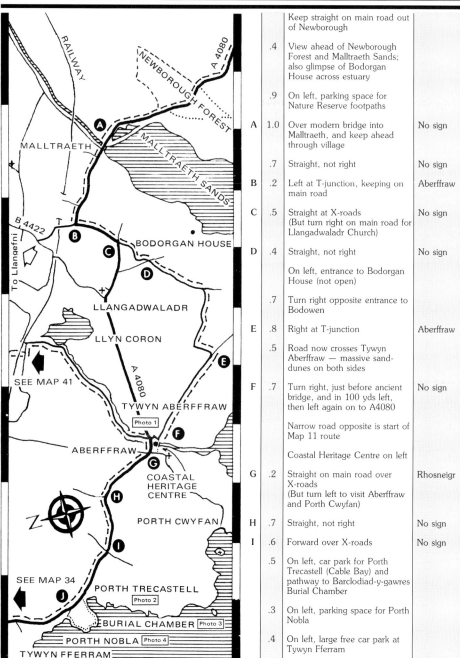

Ref	Miles	Directions	Signposted
		Keep straight on main road out of Newborough	
	.4	View ahead of Newborough Forest and Malltraeth Sands; also glimpse of Bodorgan House across estuary	
	.9	On left, parking space for Nature Reserve footpaths	
A	1.0	Over modern bridge into Malltraeth, and keep ahead through village	No sign
	.7	Straight, not right	No sign
B	.2	Left at T-junction, keeping on main road	Aberffraw
C	.5	Straight at X-roads (But turn right on main road for Llangadwaladr Church)	No sign
D	.4	Straight, not right	No sign
		On left, entrance to Bodorgan House (not open)	
	.7	Turn right opposite entrance to Bodowen	
E	.8	Right at T-junction	Aberffraw
	.5	Road now crosses Tywyn Aberffraw — massive sand-dunes on both sides	
F	.7	Turn right, just before ancient bridge, and in 100 yds left, then left again on to A4080	No sign
		Narrow road opposite is start of Map 11 route	
		Coastal Heritage Centre on left	
G	.2	Straight on main road over X-roads (But turn left to visit Aberffraw and Porth Cwyfan)	Rhosneigr
H	.7	Straight, not right	No sign
I	.6	Forward over X-roads	No sign
	.5	On left, car park for Porth Trecastell (Cable Bay) and pathway to Barclodiad-y-gawres Burial Chamber	
	.3	On left, parking space for Porth Nobla	
	.4	On left, large free car park at Tywyn Fferram	
		Total mileage on this map: 9.5	

CROWN COPYRIGHT RESERVED

On Route

Malltraeth and Trefdraeth
The correct name of the village on our route is Malltraeth Yard — there was once a boatyard here. It lies at the end of an embankment known as the Cob which was built across the Cefni Estuary in 1818, when the Afon Cefni was canalised and the surrounding marshland partially reclaimed. The parish is Trefdraeth, and the church stands on higher ground overlooking the marsh (turn right on B4422 at Point B — see map). Of soft grey stone and slate, against a dark background of trees, the 13th century Church of St. Beuno is still very much alive, and well cared-for in a tidy churchyard.

Llangadwaladr (See Page 89)

Aberffraw
In early Christian times the Court of the Welsh Princes was at Aberffraw, but no traces of the wooden buildings remain. It is now a sleepy undeveloped village, with a quiet square, a good inn and an interesting Coastal Heritage Centre, complete with audio-visual theatre, displays and a programme of guided walks — ☎ (0407) 840845/6. The Church of St. Beuno, very much restored and spoilt outside with a coating of stucco, has twin aisles divided by a 16th century arcade. The approaches to Aberffraw from the east cross the Warren — Tywyn Aberffraw — an expanse of grass and sand bisected by enormous dunes which hide the sands of Aberffraw Bay. You can drive to the foot of one line of sandhills (beware of patches of soft sand), only to find that the beach is still some way distant behind a further range. The single-span stone bridge (1731) was once the only way across the tidal Afon Ffraw, but it now serves only as a footpath, and the main road by-passes the village centre.

Porth Cwyfan
This is a remote and peaceful spot, not completely spoilt by the Defence Establishment on the western headland. On a little island in the rocky seaweed covered bay stands the tiny Church of Llangwyfan, a single cell of the 12th century, where an annual service is held in June.

Porth Trecastell
Also known as Cable Bay, as the telegraph line from Ireland ends here, Porth Trecastell has a fine sandy beach, sheltered by frowning headlands. With a car park and easy access from the road, it is often overcrowded.

Barclodiad-y-gawres Burial Chamber
A Neolithic burial chamber which is easily accessible from the footpath round the headland between Porth Trecastell and Porth Nobla. It contains several incised stones, similar to some found in Ireland. The covering mound has been elaborately restored and the chamber is only open during the summer.

1. Aberffraw

2. Porth Trecastell

3. Barclodiad-y-gawres Burial Chamber

4. Porth Nobla

Map 34

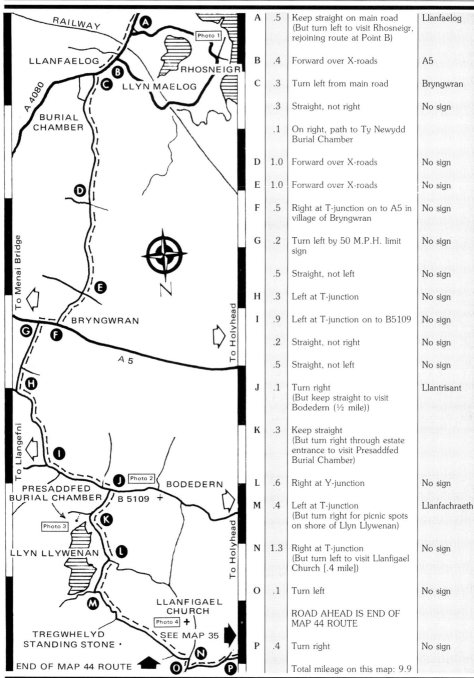

Ref	kms/Miles	Directions	Sign-posted
A	.5	Keep straight on main road (But turn left to visit Rhosneigr, rejoining route at Point B)	Llanfaelog
B	.4	Forward over X-roads	A5
C	.3	Turn left from main road	Bryngwran
	.3	Straight, not right	No sign
	.1	On right, path to Ty Newydd Burial Chamber	
D	1.0	Forward over X-roads	No sign
E	1.0	Forward over X-roads	No sign
F	.5	Right at T-junction on to A5 in village of Bryngwran	No sign
G	.2	Turn left by 50 M.P.H. limit sign	No sign
	.5	Straight, not left	No sign
H	.3	Left at T-junction	No sign
I	.9	Left at T-junction on to B5109	No sign
	.2	Straight, not right	No sign
	.5	Straight, not left	No sign
J	.1	Turn right (But keep straight to visit Bodedern (½ mile))	Llantrisant
K	.3	Keep straight (But turn right through estate entrance to visit Presaddfed Burial Chamber)	
L	.6	Right at Y-junction	No sign
M	.4	Left at T-junction (But turn right for picnic spots on shore of Llyn Llywenan)	Llanfachraeth
N	1.3	Right at T-junction (But turn left to visit Llanfigael Church (.4 mile))	No sign
O	.1	Turn left	No sign
		ROAD AHEAD IS END OF MAP 44 ROUTE	
P	.4	Turn right	No sign
		Total mileage on this map: 9.9	

CROWN COPYRIGHT RESERVED

On Route

Rhosneigr
There are no cliffs, and the sandy beaches and rocky coves make this cheerful and unpretentious resort an ideal place for family holidays. Just inland from the village lies the reed-fringed Llyn Maelog.

Ty Newydd Burial Chamber
These late Neolithic remains consist of a large coverstone resting on three uprights; unfortunately the main stone is cracked, and the added supporting pillars and the too-close official notices hardly improve the scene.

1. Rhosneigr

Bodedern
When it stood on the main Holyhead road, Bodedern was a town noted for woollen manufacture, and it still retains some of its towny atmosphere. The church has been over-restored, but there is a pleasant inn, popular with airmen from R.A.F. Valley. Near the Inn beside the main road stands an imposing pump under a classical pediment, which was presented by Lord Stanley of Alderley in 1897.

Presaddfed Burial Chamber
Another Neolithic relic, the remains of a long cairn consisting of two separate chambers, one of which has collapsed; the other has a large coverstone supported on four uprights. It stands in the centre of a field close to the reedy bird-haunted Llyn Llywenan. Visitors may have to run the gauntlet of inquisitive cattle.

2. Village Pump, Bodedern

Llanfigael
The name means 'shepherd's parish', and the little church stands alone in a group of trees, surrounded by open farmland. When we saw it in June, the peace was disturbed only by bees swarming over the porch. Plas Llanfigael, the solid Georgian farmhouse nearby, has an imposing old stone barn.

Newborough *Continued from Page 71*
This magnificent 3 mile stretch of sand, backed by Newborough Warren and the Forest, is bounded on the west by the rocky promontory of Llanddwyn Island, which is only cut off occasionally at high tide. The rocks which form this 'island', and some outcrops in the forest, are pre-Cambrian and extremely ancient. The lighthouse on the point is disused, and the lifeboat station and the Caernarfon pilots who used the tiny cottages on the Island have all gone. There is a ruin of a 16th century church, dedicated to St. Deinwen, a 5th century Saint whose shrine was a place of pilgrimage for lovers. She is commemorated by a Latin cross near the old lighthouse; a Celtic cross remembers the victims of shipwrecks, but both are modern.

The whole of the Warren, the beach above high water, Llanddwyn Island, and the shore of the Cefni Estuary as far as Malltraeth have been designated a National Nature Reserve, and the public must keep to the marked paths.

3. Presaddfed Burial Chamber

4. Llanfigael Church

Map 35

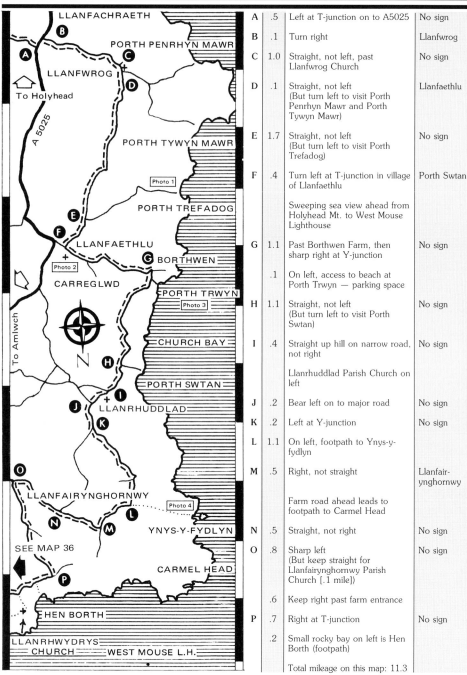

Ref	kms/Miles	Directions	Sign-posted
A	.5	Left at T-junction on to A5025	No sign
B	.1	Turn right	Llanfwrog
C	1.0	Straight, not left, past Llanfwrog Church	No sign
D	.1	Straight, not left (But turn left to visit Porth Penrhyn Mawr and Porth Tywyn Mawr)	Llanfaethlu
E	1.7	Straight, not left (But turn left to visit Porth Trefadog)	No sign
F	.4	Turn left at T-junction in village of Llanfaethlu	Porth Swtan
		Sweeping sea view ahead from Holyhead Mt. to West Mouse Lighthouse	
G	1.1	Past Borthwen Farm, then sharp right at Y-junction	No sign
	.1	On left, access to beach at Porth Trwyn — parking space	
H	1.1	Straight, not left (But turn left to visit Porth Swtan)	No sign
I	.4	Straight up hill on narrow road, not right	No sign
		Llanrhuddlad Parish Church on left	
J	.2	Bear left on to major road	No sign
K	.2	Left at Y-junction	No sign
L	1.1	On left, footpath to Ynys-y-fydlyn	
M	.5	Right, not straight	Llanfair-ynghornwy
		Farm road ahead leads to footpath to Carmel Head	
N	.5	Straight, not right	No sign
O	.8	Sharp left (But keep straight for Llanfairynghornwy Parish Church [.1 mile])	No sign
	.6	Keep right past farm entrance	
P	.7	Right at T-junction	No sign
	.2	Small rocky bay on left is Hen Borth (footpath)	
		Total mileage on this map: 11.3	

CROWN COPYRIGHT RESERVED

On Route

Porth Penrhyn Mawr
This little bay, which directly faces Holyhead, has a rather muddy, shingly beach, enclosed by rocks. There is a large farm and a few houses and bungalows, and one or two discreet caravans — a peaceful spot unlikely to be overcrowded.

Porth Tywyn Mawr
Here is a fine sandy beach facing the open sea with a large caravan site at the farm to one side of the bay, but plenty of parking space, and room for everyone.

Porth Trefadog
This is a gem — a semicircular beach of sand and shingle sheltered by weed-covered rocks, remains of an old fort on the headland to the south, and no buildings except a delightful old farmhouse, with gabled dormer windows in a mossy tiled roof.

1. Farmhouse at Porth Trefadog

Llanfaethlu
The Parish Church of St. Maethlu stands in a windy churchyard, with panoramic views of sea and farmlands. The well-cared-for interior has a barrel vaulted roof and carpeted aisle; the font is dated 1614, and there is an old box pew opposite the pulpit. The churchyard has one or two good memorials and a sundial on a wooden post. The 17th century mansion of Carreglwd in the valley is completely hidden by the only clump of trees in the district.

2. Llanfaethlu Church

Church Bay
This long rocky bay has good sandy beaches at each end, about a mile apart. At the southern end, Porth Trwyn is backed by dunes and a few bungalows; Porth Swtan to the north is more sophisticated, with some shops and a restaurant. The beach is sheltered by low cliffs, and there are even donkey rides.

Llanrhuddlad
The Parish Church (Point I) was rebuilt in 1858, with a tall spire like an oversharpened pencil.

3. Porth Trwyn

Llanfairynghornwy
This scattered parish covers the north-west corner of the Island, mainly rugged and infertile, and includes the Skerries, the rocky islands two miles off Carmel Head. The Parish Church, well inland a short distance from Point O, is medieval with a 16th century south chapel. In the same parish, near the sea between Hen Borth and Trwyn Cemlyn (see Page 79), is the delightful little Llanrhwydrys Church.

Ynys-y-fydlyn
Take the footpath from Point L, with a conifer plantation on your right, and in ¾ mile you will find a tiny shingle bay, protected on one side by a rocky island, split into two and fissured with caves. An easy walk rewarded by a scene of unusual beauty and seclusion.

4. Ynys-y-fydlyn

Map 36

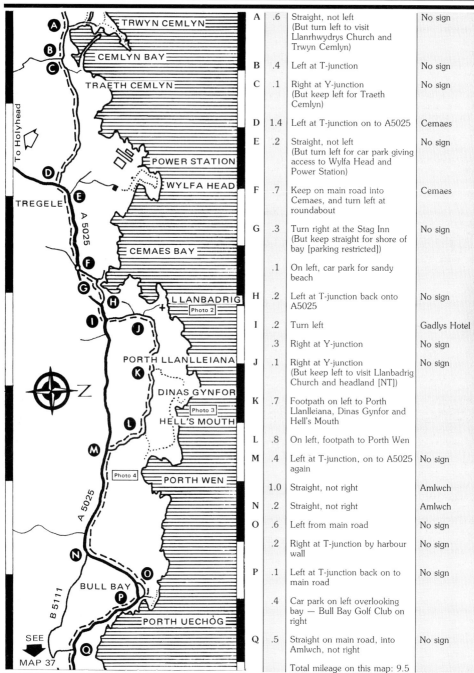

	kms Ref. Miles	Directions	Sign-posted
A	.6	Straight, not left (But turn left to visit Llanrhwydrys Church and Trwyn Cemlyn)	No sign
B	.4	Left at T-junction	No sign
C	.1	Right at Y-junction (But keep left for Traeth Cemlyn)	No sign
D	1.4	Left at T-junction on to A5025	Cemaes
E	.2	Straight, not left (But turn left for car park giving access to Wylfa Head and Power Station)	No sign
F	.7	Keep on main road into Cemaes, and turn left at roundabout	Cemaes
G	.3	Turn right at the Stag Inn (But keep straight for shore of bay [parking restricted])	No sign
	.1	On left, car park for sandy beach	
H	.2	Left at T-junction back onto A5025	No sign
I	.2	Turn left	Gadlys Hotel
	.3	Right at Y-junction	No sign
J	.1	Right at Y-junction (But keep left to visit Llanbadrig Church and headland [NT])	No sign
K	.7	Footpath on left to Porth Llanlleiana, Dinas Gynfor and Hell's Mouth	
L	.8	On left, footpath to Porth Wen	
M	.4	Left at T-junction, on to A5025 again	No sign
	1.0	Straight, not right	Amlwch
N	.2	Straight, not right	Amlwch
O	.6	Left from main road	No sign
	.2	Right at T-junction by harbour wall	No sign
P	.1	Left at T-junction back on to main road	No sign
	.4	Car park on left overlooking bay — Bull Bay Golf Club on right	
Q	.5	Straight on main road, into Amlwch, not right	No sign
		Total mileage on this map: 9.5	

CROWN COPYRIGHT RESERVED

On Route

Cemlyn Bay — Trwyn Cemlyn and Traeth Cemlyn

An enormous curving bank of shingle faces the sea and protects a landlocked lagoon, the haunt of countless wildfowl and sea birds. The headland to the west is a sandy gorse-covered waste known as Trwyn Cemlyn, with a rocky shore and a view of Wylfa Power Station. To reach it, take the left turn at Point A, past a farm road which is the easiest route to Llanrhwydrys Church (see Page 77), and a white brick pumping station, to a car park on the warren. The left fork at Point C leads to a car park at the eastern end of the shingle bank, with access to the beach (Traeth Cemlyn), and a footpath leading back along the bank to Trwyn Cemlyn. However do not walk along this bank during nesting time (April to June), and do not disturb the wildlife in the lagoon at any time. Most of the bay and its surroundings belong to the National Trust, and the lagoon is a Nature Reserve.

Wylfa Power Station

This nuclear power station was completed in 1969, and the C.E.G.B. has provided an observation tower and a picnic site nearby. Tours of the station itself are offered all the year without prior booking, from Monday to Friday, starting at 10.15 a.m. and 2 p.m. Only pre-booked parties at weekends — ☎ 0407 710471.

Cemaes Bay

A cheerful holiday village, which was once the main harbour on this stretch of coast, until overtaken by Amlwch Port. There are shops and pleasant pubs, a quiet sea-front, and a sandy beach with a convenient car park.

Llanbadrig

Standing on an exposed site near the sea is a small church, the only one in Wales dedicated to St Patrick. He is supposed to have sailed to Ireland from here. Heavily restored in oriental style by Lord Stanley of Alderley, it has been more recently vandalised, and may not be open. The headland and most of the coastline back to Cemaes Bay belong to the National Trust.

Dinas Gynfor

The footpath from Point K leads downhill past a farm entrance; keep the ruined buildings of Porth Llanlleiana on your left and bear right up the hillside. The path then circles left through the bracken to the hill-top, where Iron Age man turned the limestone outcrops into a fortress, with walls enclosing an area of 700 × 300 yards.

Porth Wen

You can follow a rough path along the cliffs from Dinas Gynfor, past the rugged cleft known as Hell's Mouth, but the easiest path to Porth Wen leads across the fields from Point L. The bay is a wide semicircle of shingle with the ruins of a brickworks, and white farm buildings on the opposite headland.

Bull Bay (See Page 81)

1. Llanrhwydrys Church (See Map 35)

2. Llandabrig Church

3. Hell's Mouth

4. Porth Wen

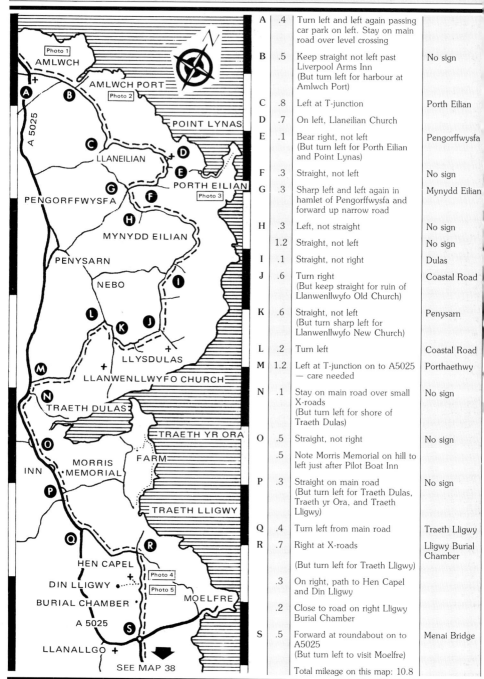

Map 37

Ref.	kms/Miles	Directions	Sign-posted
A	.4	Turn left and left again passing car park on left. Stay on main road over level crossing	
B	.5	Keep straight not left past Liverpool Arms Inn (But turn left for harbour at Amlwch Port)	No sign
C	.8	Left at T-junction	Porth Eilian
D	.7	On left, Llaneilian Church	
E	.1	Bear right, not left (But turn left for Porth Eilian and Point Lynas)	Pengorffwysfa
F	.3	Straight, not left	No sign
G	.3	Sharp left and left again in hamlet of Pengorffwysfa and forward up narrow road	Mynydd Eilian
H	.3	Left, not straight	No sign
	1.2	Straight, not left	No sign
I	.1	Straight, not right	Dulas
J	.6	Turn right (But keep straight for ruin of Llanwenllwyfo Old Church)	Coastal Road
K	.6	Straight, not left (But turn sharp left for Llanwenllwyfo New Church)	Penysarn
L	.2	Turn left	Coastal Road
M	1.2	Left at T-junction on to A5025 — care needed	Porthaethwy
N	.1	Stay on main road over small X-roads (But turn left for shore of Traeth Dulas)	No sign
O	.5	Straight, not right	No sign
	.5	Note Morris Memorial on hill to left just after Pilot Boat Inn	
P	.3	Straight on main road (But turn left for Traeth Dulas, Traeth yr Ora, and Traeth Lligwy)	No sign
Q	.4	Turn left from main road	Traeth Lligwy
R	.7	Right at X-roads (But turn left for Traeth Lligwy)	Lligwy Burial Chamber
	.3	On right, path to Hen Capel and Din Lligwy	
	.2	Close to road on right Lligwy Burial Chamber	
S	.5	Forward at roundabout on to A5025 (But turn left to visit Moelfre)	Menai Bridge
		Total mileage on this map: 10.8	

CROWN COPYRIGHT RESERVED

On Route

Bull Bay (See Map 36)
Porth Uechog — in English, Bull Bay, is an attractive small resort with a tiny rock-girt beach.

Amlwch
The Romans first found copper on Parys Mountain, 1½ miles to the south, and it was worked in Elizabethan times. A rich vein was found in 1768, and for the next 50 years Amlwch was a boom town with a population of 5,000 and 1,000 ale houses. Overseas competition ended the boom, but prospecting started again recently. Parys Mountain is a weirdly fascinating sight, with multi-coloured rocks and heaps of debris, and stagnant pools where the ore was washed. Abandoned mineshafts make the area extremely dangerous. Amlwch Port is a natural harbour which was enlarged in 1793 for ore-carrying ships; now new sea walls have been built at the harbour mouth, and a large chemical works occupies the headland to the west.

1. Amlwch Parish Church
2. Amlwch Port

Llaneilian
The Parish Church has an unusual 12th century tower, spoilt by cement rendering; the rest is mainly 15th century. The inside is interesting with a painted rood screen and a chapel to St. Eilian. At Porth Eilian a track from the roundabout near the beach leads past the cafe to several good parking places overlooking the bay, and continues to the Pilot Station and the lighthouse on Point Lynas. There are fine views from the 600ft summit of Mynydd Eilian. The ruins of the medieval Llanwenllwyfo Church lie hidden in woods behind Llysdulas House; the new church (1856) has a very sharp spire, and a unique window showing Christ in a hat. The road past the church through the grounds of Llysdulas to the shore of Traeth Dulas is not recommended.

3. Porth Eilian and Point Lynas

Traeth Dulas
This beautiful sandy estuary is almost completely landlocked; once busy with shipping, it is now a Nature Reserve, and an unspoilt area of great tranquility, best seen by taking the left turn at Point N or Point P.

Morris Memorial
The monument on the hillside above the Pilot Boat Inn commemorates three 18th century brothers who were born nearby at Pentre Eirianell; they were Welsh intellectuals and founders of the Cymmrodorion Society.

4. Hen Capel

Traeth yr Ora and Traeth Lligwy
Take the left turn at Point P, and in ¾ mile left again at a T-junction. In spite of the signs you should be able to park near the turning to Penrhyn Farm. The footpath past the farm leads to Traeth yr Ora, an absolute gem of a curving sandy beach, backed by the dunes which almost close the mouth of Traeth Dulas. The right turn at the T-junction leads to Traeth Lligwy, a larger and more crowded sandy bay, to which there is an easier approach from Point R.

Hen Capel, Din Lligwy, Lligwy Burial Chamber and Moelfre (See Page 83)

5. Din Lligwy

Map 38

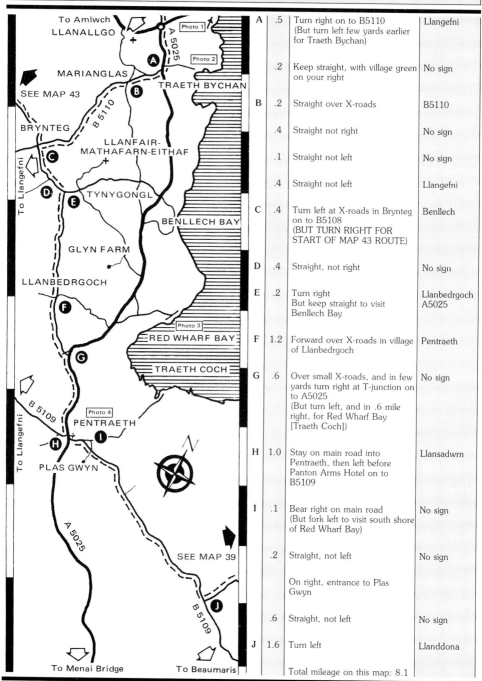

Ref	kms/Miles	Directions	Sign-posted
A	.5	Turn right on to B5110 (But turn left few yards earlier for Traeth Bychan)	Llangefni
	.2	Keep straight, with village green on your right	No sign
B	.2	Straight over X-roads	B5110
	.4	Straight not right	No sign
	.1	Straight not left	No sign
	.4	Straight not left	Llangefni
C	.4	Turn left at X-roads in Brynteg on to B5108 (BUT TURN RIGHT FOR START OF MAP 43 ROUTE)	Benllech
D	.4	Straight, not right	No sign
E	.2	Turn right But keep straight to visit Benllech Bay	Llanbedrgoch A5025
F	1.2	Forward over X-roads in village of Llanbedrgoch	Pentraeth
G	.6	Over small X-roads, and in few yards turn right at T-junction on to A5025 (But turn left, and in .6 mile right, for Red Wharf Bay [Traeth Coch])	No sign
H	1.0	Stay on main road into Pentraeth, then left before Panton Arms Hotel on to B5109	Llansadwrn
I	.1	Bear right on main road (But fork left to visit south shore of Red Wharf Bay)	No sign
	.2	Straight, not left	No sign
		On right, entrance to Plas Gwyn	
	.6	Straight, not left	No sign
J	1.6	Turn left	Llanddona
		Total mileage on this map: 8.1	

CROWN COPYRIGHT RESERVED

On Route

Hen Capel (Capel Lligwy) (see Map 37)
This is the ruin of a 12th century chapel, partly rebuilt in the 14th century, and extended in the 16th.

Din Lligwy (See Map 37)
In a woodland clearing you will find the well-preserved remains of an Iron Age village; the boundary wall encloses more than half an acre, and you can trace the outlines of two circular and seven rectangular buildings. They were last occupied in the fourth century A.D.

1. Moelfre

Lligwy Burial Chamber (See Map 37)
The enormous cover stone is supported by low uprights over a natural fissure in the rock, but the effect is sadly spoilt by the surrounding official railings.

Moelfre (See Map 37)
An attractive small resort and fishing village, with a famous lifeboat station. The Parish Church is at Llanallgo (right at Point S): in the churchyard half hidden by a tree is a memorial to the 140 people drowned in the wreck of the *Royal Charter* at Moelfre in October 1859.

Traeth Bychan
A wide sandy beach, with a view of Puffin Island, the Great Orme and the mainland — also the headquarters of the Red Wharf Bay Sailing Club.

2. Traeth Bychan

Benllech Bay
Benllech is a large and popular holiday resort. The sandy beach is enormous, and there are plenty of hotels and guest houses, and a holiday camp; the inland roads are lined with caravan sites. The old parish church, attractively secluded down a lane near Point E (see Map) has a new pulpit commemorating the bi-centenary of the poet Goronwy Owen, one-time curate of the parish. Part of Benllech has the musical-sounding name of Tynygongl. Glyn Farm (see Map) is a 17th century house with fine plaster decorations and an interesting slate chimney piece, which can be seen on written application.

Red Wharf Bay (Traeth Coch)
At low tide the sands of Traeth Coch cover ten square miles — don't try to walk across and back between two tides. The quiet village has two pubs and a few shops; there was once a quarry, shipyard and a busy quay, but only yachts are moored there now.

3. Red Wharf Bay

Pentraeth
In the 17th century Red Wharf Bay extended nearly to the village, but is now a mile inland. The left fork from Point I leads to the southern shore of the Bay, where the sluggish Afon Ceint reaches the sea — a peaceful spot of mudflats and sandy wastes. Plas Gwyn, near Point I, is a red-brick Georgian mansion (not open) in a style unusual for Anglesey, in contrast to the stone-built home farm. Two miles along B5109 inland from Pentraeth a farm road on the right leads to Llanddyfnan Church, which has a doorway with primitive medieval carvings. There is a standing stone in a field nearby.

4. The Panton Arms, Pentraeth

Map 39

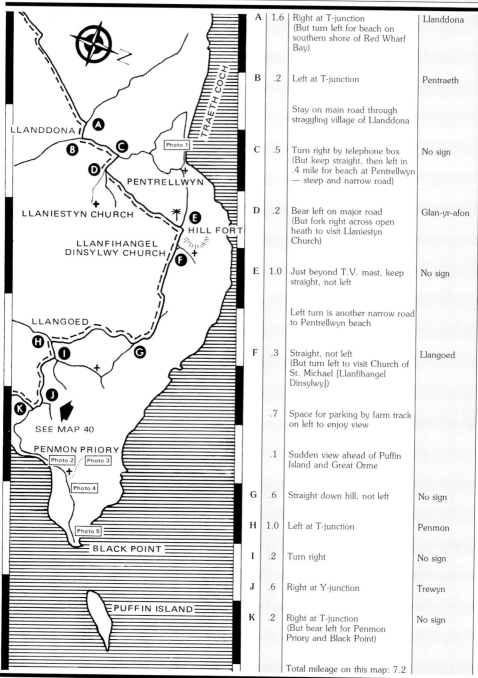

Ref.	kms / Miles	Directions	Sign-posted
A	1.6	Right at T-junction (But turn left for beach on southern shore of Red Wharf Bay)	Llanddona
B	.2	Left at T-junction Stay on main road through straggling village of Llanddona	Pentraeth
C	.5	Turn right by telephone box (But keep straight, then left in .4 mile for beach at Pentrellwyn — steep and narrow road)	No sign
D	.2	Bear left on major road (But fork right across open heath to visit Llaniestyn Church)	Glan-yr-afon
E	1.0	Just beyond T.V. mast, keep straight, not left Left turn is another narrow road to Pentrellwyn beach	No sign
F	.3	Straight, not left (But turn left to visit Church of St. Michael [Llanfihangel Dinsylwy])	Llangoed
	.7	Space for parking by farm track on left to enjoy view	
	.1	Sudden view ahead of Puffin Island and Great Orme	
G	.6	Straight down hill, not left	No sign
H	1.0	Left at T-junction	Penmon
I	.2	Turn right	No sign
J	.6	Right at Y-junction	Trewyn
K	.2	Right at T-junction (But bear left for Penmon Priory and Black Point)	No sign

Total mileage on this map: 7.2

CROWN COPYRIGHT RESERVED

On Route

Llanddona

The straggling village has some old cottages among more modern buildings. The road to the left at Point A takes you past the Wern-y-Wylan Hotel to a secluded sandy beach on the southern shore of Red Wharf Bay. The Victorian Parish Church is tucked away in the hamlet of Pentrellwyn, which you can only reach by negotiating one of the steep and narrow lanes, from Points C or E. Signs discourage through traffic, but the brave will be rewarded by another fine sandy beach, with a modern car park, shop and toilets.

1. Pentrellwyn Beach

Llaniestyn Church

You can easily miss this fine 14th century church (¼ mile across the open heath from Point D, then sharp left) as it is hidden until the last moment by a dense hedge. An impressive open porch leads through a doorway dated 1510 to a simple whitewashed interior; a massive beam supports the entrance to a 15th century chapel which has a lovely statue in low relief of St. Iestyn.

Llanfihangel Dinsylwy

The tiny Church of St. Michael nestles in a sloping churchyard beneath an Iron Age hill-fort, within sight of the sea. The church is early 15th century, much restored in 1855. Don't pick the spotted orchids in the churchyard. The only practicable path to Dinsylwy hill-fort starts from Point E and is difficult to find; the builders enclosed 17 acres on the summit by adding 8ft thick limestone walls to the natural defences.

2. Penmon Priory

Llangoed

This large parish covers the whole of the eastern tip of Anglesey, including Puffin Island. The Church (up hill from Point I) has been harshly restored, but has a good pulpit.

Puffin Island (Ynys Seiriol)

Also known as Priestholm, the island was the site of an early Christian monastic settlement; there are remains from the 7th century, and the ruin of a 12th century church. Later is was used as a signal station, and special permission is needed to land.

Penmon Priory, Cross and Dovecot (CADW)

The Church was founded by St. Seiriol, a 6th century recluse whose cell can be seen beside a well. The original Priory was burnt by the Danes; the Church was rebuilt in the 12th century, and a century later Llywelyn the Great granted the property to the Priestholm community, who rebuilt the Priory and monastic buildings. About ¼ mile behind the Priory, in the centre of a field, stands the elaborately carved Penmon Cross, dating from about A.D. 1000. The easiest route is to take the path from the car park past St. Seiriol's Well.

Penmon Dovecote was probably built around 1600 by Sir Richard Bulkeley, of Baron Hill, near Beaumaris. The Church, Priory, and Dovecot are always open without charge, but there is a toll road to Black Point.

3. Penmon Cross   *4. Penmon Dovecot*

5. Puffin Island from Black Point

Map 40

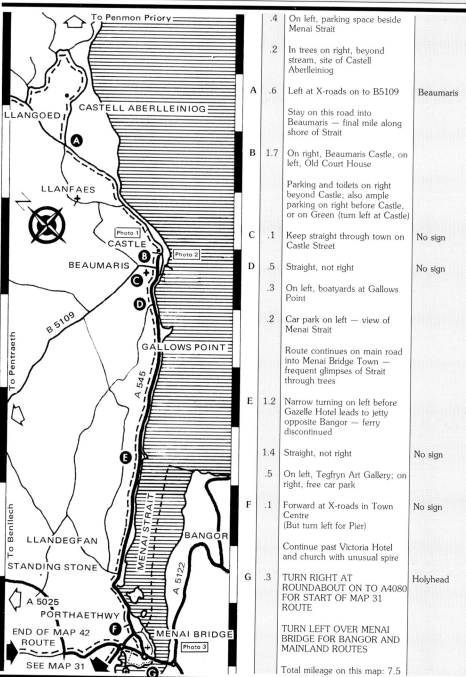

Miles	kms Ref. Miles	Directions	Sign-posted
	.4	On left, parking space beside Menai Strait	
	.2	In trees on right, beyond stream, site of Castell Aberlleiniog	
A	.6	Left at X-roads on to B5109	Beaumaris
		Stay on this road into Beaumaris — final mile along shore of Strait	
B	1.7	On right, Beaumaris Castle, on left, Old Court House	
		Parking and toilets on right beyond Castle; also ample parking on right before Castle, or on Green (turn left at Castle)	
C	.1	Keep straight through town on Castle Street	No sign
D	.5	Straight, not right	No sign
	.3	On left, boatyards at Gallows Point	
	.2	Car park on left — view of Menai Strait	
		Route continues on main road into Menai Bridge Town — frequent glimpses of Strait through trees	
E	1.2	Narrow turning on left before Gazelle Hotel leads to jetty opposite Bangor — ferry discontinued	
	1.4	Straight, not right	No sign
	.5	On left, Tegfryn Art Gallery; on right, free car park	
F	.1	Forward at X-roads in Town Centre (But turn left for Pier)	No sign
		Continue past Victoria Hotel and church with unusual spire	
G	.3	TURN RIGHT AT ROUNDABOUT ON TO A4080 FOR START OF MAP 31 ROUTE	Holyhead
		TURN LEFT OVER MENAI BRIDGE FOR BANGOR AND MAINLAND ROUTES	
		Total mileage on this map: 7.5	

CROWN COPYRIGHT RESERVED

On Route

Castell Aberlleiniog
The ruin of a medieval stone castle, on the site of a timber stronghold built in the 11th century by the Earl of Chester.

Llanfaes
This village was the site of a 13th century Franciscan Friary, but no trace of it remains, apart from relics and tombs in Beaumaris and Penmynydd churches. Llanfaes Parish Church was re-built in 1845.

Beaumaris
The town was founded by Edward I when he built the Castle in 1295, and peopled with English immigrants. For centuries it was the Island's capital, and until the building of the Menai Bridge, the main point of entry from the mainland. It has now become a pleasant holiday resort, with a leaning towards yachting, though with many reminders of its former importance. The Castle (CADW), eighth and last of Edward's Welsh castles, has a perfect symmetrical design which makes it a leading example of medieval military architecture. Unfortunately the royal funds ran low, and the Castle was left unfinished — ☏ (0248) 810361.

The Court House, opposite the Castle, was built in 1614, and was the Island's principal Assize Court until 1971; it still serves each month as a Magistrates' Court. It is a fascinating building, with its furnishings unchanged since the 18th century; in the tiny courtroom the stone-flagged public area is separated from the rest by an iron grille — no seats were provided for the common people.

The Parish Church of St. Mary and St. Nicholas, near the town centre, is nearly as old as the Castle. It contains many relics from Llanfaes Priory, including choir stalls and misericords, and the 13th century stone coffin of Princess Joan, daughter of King John, and wife of Llywelyn the Great. Just behind the Church stands Beaumaris Gaol, a grim building erected in 1829 under Robert Peel's Prison Reform Act. It was in use as the County Gaol for less than 50 years, and in 1878 the few remaining prisoners were transferred to Caernarfon; for a time it became the local police station and lock-up. Visitors are shown typical cells, and the treadwheel, the only one left in Britain, which was used to pump water into tanks on the roof. They may also see, high up on one of the outside walls, the door through which condemned men stepped out to their execution.

Beaumaris contains many examples of Georgian and earlier architecture. The Bull's Head Hotel in Castle Street, was built in 1617 on the site of an earlier hostelry. It was an important posting house; there is a fine old honeysuckle in the yard, and inside good china and brass, and other antiques. The George and Dragon Inn, just round the corner, dates from 1595, and the Tudor Rose, in Castle Street, was built in 1400 and still has much of the original timber. Do not miss a visit to the interesting little Museum of

Continued on Page 89

Menai Bridge (See Page 91)

1. Beaumaris Castle

2. Gateway, Beaumaris Castle

3. Menai Strait from the Suspension Bridge

Map 41

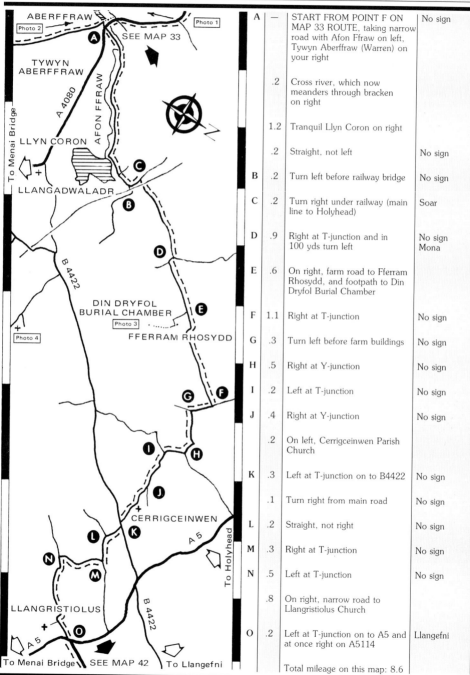

Ref	kms/Miles	Directions	Signposted
A	—	START FROM POINT F ON MAP 33 ROUTE, taking narrow road with Afon Ffraw on left, Tywyn Aberffraw (Warren) on your right	No sign
	.2	Cross river, which now meanders through bracken on right	
	1.2	Tranquil Llyn Coron on right	
	.2	Straight, not left	No sign
B	.2	Turn left before railway bridge	No sign
C	.2	Turn right under railway (main line to Holyhead)	Soar
D	.9	Right at T-junction and in 100 yds turn left	No sign Mona
E	.6	On right, farm road to Fferram Rhosydd, and footpath to Din Dryfol Burial Chamber	
F	1.1	Right at T-junction	No sign
G	.3	Turn left before farm buildings	No sign
H	.5	Right at Y-junction	No sign
I	.2	Left at T-junction	No sign
J	.4	Right at Y-junction	No sign
	.2	On left, Cerrigceinwen Parish Church	
K	.3	Left at T-junction on to B4422	No sign
	.1	Turn right from main road	No sign
L	.2	Straight, not right	No sign
M	.3	Right at T-junction	No sign
N	.5	Left at T-junction	No sign
	.8	On right, narrow road to Llangristiolus Church	
O	.2	Left at T-junction on to A5 and at once right on A5114	Llangefni
		Total mileage on this map: 8.6	

On Route

Beaumaris *Continued from Page 87*
Childhood nearby — ☏ (0248) 810448. Facing the Green and the Strait are several fine Georgian terraces, while to its north there is a fascinating audio-visual show called The Timelock, which is complete with refreshment facilities and radio-controlled model boats — ☏ (0248) 810072.

The town is perhaps best known for its yatching activity, and a visit here is often enlivened by the number of boats to be seen offshore. There are pleasure cruises to Penmon, Puffin Island (not to land), and up the Strait to Menai Bridge. Sea fishing trips are also offered — ☏ (0248) 810746.

Aberffraw (See Page 73)

Llangadwaladr (See also Map 33)
The Church of St. Cadwaladr is hidden away near the junction of A4080 with B4422 (½ mile from Point C on Map 33, and 1½ miles from Point A on Map 41). The early Welsh Princes used to worship here from their Court at Aberffraw, and a stone found in the churchyard, and now built into the north wall, is believed to have been placed there in the 7th century by Cadwaladr, himself a Prince, in memory of his grandfather Cadfan. It described him in Latin as 'Cadfan the wisest and most renowned of all Kings'. The nave was originally built in the 12th century, as shown by the blocked north door with its Norman archway; the chancel and sanctuary date from the 14th century. The finest treasure of the Church is the east window, of pre-Reformation stained glass, which shows the Saint with royal sceptre and orb. The 17th century Gothic south chapel is dedicated to the Owens of Bodowen, a house which is now a ruin overlooking the Cefni Estuary. The north chapel, re-built in 1801, belongs to the Meyrick family of Bodorgan. Their house, of the same date as the chapel, is well hidden in woods except for a distant view from the other shore.

Din Dryfol Burial Chamber
This was probably a Neolithic chamber of the 'segmented cist' type, at least 50 feet long. The chambers have been almost completely destroyed, but the remains of one can be seen, with one side-stone still in position, and a displaced cover stone resting on it; there is another single stone about 30 yards away. The site at the foot of a rocky outcrop is a short walk across the fields behind the farm.

Cerrigceinwen
There is no village in this large agricultural parish. The Church stands snugly in a sheltered hollow, and was rebuilt in the 19th century, using some old materials — the lintel of the south door is a 12th century grave slab, and the font is the same age.

Llangristiolus
Another agricultural parish which includes a stretch of the A5, and a large part of Malltraeth Marsh. You will find the church on a low hill at the end of a little turning, overlooking the marsh with the landmark of Llangaffo church spire on the ridge 3 miles to the south. It was rebuilt in the 13th century, and restored in 1832, and possesses another good 12th century font.

1. Aberffraw Church

2. Old Bridge, Aberffraw

3. Din Dryfol Burial Chamber

4. Trefdraeth Church (see page 73)

Map 42

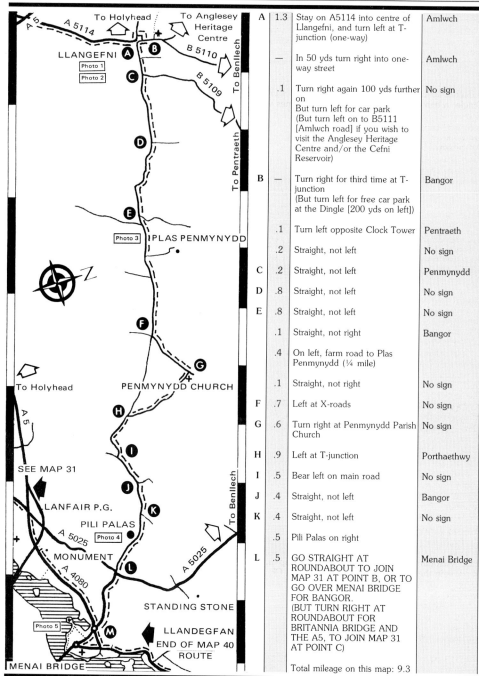

	kms Ref. Miles	Directions	Sign-posted
A	1.3	Stay on A5114 into centre of Llangefni, and turn left at T-junction (one-way)	Amlwch
	—	In 50 yds turn right into one-way street	Amlwch
	.1	Turn right again 100 yds further on But turn left for car park (But turn left on to B5111 [Amlwch road] if you wish to visit the Anglesey Heritage Centre and/or the Cefni Reservoir)	No sign
B	—	Turn right for third time at T-junction (But turn left for free car park at the Dingle [200 yds on left])	Bangor
	.1	Turn left opposite Clock Tower	Pentraeth
	.2	Straight, not left	No sign
C	.2	Straight, not left	Penmynydd
D	.8	Straight, not left	No sign
E	.8	Straight, not left	No sign
	.1	Straight, not right	Bangor
	.4	On left, farm road to Plas Penmynydd (¼ mile)	
	.1	Straight, not right	No sign
F	.7	Left at X-roads	No sign
G	.6	Turn right at Penmynydd Parish Church	No sign
H	.9	Left at T-junction	Porthaethwy
I	.5	Bear left on main road	No sign
J	.4	Straight, not left	Bangor
K	.4	Straight, not left	No sign
	.5	Pili Palas on right	
L	.5	GO STRAIGHT AT ROUNDABOUT TO JOIN MAP 31 AT POINT B, OR TO GO OVER MENAI BRIDGE FOR BANGOR. (BUT TURN RIGHT AT ROUNDABOUT FOR BRITANNIA BRIDGE AND THE A5, TO JOIN MAP 31 AT POINT C)	Menai Bridge
		Total mileage on this map: 9.3	

CROWN COPYRIGHT RESERVED

On Route

Llangefni
This busy market town is now the administrative centre of the Island. The cattle market has been moved from the town centre and is now held in the new cattle mart, but the usual motley collection of stalls can be found in the Square near the Bull Hotel. The Parish Church of St. Cyngar stands well sheltered by trees beside the car park at the foot of the Dingle, a beautiful wooded valley which comes very close to the centre of the town. There is a footpath which follows the banks of the sparkling Afon Cefni for a mile or more.

1. Parish Church, Llangefni

2. The Dingle, Llangefni

Anglesey Heritage Centre
(See Route Directions from Llangefni)
Not open at the time of writing, but do enquire in Llangefni for further details as it should be well worth visiting. It will contain a Wildlife Gallery and the Charles Tunnicliffe Collection, comprising the majority of this well-known wildlife artist's works.

Cefni Reservoir
(See Route Directions from Llangefni)
A relatively small reservoir, the surrounds of which have been planted by the Forestry Commission. There is a car park and picnic site on the B5111, at the north-eastern end, and visitors can enjoy a pleasant walk along forest tracks. Day fishing permits (for trout) may be purchased in Llangefni, and there is also a bird hide near the car park.

3. Near Plas Penmynydd

Penmynydd (See Page 138)

Llandegfan
This parish includes the stretch of the Beaumaris – Menai Bridge road known as the 'Millionaires Mile', by reason of the many Victorian mansions hidden in the trees beside it. The village, on the higher ground to the north has modern housing and enjoys magnificent views of Snowdonia. There is a fine standing stone, or 'maen hir', on a hill top above the village — turn left at Point L on A5025, then right in ¾ mile, and you will find the stone in a field ¼ mile on your left.

Pili Palas
Here is a delightful display of native and tropical butterflies, and a variety of other insects, all in a controlled environment through which visitors may wander. There is also a gift shop and cafe — ☎ (0248) 712474.

4. At Pili Palas

Menai Bridge Town (Porthaethwy)
(See also Maps 31 and 40)
Telford's suspension bridge gave its name to the little Victorian market town which grew up in its shadow in the Parish of Llandysilio. The old Church of St. Tysilio is on Church Island, easily reached by a footpath from a car park on the roadside. This path takes you through Coed Cyrnol, a dense wood of Scots pines, and over a causeway to the tiny 14th century church. The Belgian promenade, so called because it was built by Flemish refugees during the 1914–18 war, follows the shore from the island to the suspension bridge and provides a peaceful walk with a fine view of the Strait and the Britannia Bridge.

5. Menai Strait from the Belgian Promenade

Map 43

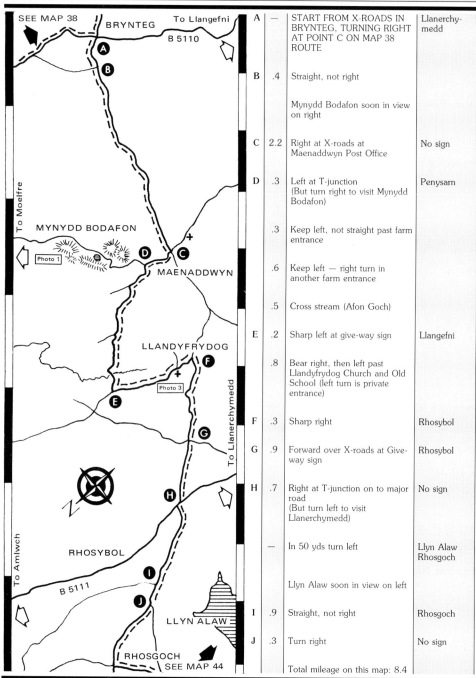

Ref	kms/Miles	Directions	Signposted
A	—	START FROM X-ROADS IN BRYNTEG, TURNING RIGHT AT POINT C ON MAP 38 ROUTE	Llanerchy-medd
B	.4	Straight, not right	
		Mynydd Bodafon soon in view on right	
C	2.2	Right at X-roads at Maenaddwyn Post Office	No sign
D	.3	Left at T-junction (But turn right to visit Mynydd Bodafon)	Penysarn
	.3	Keep left, not straight past farm entrance	
	.6	Keep left — right turn in another farm entrance	
	.5	Cross stream (Afon Goch)	
E	.2	Sharp left at give-way sign	Llangefni
	.8	Bear right, then left past Llandyfrydog Church and Old School (left turn is private entrance)	
F	.3	Sharp right	Rhosybol
G	.9	Forward over X-roads at Give-way sign	Rhosybol
H	.7	Right at T-junction on to major road (But turn left to visit Llanerchymedd)	No sign
	—	In 50 yds turn left	Llyn Alaw Rhosgoch
		Llyn Alaw soon in view on left	
I	.9	Straight, not right	Rhosgoch
J	.3	Turn right	No sign
		Total mileage on this map: 8.4	

CROWN COPYRIGHT RESERVED

On Route

Mynydd Bodafon

This sudden outcrop of rocky, heather-clad hills, surrounding a tranquil lake, must be visited for the panoramic view from the eastern summit — there is a convenient car park at the foot and a clearly marked path to the top. From here you can see nearly the whole of Anglesey, and to the south many miles of the Welsh mainland, from the Great Orme to the Lleyn Peninsula, with the brooding peaks of Snowdonia in the background.

1. Mynydd Bodafon

Llandyfrydog

Church and old school house make an attractive tree-shaded group in dark grey stone and slate. The church is mainly the result of Victorian restoration, but has a 14th century chancel arch, an ancient font, and several interesting gravestones and a sundial in the churchyard. The school was built early in the 19th century by the local farming community, and was probably the earliest voluntary school in Wales. It once had 80 pupils, but has now been converted to a pleasant house.

Llanerchymedd

Once a busy market town, Llanerchymedd is now a quiet place of wide streets, and a small square at the road junction from which you enter the Parish Church through an imposing lych gate. The church, except for the squat stone tower, was rebuilt in 1856.

2. Llandyfrydog Church

Holyhead *Continued from Page 97*

housed in the former St Elbod's Church in Rhosygaer Avenue.

The Parish Church was founded about A.D. 550 by St. Cybi, the son of a Cornish King, and built within the walls of a third century Roman coastal fort, of which three of the sides and parts of the circular corner towers remain. The present Church, large and airy, was built between the 13th and 16th centuries, and restored by Sir Gilbert Scott in the 1870's; it contains some fine carving and glass.

On a side road between Holyhead and Trearddur Bay you will find the Trefignath Burial Chamber, the remains of a Neolithic 'segmented cist', and half a mile nearer the town, the Bronze Age Ty Mawr Standing Stone (See Map 45).

Penrhos Nature Reserve (See Map 45)

Some years ago local policeman and naturalist, Ken Williams, persuaded Rio Tinto Zinc to allow the Penrhos Estate to the east of Holyhead, which had been the home of the Stanleys of Alderley, to be developed as a Nature Reserve, as the land was not required for the new aluminium smelting works. It has been open to the public since 1973; the area provides a great variety of habitats for sea and land birds, and visitors can wander at will, or just sit and watch.

3. Fishing Boats at Holyhead

Map 44

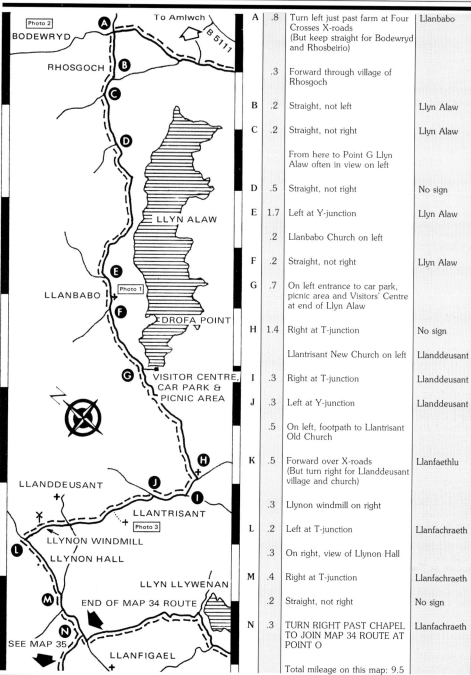

Ref.	kms / Miles	Directions	Sign-posted
A	.8	Turn left just past farm at Four Crosses X-roads (But keep straight for Bodewryd and Rhosbeirio)	Llanbabo
	.3	Forward through village of Rhosgoch	
B	.2	Straight, not left	Llyn Alaw
C	.2	Straight, not right	Llyn Alaw
		From here to Point G Llyn Alaw often in view on left	
D	.5	Straight, not right	No sign
E	1.7	Left at Y-junction	Llyn Alaw
	.2	Llanbabo Church on left	
F	.2	Straight, not right	Llyn Alaw
G	.7	On left entrance to car park, picnic area and Visitors' Centre at end of Llyn Alaw	
H	1.4	Right at T-junction	No sign
		Llantrisant New Church on left	Llanddeusant
I	.3	Right at T-junction	Llanddeusant
J	.3	Left at Y-junction	Llanddeusant
	.5	On left, footpath to Llantrisant Old Church	
K	.5	Forward over X-roads (But turn right for Llanddeusant village and church)	Llanfaethlu
	.3	Llynon windmill on right	
L	.2	Left at T-junction	Llanfachraeth
	.3	On right, view of Llynon Hall	
M	.4	Right at T-junction	Llanfachraeth
	.2	Straight, not right	No sign
N	.3	TURN RIGHT PAST CHAPEL TO JOIN MAP 34 ROUTE AT POINT O	Llanfachraeth
		Total mileage on this map: 9.5	

CROWN COPYRIGHT RESERVED

On Route

Bodewryd
Keep straight, not left, at Point A, and in just over a mile you will pass Bodewryd Church on your left — small and neat in a tidy churchyard; then to the right you will see the gabled Bodewryd Dovecot. Built in the 18th century, the dovecot fell into decay, but was presented to the local borough council who undertook its restoration in 1979. Further along the same road, after about three quarters of a mile, you will come to the disused Rhosbeirio Church.

Llanbabo
This little creeper covered church has a delightful setting close to the Alaw Reservoir, with an ancient yew in the tiny churchyard, and close to a stream and an old stone bridge. A fine 14th century low relief carving depicts St. Pabo as crowned king with a sceptre. Parts of the church have survived from the 12th and 14th centuries, and some of the roof timbers are medieval.

Llyn Alaw
This reservoir, nearly three miles long and half a mile wide, has been formed by the flooding of an area of marsh and farmland previously drained by the Afon Alaw. There is a Visitors' Centre, car park and picnic place at Bod Deiniol (near Point G), a subsidiary car park a short distance eastwards, beyond the dam, and a further car park and picnic place, with access to a bird hide, at Gwredog north of Llanerchymedd. The Visitors' Centre has an exhibition covering the reservoir's history and function, and it is possible to walk from here round to Drofa Point. Unlike lakes and reservoirs in mountain areas, this reservoir is relatively shallow, and this fact coupled with the rich inflow of nutrients has resulted in it becoming not only one of Wales' most productive brown and rainbow trout fisheries, but also an important site for wildfowl and waders. Fishing permits are obtainable from a coin-operated dispenser at the Visitors' Centre.

Llantrisant
Hamlet in unexciting country south of Llyn Alaw. The new church at its centre is not of great interest to visitors, but the old church, left untouched by the Victorians, could be worth finding. It lies down a farm road, and is a late 14th century building with a 17th century south chapel. About a mile to the north of the new church, on the bank of the little Afon Alaw there is a burial mound, Bedd Branwen, the legendary grave of the beautiful Queen Branwen. This lady was the daughter of Llyr, one of the great figures of the collection of Welsh folk tales from the Dark Ages, known as *The Mabinogion*.

Llanddeusant
This minute village in an undramatic Anglesey setting has a large and somewhat forbidding Victorian church, complete with tower and little conical spire. Llynon windmill, still standing well to the west of the village, was the last working windmill on the island of Anglesey, and is a reminder of the times when the many mills of this type were an outstanding feature of the Anglesey skyline.

1. Llanbabo Church

2. Bodewryd Dovecot

3. Llantrisant Old Church

Map 45

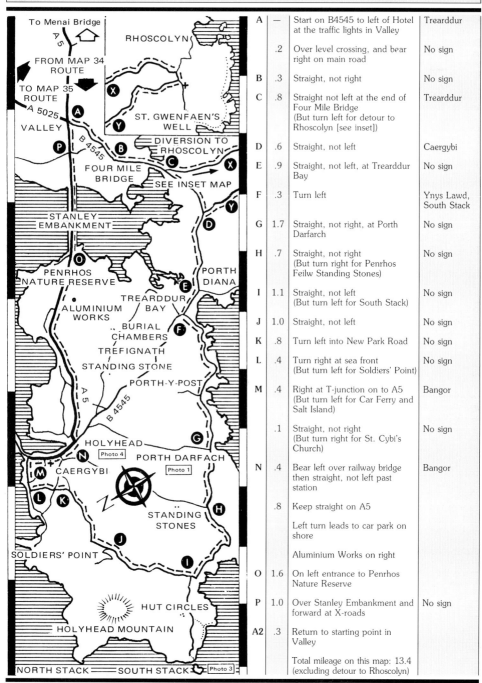

Ref	kms/Miles	Directions	Sign-posted
A	—	Start on B4545 to left of Hotel at the traffic lights in Valley	Trearddur
	.2	Over level crossing, and bear right on main road	No sign
B	.3	Straight, not right	No sign
C	.8	Straight not left at the end of Four Mile Bridge (But turn left for detour to Rhoscolyn [see inset])	Trearddur
D	.6	Straight, not left	Caergybi
E	.9	Straight, not left, at Trearddur Bay	No sign
F	.3	Turn left	Ynys Lawd, South Stack
G	1.7	Straight, not right, at Porth Darfarch	No sign
H	.7	Straight, not right (But turn right for Penrhos Feilw Standing Stones)	No sign
I	1.1	Straight, not left (But turn left for South Stack)	No sign
J	1.0	Straight, not left	No sign
K	.8	Turn left into New Park Road	No sign
L	.4	Turn right at sea front (But turn left for Soldiers' Point)	No sign
M	.4	Right at T-junction on to A5 (But turn left for Car Ferry and Salt Island)	Bangor
	.1	Straight, not right (But turn right for St. Cybi's Church)	No sign
N	.4	Bear left over railway bridge then straight, not left past station	Bangor
	.8	Keep straight on A5	
		Left turn leads to car park on shore	
		Aluminium Works on right	
O	1.6	On left entrance to Penrhos Nature Reserve	
P	1.0	Over Stanley Embankment and forward at X-roads	No sign
A2	.3	Return to starting point in Valley	
		Total mileage on this map: 13.4 (excluding detour to Rhoscolyn)	

CROWN COPYRIGHT RESERVED

On Route

Rhoscolyn
The detour of about 4 miles between Points C and D takes you to Rhoscolyn beach, a horseshoe of firm sand between rocky headlands. The narrow lane to the beach car park is a left turn about 1.8 miles from Point C; don't be put off by signs saying 'no passing places'. The headland to the west has some spectacular multi-coloured cliffs and rock formations, and St. Gwenfaen's Well, a spring named after the saint to whom the tiny church is dedicated. The easiest path to the cliffs follows the farm road from the church, through the farmyard, then down a track between stone walls.

1. Porth Darfach

Trearddur Bay
The series of sandy bays and rocky coves, including Trearddur Bay itself, which stretch from Porth Diana (left at Point E) to Porth Darfach (Point G) are deservedly popular, and parking near the beaches may be difficult. Porth Darfach once had a landing stage used as an alternative to Holyhead by the Irish packets when winds were contrary.

Penrhos Feilw Standing Stones
Two stones, each 10 feet high and 11 feet apart which date from the Bronze Age, and are believed to have been part of a stone cist, in the centre of a stone circle.

2. Penrhos Feilw Standing Stones

South Stack
The lighthouse was built in 1808 on a small island, and visitors can reach it by a steep path, many steps, and a suspension bridge. The road to South Stack from Point I passes a group of hut circles, the remains of an Iron Age settlement. About 20 round or rectangular buildings can be traced in the bracken on the hillside. From the car park a path leads to the cliffs, with spectacular views of the rugged coastline, including South Stack. These cliffs are part of a bird sanctuary under the care of the RSPB. During May and June thousands of puffins and razor-bills nest here together with the rare choughs.

Holyhead Mountain
On the summit of this dramatic hill, only 720ft high but a landmark for miles around, is the Iron Age hill-fort of Caer y Twr. The easiest path to it starts from the South Stack road.

3. South Stack

Holyhead (Caer Gybi)
A regular packet service to Ireland from Holyhead by sailing boat started in the 17th century. The Admiralty Pier on Salt Island, now used by the car ferry, was built in 1821 and the Doric Arch commemorates a visit in that year by George IV, and marks the end of the A5. The enormous breakwater, 1½ miles long, was started in 1845, using local stone. You will find the landward end at Soldiers' Point (turn left at Point L). Returning along the Promenade beside Newry Beach, you pass the Trinity House Depot with its stock of replacement buoys. The story of this great harbour, and of Holyhead in general, is told in the Holyhead Maritime Museum, which is
Continued on Page 93

Penrhos Nature Reserve (See Page 93)

4. St. Cybi's Church, Holyhead

LLEYN PENINSULA KEY MAP

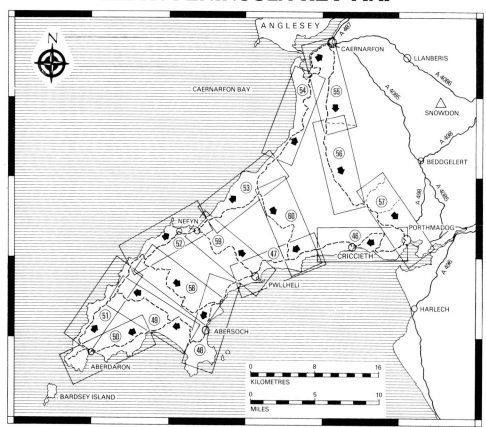

CROWN COPYRIGHT RESERVED

Caernarfon Castle

EXPLORING THE LLEYN PENINSULA

Portmeirion

The long and varied coastline of the Lleyn Peninsula is similar in character to that of Anglesey. Nearly all the main resorts are in the south where there are many magnificent beaches, but from Abersoch to the western tip of the peninsula — the 'Land's End of Wales' — the coast becomes increasingly rugged, and this feature dominates the north-western coast as far as Morfa Nefyn. But even so the cliffs and rocky headlands are interspersed with a number of sandy beaches and coves, many of which are worth the often lengthy walks from our route. Our main route follows as close as possible to the coast, while cross routes explore the unspoilt and ever narrowing interior.

Map 46

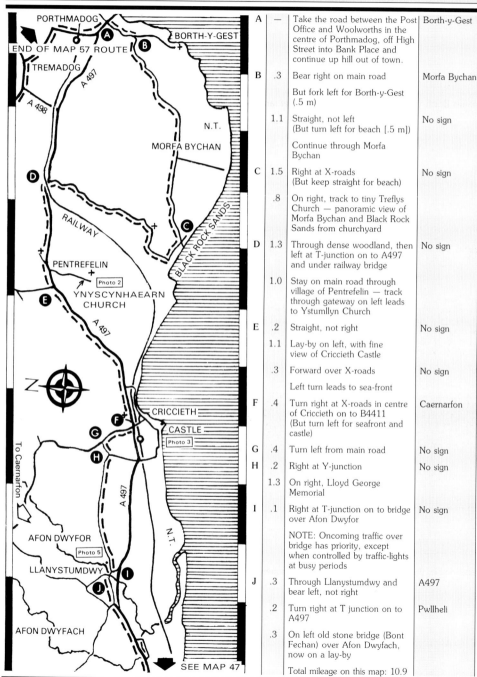

Ref	kms/Miles	Directions	Sign-posted
A	—	Take the road between the Post Office and Woolworths in the centre of Porthmadog, off High Street into Bank Place and continue up hill out of town.	Borth-y-Gest
B	.3	Bear right on main road	Morfa Bychan
		But fork left for Borth-y-Gest (.5 m)	
	1.1	Straight, not left (But turn left for beach [.5 m])	No sign
		Continue through Morfa Bychan	
C	1.5	Right at X-roads (But keep straight for beach)	No sign
	.8	On right, track to tiny Treflys Church — panoramic view of Morfa Bychan and Black Rock Sands from churchyard	
D	1.3	Through dense woodland, then left at T-junction on to A497 and under railway bridge	No sign
	1.0	Stay on main road through village of Pentrefelin — track through gateway on left leads to Ystumllyn Church	
E	.2	Straight, not right	No sign
	1.1	Lay-by on left, with fine view of Criccieth Castle	
	.3	Forward over X-roads	No sign
		Left turn leads to sea-front	
F	.4	Turn right at X-roads in centre of Criccieth on to B4411 (But turn left for seafront and castle)	Caernarfon
G	.4	Turn left from main road	No sign
H	.2	Right at Y-junction	No sign
	1.3	On right, Lloyd George Memorial	
I	.1	Right at T-junction on to bridge over Afon Dwyfor	No sign
		NOTE: Oncoming traffic over bridge has priority, except when controlled by traffic-lights at busy periods	
J	.3	Through Llanystumdwy and bear left, not right	A497
	.2	Turn right at T junction on to A497	Pwllheli
	.3	On left old stone bridge (Bont Fechan) over Afon Dwyfach, now on a lay-by	
		Total mileage on this map: 10.9	

CROWN COPYRIGHT RESERVED

On Route

Porthmadog (See page 123)

Borth-y-Gest
A largely unspoilt little seaside resort, clustered around a small bay, and looking out over the Afon Glaslyn estuary, with its multitude of sailing dinghies and other boats. There are small sandy coves tucked away nearby and the wide range of accommodation makes Borth-y-Gest an ideal place for a quiet family holiday. There is a pleasant walk north-westwards passing between Cist Cerrig, three upright stones which are the remains of a Stone Age burial chamber, and Moel-y-Gest, a rocky hill with fine views from its summit.

Morfa Bychan
This is a modern development of bungalows and caravan sites behind the famous Black Rock Sands — more than a mile of firm clean sand on which you may safely drive your car; two access points are shown in the route directions. Here also is the Porthmadog Golf Club's course, laid out on linksland which is mainly National Trust property.

Pentrefelin
This hamlet on the A497 has a simple modern church which, like the nearby rectory, was designed by Clough Williams Ellis in 1912. On the south side of the road, near the centre of the village, is a standing stone which must be one of the tallest and slimmest in all Wales. The early Victorian 'old' church of Ynyscynhaearn, with its box pews and three-decker pulpit, was still standing at the end of a long farm track when we last called here, but was in a bad state of repair. We hope that it has fared better since — it certainly deserves to do so.

Criccieth
Unspoilt by sea-front shops and 'amusements', Criccieth is a quietly attractive resort, dominated by its castle ruins on a theatrical mound. To the east of the castle a gracefully curving promenade surrounds a shallow bay with sand and shingle beach; to the west a simple Marine Parade of Victorian hotels and guest houses. The town centre, with its well-kept green, has a village atmosphere. There is a Victorian parish church (on right of main road, before Point F); a turning to the right, also just before Point F, leads up hill past an older and less pretentious church towards the golf course on the slopes of Mynydd Ednyfed — worth exploring for the panoramic views.

The Castle (CADW) was built in the time of Llywelyn the Great (early 13c), and strengthened and extended by the English after Edward I had conquered the district in 1284. The English occupation continued fairly peacefully until the reign of Henry IV, when in spite of repairs to the Castle and reinforcement of the garrison, it fell to the Welsh during the rising inspired by Owain Glyndwr, and was burnt and left derelict. Since the 1930s it has been excavated and restored. As usual the official guide is excellent, and tells the whole interesting story — ☏ (0766) 522227.

Llanystumdwy (See Page 103)

1. Porthmadog Harbour

2. Ynyscnhaearn Church

3. Marine Parade, Criccieth

4. Lloyd George Statue

5. Lloyd George Memorial, Llanystumdwy

Map 47

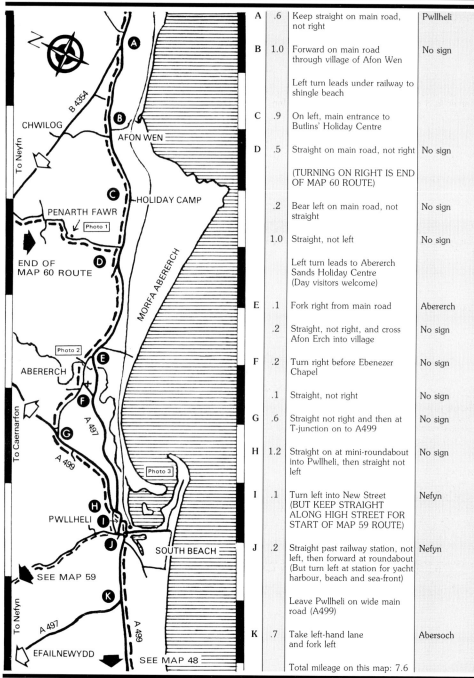

Ref.	kms / Miles	Directions	Sign-posted
A	.6	Keep straight on main road, not right	Pwllheli
B	1.0	Forward on main road through village of Afon Wen	No sign
		Left turn leads under railway to shingle beach	
C	.9	On left, main entrance to Butlins' Holiday Centre	
D	.5	Straight on main road, not right	No sign
		(TURNING ON RIGHT IS END OF MAP 60 ROUTE)	
	.2	Bear left on main road, not straight	No sign
	1.0	Straight, not left	No sign
		Left turn leads to Abererch Sands Holiday Centre (Day visitors welcome)	
E	.1	Fork right from main road	Abererch
	.2	Straight, not right, and cross Afon Erch into village	No sign
F	.2	Turn right before Ebenezer Chapel	No sign
	.1	Straight, not right	No sign
G	.6	Straight not right and then at T-junction on to A499	No sign
H	1.2	Straight on at mini-roundabout into Pwllheli, then straight not left	No sign
I	.1	Turn left into New Street (BUT KEEP STRAIGHT ALONG HIGH STREET FOR START OF MAP 59 ROUTE)	Nefyn
J	.2	Straight past railway station, not left, then forward at roundabout (But turn left at station for yacht harbour, beach and sea-front)	Nefyn
		Leave Pwllheli on wide main road (A499)	
K	.7	Take left-hand lane and fork left	Abersoch
		Total mileage on this map: 7.6	

CROWN COPYRIGHT RESERVED

On Route

Llanystumdwy (See Map 46)
The name means 'the church at the bend of the Dwy river', and the river, the Afon Dwyfor, is very much in evidence, as the narrow stone bridge in the centre of the village causes severe congestion at busy times. Llanystumdwy is best known for its associations with David Lloyd George, 1st Earl of Dwyfor, who spent his childhood with his widowed mother in a cottage opposite the Feathers Inn. His uncle, the village shoemaker, had his workshop next door. David Lloyd George became a solicitor, and practiced in Manchester and in partnership with his brother in Porthmadog; he was first elected to Parliament as the member for Caernarfon Boroughs in 1890. For many years his home was a house called Brynawelon at Criccieth, and his grave and memorial are at Llanystumdwy.
The memorial, an attractive circular composition in dark grey stone, and the entrance gates to the Museum opposite, were designed by Clough Williams Ellis. The woods in which the memorial stands slope steeply down to the Dywfor, and a footpath beside the river makes a beautiful walk. The Lloyd George Memorial Museum contains many mementoes of this famous politician.

Penarth Fawr (See Page 129)

Abererch
This is a quietly attractive grey and white village, with some unobtrusive modern development, on the banks of the Afon Erch. A restored medieval church and the red and white Ebenezer Chapel face each other at the top of the village (Point F). A turning to the left from the main road before you come to the village leads to the Abererch Sands Holiday Centre, a caravan site in the dunes behind the enormous beach of Morfa Abererch.

Pwllheli
There is little to remind you of the sea as you enter Pwllheli, the busy market centre of the Lleyn, and still a railway terminus. There are only one or two good buildings in the old town; of the many chapels the best is 'Penlan', and the parish church was built in the 'Early Decorated' style in 1887. But take the wide road past the station entrance, and in half a mile you will come to South Beach, a wide promenade behind a long shingle beach. If you turn left just before reaching the promenade, and drive another half mile through a council estate, you will come to the yacht harbour, with a busy boatyard, and a neat caravan site. Nearby stands the Gimblet Rock, an imposing mass of stone, but much reduced from its original size by quarrying. At one time Pwllheli harbour was busy with trading vessels, but it slowly silted up; in 1903 it was cleared with the help of a Government grant of £70,000, and it is now a popular yachting base.

1. Penarth Fawr (see page 129)

2. Abererch

3. Pwllheli Harbour

Map 48

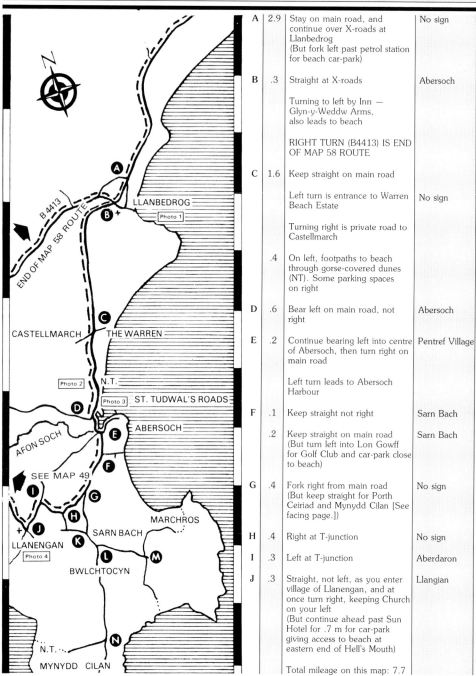

Ref	kms/Miles	Directions	Sign-posted
A	2.9	Stay on main road, and continue over X-roads at Llanbedrog (But fork left past petrol station for beach car-park)	No sign
B	.3	Straight at X-roads Turning to left by Inn — Glyn-y-Weddw Arms, also leads to beach RIGHT TURN (B4413) IS END OF MAP 58 ROUTE	Abersoch
C	1.6	Keep straight on main road Left turn is entrance to Warren Beach Estate Turning right is private road to Castellmarch	No sign
	.4	On left, footpaths to beach through gorse-covered dunes (NT). Some parking spaces on right	
D	.6	Bear left on main road, not right	Abersoch
E	.2	Continue bearing left into centre of Abersoch, then turn right on main road Left turn leads to Abersoch Harbour	Pentref Village
F	.1	Keep straight not right	Sarn Bach
	.2	Keep straight on main road (But turn left into Lon Gowff for Golf Club and car-park close to beach)	Sarn Bach
G	.4	Fork right from main road (But keep straight for Porth Ceiriad and Mynydd Cilan [See facing page.])	No sign
H	.4	Right at T-junction	No sign
I	.3	Left at T-junction	Aberdaron
J	.3	Straight, not left, as you enter village of Llanengan, and at once turn right, keeping Church on your left (But continue ahead past Sun Hotel for .7 m for car-park giving access to beach at eastern end of Hell's Mouth)	Llangian
		Total mileage on this map: 7.7	

CROWN COPYRIGHT RESERVED

On Route

Llandbedrog (See page 125)

Abersoch

Safe moorings for hundreds of yachts, and the boatyards to service them, explain the growing popularity of Abersoch with sailing folk; others are attracted by the very fine sandy beaches and the sporting golf course. The tidy complex of bungalows and caravans at the Warren has its own shops and services; the beach is long, wide and clean, and day visitors are welcome. The same beach can also be reached by footpaths across National Trust land nearer the village. Standing back from the road opposite the entrance to the Warren is the Jacobean manor house of Castellmarch (private). The other main beach is backed by the golf course, and is easily reached from Point F.

Sarn Bach, Bwlchtocyn, Porth Ceiriad and Mynydd Cilan

The complex of lanes southwards from Point G is well worth exploring, and there are several parking places which give access to the coast. Keep straight, not right, at Point G, and in .5 m keep straight again through the hamlet of Sarn Bach at Point K (see map). At Point L (.2 m) you can turn left (sign Marchros), and left again at Point M (.5 m) — this will take you to the southern end of the main Abersoch beach. At Point M bear left at Y-junction just past a letter box on the right. If you turn right at M the road has few parking places. After the Y-junction the road runs down to the beach with parking and toilets.

If you keep straight at Point L through Bwlchtocyn, in 1 mile at Point N there is a right turn (sign Mynydd Cilan) leading to open moorland (NT) which stretches as far as the rocky coast overlooking the south-eastern end of Porth Neigwl. Straight on from Point N takes you to the southern headlands of Trwyn Cilan and Trwyn Llech-y-doll.

Llanengan

The fine parish church dates from the 15th and early 16th centuries. The three bells bear 17th century dates, and are believed to have come from the Abbey of St. Mair on Bardsey, with which Llanengan was traditionally associated; it was no doubt a point of call for Bardsey pilgrims. In the church there is a beautiful screen between nave and chancel, and an offertory chest carved from a single baulk of timber, known as Cyff Engan.

The Sun Hotel is a pleasant free house; in .7 mile down the road past the inn you will find a car park from which a footpath leads to the beach at the south-eastern end of Porth Neigwl (see page 107).

1. Trwyn Llanbedrog

2. Abersoch

3. Abersoch — Mouth of Afon Soch

4. Llanengan Church

Map 49

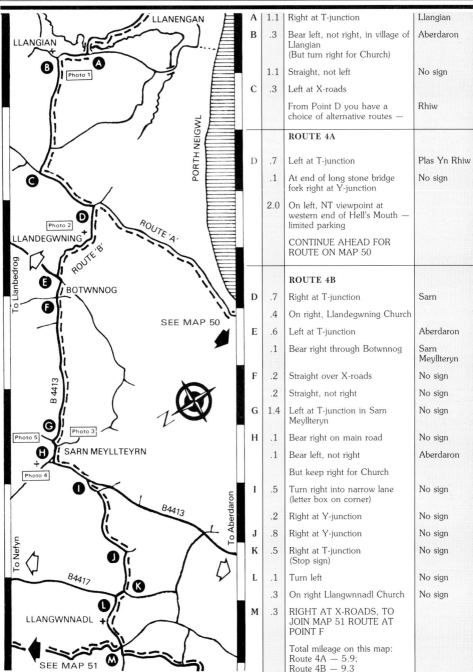

Ref	kms / Miles	Directions	Sign-posted
A	1.1	Right at T-junction	Llangian
B	.3	Bear left, not right, in village of Llangian (But turn right for Church)	Aberdaron
	1.1	Straight, not left	No sign
C	.3	Left at X-roads	
		From Point D you have a choice of alternative routes —	Rhiw
		ROUTE 4A	
D	.7	Left at T-junction	Plas Yn Rhiw
	.1	At end of long stone bridge fork right at Y-junction	No sign
	2.0	On left, NT viewpoint at western end of Hell's Mouth — limited parking	
		CONTINUE AHEAD FOR ROUTE ON MAP 50	
		ROUTE 4B	
D	.7	Right at T-junction	Sarn
	.4	On right, Llandegwning Church	
E	.6	Left at T-junction	Aberdaron
	.1	Bear right through Botwnnog	Sarn Meyllteryn
F	.2	Straight over X-roads	No sign
	.2	Straight, not right	No sign
G	1.4	Left at T-junction in Sarn Meyllteryn	No sign
H	.1	Bear right on main road	No sign
	.1	Bear left, not right	Aberdaron
		But keep right for Church	
I	.5	Turn right into narrow lane (letter box on corner)	No sign
	.2	Right at Y-junction	No sign
J	.8	Right at Y-junction	No sign
K	.5	Right at T-junction (Stop sign)	No sign
L	.1	Turn left	No sign
	.3	On right Llangwnnadl Church	No sign
M	.3	RIGHT AT X-ROADS, TO JOIN MAP 51 ROUTE AT POINT F	
		Total mileage on this map: Route 4A — 5.9; Route 4B — 9.3	

CROWN COPYRIGHT RESERVED

On Route

Porth Neigwl (Hell's Mouth)

This great bay, with 3½ miles of almost deserted sand, has a horrid reputation from the days of sail when the combination of south-westerly gales and treacherous offshore currents claimed many victims. Today it looks harmless enough, particularly when the sun shines. For the motorist the best access point for the beach is near Llanengan (see page 105).

Llangian

Some years ago Llangian earned the title of 'Best Kept Village in Wales', and that standard is still maintained, with spruce cottages and colourful gardens. The simple church, dating from the 13th and 15th centuries, with some modern addition, has a particular treasure in the churchyard. This is a rough stone pillar with a Latin inscription saying that the remains of 'Melius the doctor, son of Martinus, lie here'. It dates from the 5th or 6th century A.D., and is the only record in Britain of an early Christian burial which mentions the deceased's profession.

Llandegwning

There is hardly any village — just a charming miniature church with a conical spire, set on a small tower which is octagonal below and round above.

Sarn Meyllteryn

Pleasantly sited in a wooded valley, this village boasts three inns — the Pen-Y-Bont Hotel and the Penrhyn Arms on the main road, and the whitewashed Ty-Newydd Inn on the hillside to the left of our route. No doubt it was once a more important place than it is now. The sharply-pointed church (mid-19th century) has a beautiful position overlooking the valley on the side road from Point H.

'Arthur's Quoit' and Penllech Church

The best way to visit Cefnamwlch Burial Chamber (popularly known as 'Arthur's Quoit'), and the old Penllech Church, is to continue from Point H past Sarn Meyllteryn Church. In 1.2 m you will see the stones which formed the framework of the Iron Age burial chamber in a field to your left. In a further .3 m turn left on to B4417; then in another .2 m you will see a farm track on the right which leads to the church, now neglected and alone except for the adjacent farmyard. Another 1.2 m forward on B4417 brings you to cross-roads (Point L), where you turn right to rejoin our route.

Llangwnnadl

Again there is no obvious village, but this unusual three-aisled church is still active and well cared-for. Spacious and airy, it was built in the 15th and 16th centuries on the site of a 6th century church. The sanctuary bell is a reproduction of the original 16th century bell now in the Cardiff Museum. In the south wall there is a 6th century stone with an inscribed Celtic cross, said to be the headstone of the founder's grave.

1. Cottages at Llangian

2. Llandegwning Church

3. Ty-Newydd Inn, Sarn Meyllteryn

4. Sarn Meyllteryn Church

5. Penrhyn Arms Hotel, Sarn Meyllteryn

Miles	Map 50	kms Ref Miles		Directions	Sign-posted
	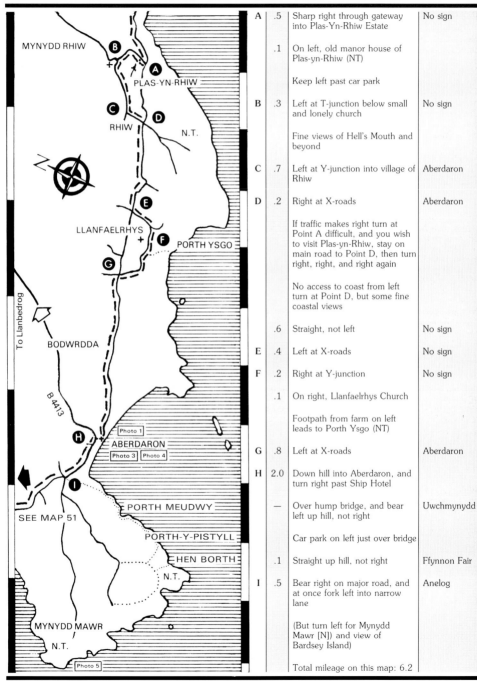	A	.5	Sharp right through gateway into Plas-Yn-Rhiw Estate	No sign
			.1	On left, old manor house of Plas-yn-Rhiw (NT)	
				Keep left past car park	
		B	.3	Left at T-junction below small and lonely church	No sign
				Fine views of Hell's Mouth and beyond	
		C	.7	Left at Y-junction into village of Rhiw	Aberdaron
		D	.2	Right at X-roads	Aberdaron
				If traffic makes right turn at Point A difficult, and you wish to visit Plas-yn-Rhiw, stay on main road to Point D, then turn right, right, and right again	
				No access to coast from left turn at Point D, but some fine coastal views	
			.6	Straight, not left	No sign
		E	.4	Left at X-roads	No sign
		F	.2	Right at Y-junction	No sign
			.1	On right, Llanfaelrhys Church	
				Footpath from farm on left leads to Porth Ysgo (NT)	
		G	.8	Left at X-roads	Aberdaron
		H	2.0	Down hill into Aberdaron, and turn right past Ship Hotel	
			—	Over hump bridge, and bear left up hill, not right	Uwchmynydd
				Car park on left just over bridge	
			.1	Straight up hill, not right	Ffynnon Fair
		I	.5	Bear right on major road, and at once fork left into narrow lane	Anelog
				(But turn left for Mynydd Mawr [N]) and view of Bardsey Island)	
				Total mileage on this map: 6.2	

CROWN COPYRIGHT RESERVED

On Route

Rhiw
This village on the slopes of Mynydd Rhiw is the highest in the Lleyn. Below the village the 16th century manor house of Plas-yn-Rhiw looks out beyond its beautiful woodland gardens across Porth Neigwl to the distant Welsh hills. It was given to the National Trust by the three daughters of William and Constance Keating in memory of their parents. The house and gardens are open to visitors — ☎ (0758) 88219. The Misses Keating have also been generous benefactors in giving the National Trust several areas of coastline in the district.

Aberdaron
This attractive little fishing and holiday village is situated in cliff-girt country with much gorse and heather, in a sheltered bay at the western end of the Lleyn Peninsula. It has bright painted plaster and pebble-dashed cottages, steep hills, a sparkling stream, a medieval hump-back bridge and a mile-long sandy beach. It was the last mainland stage for pilgrims on their long journey to the Abbey of St Mary on Bardsey Island, and their 14th century rest-house, Y-Gegin Fawr (*The Old Kitchen*), is now a cafe and souvenir shop. The nearby Post Office was designed by Clough Williams-Ellis, of Portmeirion fame. The large church on the cliff-edge above the beach dates from the 12th and 15th centuries, and has a late Norman doorway, weathered by centuries of storms. This building once gave sanctuary to the fugitive Gruffydd ap Rhys ap Tewdwr, during his successful flight from the allies of Henry I. Just under two miles to the north-east, the hill Mynydd Ystum is crowned by the earthworks of an Iron Age settlement, Castell Odo.

Walk south-west from Aberdaron along cliff paths, above the minute inlets of Porth Meudwy, Porth y Pistyll and Hen Borth, for fine views eastwards towards the mountains of Snowdonia.

Mynydd Mawr
Turn left at Point I and keep straight for 1½ miles to a gate on to National Trust property which embraces the whole of Mynydd Mawr (Big Mountain) and the headland of Braich-y-Pwll — the 'Land's End' of Wales. A concrete road zig-zags up hill to a car park on the summit from which the views are tremendous — Bardsey Island two miles SSW, and a panorama of the coastline of Lleyn, and the Welsh mainland. Footpaths lead across the rocky moorland to the cliffs, and on the eastern side of the headland it is possible, but dangerous, to scramble down to the shore to find the remains of an ancient church. Here also is Ffynnon Fair (St. Mary's Well), which is said always to yield fresh water, although covered by each tide.

Bardsey Island (Ynys Enlli)
The sound between the mainland and Bardsey Island is a notorious tide-race, and one possible translation of the Welsh name is 'Isle of Tides (or Eddies)'. The English name may have been derived from 'Birdsey'; appropriately the Island is now a bird

Continued on Page 111

1. Norman Doorway, Aberdaron Church

2. Roman Tombstone, Langian (see p. 107)

3. The Ship Hotel, Aberdaron

4. Y-Gegin Fawr, Aberdaron

5. Bardsey Island

Map 51

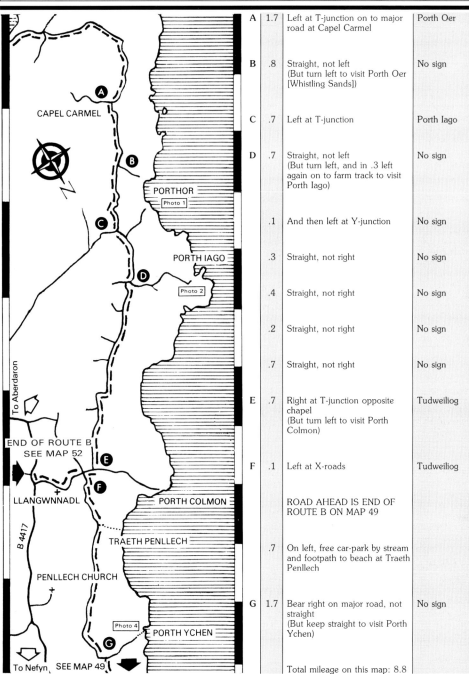

Ref.	kms / Miles	Directions	Signposted
A	1.7	Left at T-junction on to major road at Capel Carmel	Porth Oer
B	.8	Straight, not left (But turn left to visit Porth Oer [Whistling Sands])	No sign
C	.7	Left at T-junction	Porth Iago
D	.7	Straight, not left (But turn left, and in .3 left again on to farm track to visit Porth Iago)	No sign
	.1	And then left at Y-junction	No sign
	.3	Straight, not right	No sign
	.4	Straight, not right	No sign
	.2	Straight, not right	No sign
	.7	Straight, not right	No sign
E	.7	Right at T-junction opposite chapel (But turn left to visit Porth Colmon)	Tudweiliog
F	.1	Left at X-roads	Tudweiliog
		ROAD AHEAD IS END OF ROUTE B ON MAP 49	
	.7	On left, free car-park by stream and footpath to beach at Traeth Penllech	
G	1.7	Bear right on major road, not straight (But keep straight to visit Porth Ychen)	No sign
		Total mileage on this map: 8.8	

CROWN COPYRIGHT RESERVED

On Route

Bardsey Island *Continued from Page 109*
sanctuary, and is visited mainly by students of bird life and the lighthouse keepers. At one time it supported a small farming and fishing community. Only a ruined tower and a few stones now remain of the ancient Abbey of St. Mair (Mary), which was founded by St. Cadfan in the 6th century. The monks of Bangor-is-Coed, near Chester, came here for refuge when they were expelled by the Saxons, and the Abbey was a place of pilgrimage for hundreds of years. Ancient poets claimed that over 20,000 'saints', or holy men, are buried on the island.

Porthor (or Porth Oer) — Whistling Sands Bay
The sand of the bay is said to produce a whistling sound if it is walked on when dry — hence the popular name. Take the turning to the left at Point B; in ¼ mile there is a large car park, from which it is only a short walk down a fairly steep path to the beach.

Porth Iago
This is a delightful spot — a cove barely 100 yards across with a beach of golden sand between rocky headlands. It faces south-west and is a perfect sun-trap. To find it take the left turn at Point D, and in about ¼ mile turn left on to a fairly rough farm track (signed), pay a parking fee at the farm and continue to an ample grass car park just above the beach — less than a mile altogether from the main route.

Port Colmon
A drive of nearly a mile along a good road from Point E brings you to a rocky harbour where you can park. Here you can sit and enjoy the coastal scenery, or walk to your right along the cliff-top to a stretch of sandy beach, which is one end of Traeth Penllech (see below).

Traeth Penllech
About a mile in length, this beach of firm sand can be reached from Porth Colmon, or by a footpath from the car park on our route (see Route Directions). For about ¼ mile the path follows a stream which suddenly cascades down to the sea through the ravine it has cut for itself in the low rocky cliff. There is an easy climb down to the beach.

Porth Ychen
Less than ½ mile down the turning from Point G will be found a group of cottages where there is some parking space (but be careful not to obstruct the residents' entrances). Straight ahead is a footpath across a stretch of gorse and heather covered moorland which leads to a tiny rocky bay with a weed-strewn shingle beach.

Penllech Church (See page 107)

1. Porthor — 'The Whistling Sands'

2. Porth Iago

3. 'Arthur's Quoit'

4. Porth Ychen

Map 52

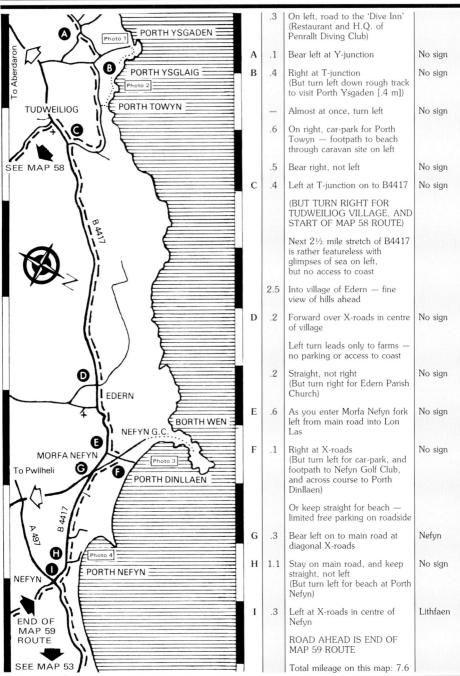

Miles	kms Ref. Miles	Directions	Signposted
	.3	On left, road to the 'Dive Inn' (Restaurant and H.Q. of Penrallt Diving Club)	
A	.1	Bear left at Y-junction	No sign
B	.4	Right at T-junction (But turn left down rough track to visit Porth Ysgaden [.4 m])	No sign
	—	Almost at once, turn left	No sign
	.6	On right, car-park for Porth Towyn — footpath to beach through caravan site on left	
	.5	Bear right, not left	No sign
C	.4	Left at T-junction on to B4417 (BUT TURN RIGHT FOR TUDWEILIOG VILLAGE, AND START OF MAP 58 ROUTE)	No sign
		Next 2½ mile stretch of B4417 is rather featureless with glimpses of sea on left, but no access to coast	
	2.5	Into village of Edern — fine view of hills ahead	
D	.2	Forward over X-roads in centre of village	No sign
		Left turn leads only to farms — no parking or access to coast	
	.2	Straight, not right (But turn right for Edern Parish Church)	No sign
E	.6	As you enter Morfa Nefyn fork left from main road into Lon Las	No sign
F	.1	Right at X-roads (But turn left for car-park, and footpath to Nefyn Golf Club, and across course to Porth Dinllaen)	No sign
		Or keep straight for beach — limited free parking on roadside	
G	.3	Bear left on to main road at diagonal X-roads	Nefyn
H	1.1	Stay on main road, and keep straight, not left (But turn left for beach at Porth Nefyn)	No sign
I	.3	Left at X-roads in centre of Nefyn	Lithfaen
		ROAD AHEAD IS END OF MAP 59 ROUTE	
		Total mileage on this map: 7.6	

CROWN COPYRIGHT RESERVED

On Route

Porth Ysgaden

A very rough track to the left from Point B takes you to Porth Ysgaden, known as the 'Herring Harbour', since it was once the base for a local fishing industry. The harbour buildings are now in ruins, but large mooring rings can still be seen on the rocks. A few local crab and lobster fishermen still keep their boats and gear down here. The surrounding coastline is extremely rocky, and it is a wild and dangerous place in a westerly gale. Footpaths eastwards over the cliffs lead to the next cove — Porth Ysglaig — and continue on to Porth Towyn (see below).

1. *Porth Ysgaden*

Porth Towyn

This is a popular sandy beach, and notices restrict parking in the road nearby, but there is a car park at the farm, from which a short footpath through a caravan site takes you down to the seashore.

Tudweiliog (See page 125)

Morfa Nefyn and Porth Dinllaen

As you approach Morfa Nefyn on the main road, there is nothing to suggest, apart from the name (Morfa means 'bog' or 'sea-marsh') that the sea is anywhere near. In fact the beach known as Porth Dinllaen, more than a mile of firm yellow sand, is only a few hundred yards from Point F. In the shelter of the headland at the western end of the beach is the peaceful hamlet of Porth Dinllaen, which the casual visitor can reach only by walking across the sands from Morfa Nefyn at low tide, or by a footpath across the golf course, which starts from the car park at Point F. Only residents who have a key to the golf course gate may take their cars on to the headland; suitable vehicles can drive over the sands at low tide.

2. *Porth Towyn*

There are traces of an Iron Age promontory fort on the headland. The unique situation of Porth Dinllaen makes it a wonderfully peaceful spot, and the houses there are much sought after; there is even a prosperous little inn. The ubiquitous William Madocks, M.P., of Porthmadog fame, was the author of a scheme to turn Porth Dinllaen into a port for the Irish Mail — thankfully it came to nothing, but not before the almost straight road from the south coast of Lleyn had been specially built to carry the anticipated mail traffic.

3. *Porth Dinllaen*

Porth Nefyn

At the eastern end of Porth Dinllaen the headland of Penrhyn Nefyn separates it from the next bay — Porth Nefyn, another fine sandy beach. This is easily reached by the rather insignificant turning on the left at Point H.

Nefyn (See page 127)

4. *The Rivals from Porth Nefyn*

Map 53

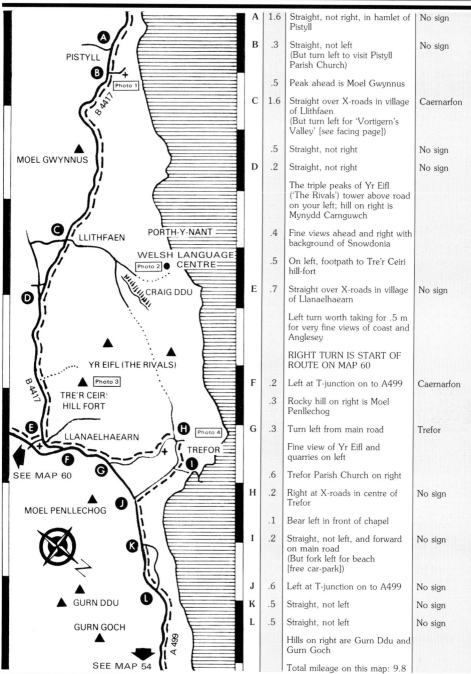

Ref.	kms & Miles	Directions	Signposted
A	1.6	Straight, not right, in hamlet of Pistyll	No sign
B	.3	Straight, not left (But turn left to visit Pistyll Parish Church)	No sign
	.5	Peak ahead is Moel Gwynnus	
C	1.6	Straight over X-roads in village of Llithfaen (But turn left for 'Vortigern's Valley' [see facing page])	Caernarfon
	.5	Straight, not right	No sign
D	.2	Straight, not right	No sign
		The triple peaks of Yr Eifl ('The Rivals') tower above road on your left; hill on right is Mynydd Carnguwch	
	.4	Fine views ahead and right with background of Snowdonia	
	.5	On left, footpath to Tre'r Ceiri hill-fort	
E	.7	Straight over X-roads in village of Llanaelhaearn	No sign
		Left turn worth taking for .5 m for very fine views of coast and Anglesey	
		RIGHT TURN IS START OF ROUTE ON MAP 60	
F	.2	Left at T-junction on to A499	Caernarfon
	.3	Rocky hill on right is Moel Penllechog	
G	.3	Turn left from main road	Trefor
		Fine view of Yr Eifl and quarries on left	
	.6	Trefor Parish Church on right	
H	.2	Right at X-roads in centre of Trefor	No sign
	.1	Bear left in front of chapel	
I	.2	Straight, not left, and forward on main road (But fork left for beach [free car-park])	No sign
J	.6	Left at T-junction on to A499	No sign
K	.5	Straight, not left	No sign
L	.5	Straight, not left	No sign
		Hills on right are Gurn Ddu and Gurn Goch	
		Total mileage on this map: 9.8	

CROWN COPYRIGHT RESERVED

On Route

Pistyll

The simple rectangular parish church of St. Beuno is at least partly 12th century, but high in the wall by the altar window there is a faint inscription which is thought to be the date 1050. Note the strong buttressing of the west front and the massive roof timbers; it was thatched until about 100 years ago. There are traces of wall paintings and a leper's window. At one time there were only three windows, all in the chancel, which made it very dark inside, but the congregation were no doubt illiterate, and had no need of light for reading. When we called soon after the harvest festival the church was still delightfully filled with the scent of hay and wild flowers strewn on the floor and used for decoration.

1. St. Beuno's Church, Pistyll

Llithfaen

In this exposed hillside village the turning to the left from the cross-roads at Point C leads to 'Vortigern's Valley'. Vortigern was the 'Great Prince' of the 5th century, who summoned Hengist and Horsa to his aid, and is supposed to have died here. In ½ mile you will come to a car park and picnic area (Forestry Commission); do not attempt to drive further, but take the footpath through the plantation on to the high slopes overlooking the sea and a long shingle beach with the remains of an abandoned pier. Behind this beach, which is called Porth y Nant, stands the Nant Gwrtheyrn Welsh Language Centre. This provides a wide range of facilities — ☏ (0758) 85334. Prominent across the valley is the sheer rock face of Craig Ddu (Black Crag), from which rise the steep slopes of Yr Eifl, scarred with disused quarries.

2. Vortigern's Valley

Yr Eifl — 'The Rivals'

These three peaks are a prominent landmark, with their height somewhat exaggerated by the nearness of the sea and the low ground to the south. Properly the Welsh name means 'The Forks' — 'The Rivals' is a fancy name thought up by the English. The central peak is the highest (1,850 ft), and the one nearest the sea the lowest (1,458 ft), its slopes ending in the rugged headland of Trwyn-y-Gorlech above Porth-y-Nant. The eastern peak above Llanaelhaearn (1,591 ft) is crowned by an ancient hill fort — 'Tre'r Ceiri — to which there is a fairly easy footpath from the main road (see Route Directions). The view from the summit on a clear day is one of the best in Wales, taking in most of the Lleyn, Anglesey and Snowdonia, with even a glimpse of the Isle of Man when conditions are favourable. Tre'r Ceiri is a group of cytiau (hut circles), stone walled structures which were once roofed with poles and bracken. The settlement covered more than 5 acres, and was surrounded by walls which still rise to 15 ft in places.

3. Tre'r Ceiri Hill Fort

Llanaelhaearn (See page 129)

Trefor (See page 117)

4. Yr Eifl

Map 54

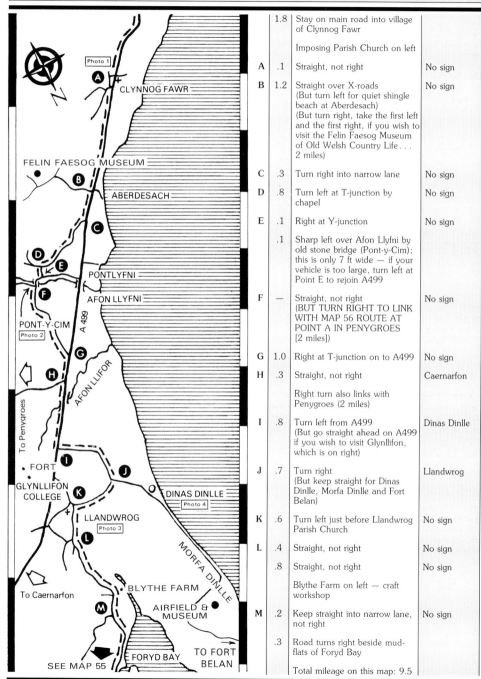

	kms Ref. Miles	Directions	Sign-posted
	1.8	Stay on main road into village of Clynnog Fawr Imposing Parish Church on left	
A	.1	Straight, not right	No sign
B	1.2	Straight over X-roads (But turn left for quiet shingle beach at Aberdesach) (But turn right, take the first left and the first right, if you wish to visit the Felin Faesog Museum of Old Welsh Country Life... 2 miles)	No sign
C	.3	Turn right into narrow lane	No sign
D	.8	Turn left at T-junction by chapel	No sign
E	.1	Right at Y-junction	No sign
	.1	Sharp left over Afon Llyfni by old stone bridge (Pont-y-Cim); this is only 7 ft wide — if your vehicle is too large, turn left at Point E to rejoin A499	
F	—	Straight, not right (BUT TURN RIGHT TO LINK WITH MAP 56 ROUTE AT POINT A IN PENYGROES [2 miles])	No sign
G	1.0	Right at T-junction on to A499	No sign
H	.3	Straight, not right Right turn also links with Penygroes (2 miles)	Caernarfon
I	.8	Turn left from A499 (But go straight ahead on A499 if you wish to visit Glynllifon, which is on right)	Dinas Dinlle
J	.7	Turn right (But keep straight for Dinas Dinlle, Morfa Dinlle and Fort Belan)	Llandwrog
K	.6	Turn left just before Llandwrog Parish Church	No sign
L	.4	Straight, not right	No sign
	.8	Straight, not right Blythe Farm on left — craft workshop	No sign
M	.2	Keep straight into narrow lane, not right	No sign
	.3	Road turns right beside mud-flats of Foryd Bay	
		Total mileage on this map: 9.5	

CROWN COPYRIGHT RESERVED

On Route

Trefor (See Map 53)
Many of the typical quarrymen's cottages have been refurbished as holiday homes, and are bright with new paint. The quarries themselves, on the slopes of Yr Eifl to the west of the village, and Gurn Ddu to the east, have declined, and the pier from which the stone was loaded on to coasters is derelict. The beach at Trefor is mainly mud and shingle, but there are patches of sand.

Clynnog Fawr
The magnificent late-Perpendicular church dedicated to St. Beuno was built as a collegiate church not later than the reign of the Tudor Henry VIII on the site of an earlier building. St. Beuno, probably the most important Welsh saint after St. David, came to Clynnog towards the end of his life in AD 635. The vast interior has the feeling of a cathedral, and contains some fine examples of wood carving in the roof timbers, rood screen and misericord seats. Relics include a massive oaken strong-box known as 'The Chest of Beuno', and a pair of dog-tongs. The holy water of St. Beuno's Well, on the side of the main road about 300 yards south-west of the church, was said to cure all ills. Just visible from the main road, and close to the sea on private ground, there is a fine cromlech or burial chamber.

Felin Faesog Museum of Old Welsh Country Life
Turn right at Point B to visit this 17th century watermill on the little Afon Desach, close to the hamlet of Tai'n Lon. Its contents includes kitchen and bedroom displays and various items illustrating the old Welsh way of life. These relate to farming, blacksmithing, printing, cobbling and joinery. There are also old prams, washing machines and one of the first vacuum cleaners, and of special interest is the machinery of the old mill itself. There is a cafe and shop — ☎ (0286) 86311.

Pont-y-Cim
The ancient single-span bridge once carried the main route from Caernarfon into the Lleyn, but was long ago by-passed by the main road through Pontlyfni. The bridge carries the date 1612, and is only 7 ft wide between parapets — just enough for a private car. It spans the Afon Llyfni which yields good salmon and trout fishing. Pontlyfni has some seaside bungalows and caravans, but the beach is stony and often covered with strong smelling seaweed.

Glynllifon
Formerly in the hands of the Lords Newborough, the 19th century mansion of Glynllifon (the third house on the present site) was opened as the Caernarfonshire Agricultural Institute in 1954, and the attractive gardens and grounds and the associated
Continued on Page 134

Llandwrog (See Page 119)
Dinas Dinlle (See Page 119)
Fort Belan (See Page 134)

1. St. Beuno's Church, Clynnog Fawr

2. Pont-y-Cim

3. Almshouses at Llandwrog

4. Yr Eifl from Dinas Dinlle

Map 55

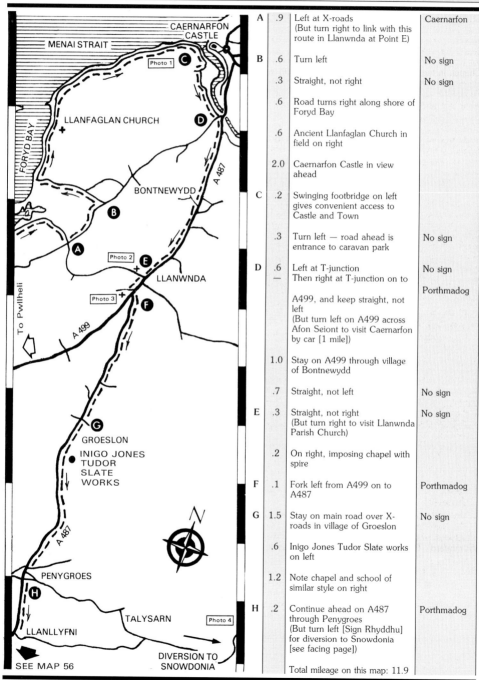

Ref	kms/Miles	Directions	Sign-posted
A	.9	Left at X-roads (But turn right to link with this route in Llanwnda at Point E)	Caernarfon
B	.6	Turn left	No sign
	.3	Straight, not right	No sign
	.6	Road turns right along shore of Foryd Bay	
	.6	Ancient Llanfaglan Church in field on right	
	2.0	Caernarfon Castle in view ahead	
C	.2	Swinging footbridge on left gives convenient access to Castle and Town	
	.3	Turn left — road ahead is entrance to caravan park	No sign
D	.6	Left at T-junction Then right at T-junction on to A499, and keep straight, not left (But turn left on A499 across Afon Seiont to visit Caernarfon by car [1 mile])	No sign / Porthmadog
	1.0	Stay on A499 through village of Bontnewydd	
	.7	Straight, not left	No sign
E	.3	Straight, not right (But turn right to visit Llanwnda Parish Church)	No sign
	.2	On right, imposing chapel with spire	
F	.1	Fork left from A499 on to A487	Porthmadog
G	1.5	Stay on main road over X-roads in village of Groeslon	No sign
	.6	Inigo Jones Tudor Slate works on left	
	1.2	Note chapel and school of similar style on right	
H	.2	Continue ahead on A487 through Penygroes (But turn left [Sign Rhyddhu] for diversion to Snowdonia [see facing page])	Porthmadog
		Total mileage on this map: 11.9	

CROWN COPYRIGHT RESERVED

On Route

Llandwrog (See Page 116)
A Gothic village built by Lord Newborough in the 1830's; the church with an impressive spire and a Gothic revival interior dates from 1860 — there are some beautiful monuments near the altar in the Wynne Chapel. In the village close to the church is a group of almshouses set in an attractive curve, while at Blythe Farm, about a mile beyond on our route, there is a craft workshop producing models in slate and resin — ☎ (0286) 831050.

Dinas Dinlle (See Page 116)
On this mound by the sea were some early British defence works; the Romans came and built a fort with double ramparts, and a causeway to connect it with Segontium, their base at Caernarfon — in fact it formed the seaward end of Watling Street, the trunk route which was vital for the military control of the country. Nearby a few modern bungalows, cafes and guest houses show little respect for history. A dead straight road continues northwards for more than a mile beside the lonely shingle beach to an an airfield from Which 'Snowdon Pleasure Flights' are available from Easter to September — ☎ (0286) 830800, and there is also an interesting Air Museum, the main theme of which is Mountain Rescue — a service which orginated here many years ago, when it was an RAF airfield.

Fort Belan (See Page 116 and 134)

Llanfaglan Church (See also page 17)
The community once served by this medieval church has gone, and it now stands alone, sheltered by trees within the churchyard wall and surrounded by open fields. It escaped the restoring zeal of the 19th century, but is still in good repair, and used for the occasional service and burial. The lintel inside the door is a late Roman tombstone, and there are other Roman stones in the walls — evidence that this site was a place of worship long before the present building.

Groeslon
Not an outstandingly interesting village, but on the left, not far beyond, will be found the Inigo Jones Tudor Slateworks, which has an interesting slate showroom and (in summer) a cafe — ☎ (0286) 830242.

Caernarfon (See pages 17 and 19)

Llanwnda
The Normanesque Parish Church (1848) is notable mainly for the large and ornate memorials in the churchyard. The prominent chapel with a spire on your right just before Point F is late Victorian.

Diversion to Nantlle and Snowdonia
We strongly recommend you to turn aside in Penygroes into the Nantlle valley, passing on your way the terraced miners' cottages and slate quarries of Talysarn. The road passes Llyn Nantlle and climbs through a mountain pass until you come in sight of the western slopes of Snowdon itself rising from the village of Rhyd-ddu, the starting point of one of the routes to the summit. (See Map 6, page 14.) The distance from Penygroes to Rhyd-ddu is about 7½ miles.

1. Caernarfon Castle

2. Monument in Llanwnda Churchyard

3. Chapel at Llanwnda

4. Snowdon from the Nantlle—Rhyd-ddu Road

Map 56

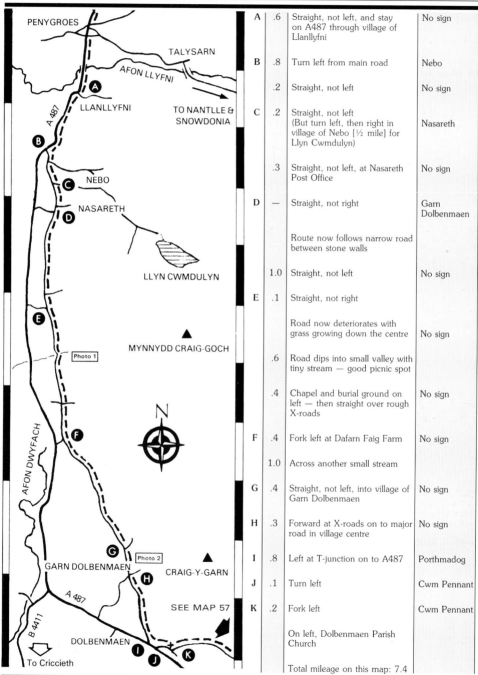

Ref.	kms / Miles	Directions	Sign-posted
A	.6	Straight, not left, and stay on A487 through village of Llanllyfni	No sign
B	.8	Turn left from main road	Nebo
	.2	Straight, not left	No sign
C	.2	Straight, not left (But turn left, then right in village of Nebo [½ mile] for Llyn Cwmdulyn)	Nasareth
	.3	Straight, not left, at Nasareth Post Office	No sign
D	—	Straight, not right	Garn Dolbenmaen
		Route now follows narrow road between stone walls	
	1.0	Straight, not left	No sign
E	.1	Straight, not right	
		Road now deteriorates with grass growing down the centre	No sign
	.6	Road dips into small valley with tiny stream — good picnic spot	
	.4	Chapel and burial ground on left — then straight over rough X-roads	No sign
F	.4	Fork left at Dafarn Faig Farm	No sign
	1.0	Across another small stream	
G	.4	Straight, not left, into village of Garn Dolbenmaen	No sign
H	.3	Forward at X-roads on to major road in village centre	No sign
I	.8	Left at T-junction on to A487	Porthmadog
J	.1	Turn left	Cwm Pennant
K	.2	Fork left	Cwm Pennant
		On left, Dolbenmaen Parish Church	
		Total mileage on this map: 7.4	

CROWN COPYRIGHT RESERVED

On Route

Llanllyfni
An unexceptional quarrying village astride the A487, with several chapels including one, the Capel Ebenezer, which has an unspoilt early 19th century interior complete with box pews. To the north-east of the village the earthworks of a defended Iron Age settlement, Caer Engan, overlook the swift-flowing Afon Llyfni.

Llyn Cwmdulyn
This little reservoir at the end of a rough track beyond the village of Nebo (see Route Directions) nestles at the foot of a sheer rock face — Craig Cwmdulyn. The peak to the east immediately behind the lake is Garnedd Goch (2,301 ft), and the one to the south is Mynydd Craig Goch (1,996 ft).

1. Our Route near Point E

Dolbenmaen and Garn Dolbenmaen
These are quite separate villages — Garn Dolbenmaen is much the larger and stands some way up the hillside away from A487; it has a wide main street with some attractively grouped buildings. Dolbenmaen has been by-passed more recently, and is little more than a hamlet; the tiny church has an 18th century lych-gate.

Diversion to Cwm Pennant (See Page 122)
This delectable valley with oak and ash much in evidence, stretches north (from Point A) into the mountains for more than 4 miles, closely following the Afon Dwyfor back towards its source. There are interesting remains of old mines, but farming is the only occupation here today. The head of the valley is dominated on the east by lofty Moel Hebog, and on the north and west by the Nantlle Ridge, which incorporates the summits of Garnedd-goch, Trum y Ddysgl and Y Garn. From the end of the public road at Beudy'r Ddol there is a track running north-east over the Bwlch-y-ddwy-elor, and down through part of the Beddgelert Forest to Rhyd-Ddu, but most who come here will be content with the tranquil charms of the valley itself. Let us leave the last words to the much-quoted Eifion Wyn — 'O God, why didst Thou make Cwm Pennant so beautiful and the life of an old shepherd so short?' Although it is possible to drive right up this valley, it would be preferable to explore it on foot, using the Ordnance Survey's Landranger Sheet 115, or if possiblle, their large scale Outdoor Leisure Map 17.

2. Garn Dolbenmaen

Brynkir Woollen Mills (See Page 122)
A working woollen mill where visitors may see machines in action, and then browse in the mill shop, where mill products on display include blankets, bedspreads, travelling rugs, tweeds and flannels. There is also a water wheel to be seen — ☎ (0766) 75236.

Diversion to Llyn Cwmystradlyn
(See Page 122)
This reservoir in a remote mountain valley is about 2½ miles from the main road. On your way you will pass the gaunt ruin of Ynyspandy slate mill.

3. In Cwm Pennant

Map 57

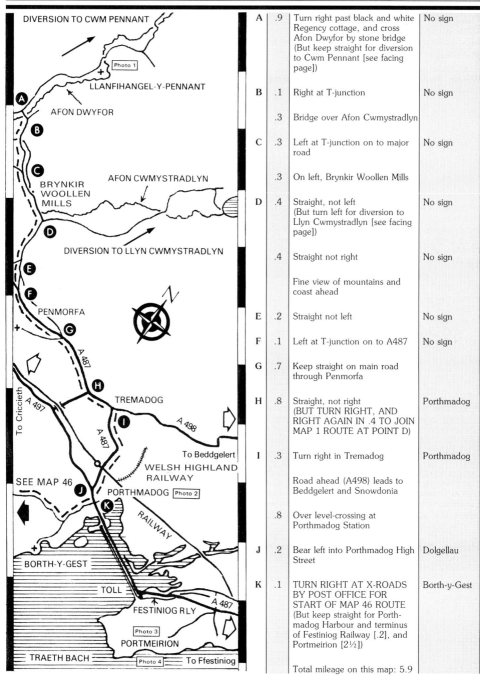

Ref	kms/Miles	Directions	Sign-posted
A	.9	Turn right past black and white Regency cottage, and cross Afon Dwyfor by stone bridge (But keep straight for diversion to Cwm Pennant [see facing page])	No sign
B	.1	Right at T-junction	No sign
	.3	Bridge over Afon Cwmystradlyn	
C	.3	Left at T-junction on to major road	No sign
	.3	On left, Brynkir Woollen Mills	
D	.4	Straight, not left (But turn left for diversion to Llyn Cwmystradlyn [see facing page])	No sign
	.4	Straight not right	No sign
		Fine view of mountains and coast ahead	
E	.2	Straight not left	No sign
F	.1	Left at T-junction on to A487	No sign
G	.7	Keep straight on main road through Penmorfa	
H	.8	Straight, not right (BUT TURN RIGHT, AND RIGHT AGAIN IN .4 TO JOIN MAP 1 ROUTE AT POINT D)	Porthmadog
I	.3	Turn right in Tremadog	Porthmadog
		Road ahead (A498) leads to Beddgelert and Snowdonia	
	.8	Over level-crossing at Porthmadog Station	
J	.2	Bear left into Porthmadog High Street	Dolgellau
K	.1	TURN RIGHT AT X-ROADS BY POST OFFICE FOR START OF MAP 46 ROUTE (But keep straight for Porthmadog Harbour and terminus of Festiniog Railway [.2], and Portmeirion [2½])	Borth-y-Gest
		Total mileage on this map: 5.9	

CROWN COPYRIGHT RESERVED

On Route

For Diversions to: Cwm Pennant, Brynkir Woollen Mills and Llyn Cwmystradlyn (See Page 121)

Penmorfa

Its name means *head of the marsh*, and until William Madocks built his famous embankments, Penmorfa was indeed on the edge of marshy estuary country. It was here that Madocks first bought a small farm in 1797, and the nearby 'new town' of Tremadog was the result of his earliest reclamation activities.

Much of the small village of Penmorfa now lies on the A487, but the church will be found half a mile to the south. This attractively situated building has some 15th century glass in its west window, and also a memorial to Sir John Owen, a royalist leader in the Civil War, who was once condemned to death, but who secured a reprieve and lived to see the restoration of Charles II, the son of the monarch whose cause he had served so well. Close to the church there is an interesting pottery and farm museum at Tyn Llan Farm, which also has a cafe.

Tremadog

This little town was developed by William Madocks, M.P., the founder of Porthmadog, as part of his scheme to make Porth Dinllaen on the north coast of Lleyn the port for a new mail route to Ireland. It was built during the first years of the 19th century on reclaimed land, and the buildings facing the open square have an attractive unity of design — a good example of early town planning. High in the woods to the east of Tremadog is the Regency house of Tan-yr-Allt, built by Madocks and later rented by the poet Shelley. T. E. Lawrence, of World War I desert fame, was born in Tremadog.

Porthmadog

Early in the 19th century, while already working on the creation of nearby Tremadog, William Madocks, M.P. for Boston in Lincolnshire, gained the approval of Parliament for the building of a mile-long embankment across the mouth of the Glaslyn Estuary. This embankment, which for many years has carried both road and narrow gauge railway, and which is known as The Cob, reclaimed nearly seven thousand acres from the sea and made Porthmadog a major port for the then rapidly growing slate industry. Boston Lodge at its eastern end was named after the M.P.'s constituency, and the workshops of the Ffestiniog Narrow Gauge Railway are located here. The picturesque trading schooners and ketches have long since departed — all except one, the sailing ketch *Garlandstone*, now moored to the quayside as the main exhibit of Porthmadog's interesting Maritime Museum.

The harbour is now filled with yachts and other pleasure craft, and modern houses and flats have been built on the quays. The other relic of the slate industry, and now very much alive, is the Ffestiniog
Continued on Page 138

Ffestiniog Railway (See page 13)

1. Llanfihangel-y-Pennant Church

2. Porthmadog Harbour

3. Portmeirion Village (see pages 127 and 129)

4. Portmeirion Hotel (see page 129)

Map 58

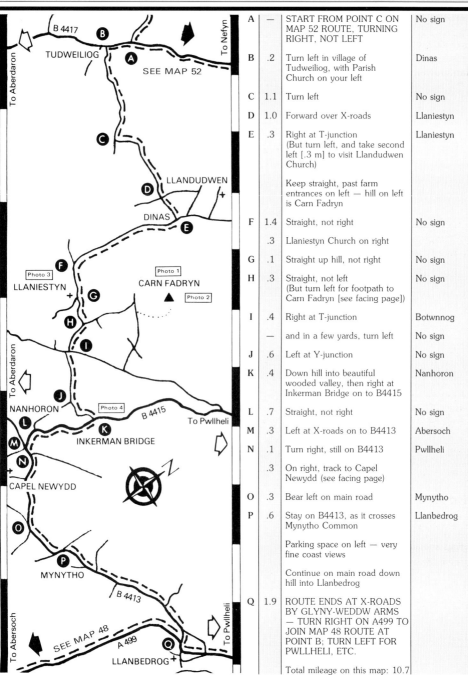

Ref	kms Miles	Directions	Sign-posted
A	—	START FROM POINT C ON MAP 52 ROUTE, TURNING RIGHT, NOT LEFT	No sign
B	.2	Turn left in village of Tudweiliog, with Parish Church on your left	Dinas
C	1.1	Turn left	No sign
D	1.0	Forward over X-roads	Llaniestyn
E	.3	Right at T-junction (But turn left, and take second left [.3 m] to visit Llandudwen Church)	Llaniestyn
		Keep straight, past farm entrances on left — hill on left is Carn Fadryn	
F	1.4	Straight, not right	No sign
	.3	Llaniestyn Church on right	
G	.1	Straight up hill, not right	No sign
H	.3	Straight, not left (But turn left for footpath to Carn Fadryn [see facing page])	No sign
I	.4	Right at T-junction	Botwnnog
	—	and in a few yards, turn left	No sign
J	.6	Left at Y-junction	No sign
K	.4	Down hill into beautiful wooded valley, then right at Inkerman Bridge on to B4415	Nanhoron
L	.7	Straight, not right	No sign
M	.3	Left at X-roads on to B4413	Abersoch
N	.1	Turn right, still on B4413	Pwllheli
	.3	On right, track to Capel Newydd (see facing page)	
O	.3	Bear left on main road	Mynytho
P	.6	Stay on B4413, as it crosses Mynytho Common	Llanbedrog
		Parking space on left — very fine coast views	
		Continue on main road down hill into Llanbedrog	
Q	1.9	ROUTE ENDS AT X-ROADS BY GLYNY-WEDDW ARMS — TURN RIGHT ON A499 TO JOIN MAP 48 ROUTE AT POINT B; TURN LEFT FOR PWLLHELI, ETC.	
		Total mileage on this map: 10.7	

CROWN COPYRIGHT RESERVED

On Route

Tudweiliog
An exposed village on a hill-top, with a pleasant-looking inn, and a dull Victorian church, rebuilt by Sir Gilbert Scott in 1850.

Llandudwen Church
This is a tiny medieval church, beautifully kept and standing alone in open farmland within a close-mown walled enclosure — a visual gem well worth the short detour. The contents of this attractive little building, which is dedicated to St Tudwen, the great-aunt of St David, include an octagonal font probably made in the 10th century, and some early 19th century glass.

Llaniestyn
In a wooded valley at the foot of Carn Fadryn, this peaceful village has another well-cared-for medieval church, distinguished by an unusual musicians' gallery. It also has a good 16th century font and a number of attractive monuments.

Carn Fadryn
There is an Iron Age fort on the top of this prominent, conical-shaped hill, and a large flat stone known as Arthur's Table or the King's Table (*Bwrdd y Brenin*). Local legend tells of a pot of gold hidden beneath the stone, and it is also thought to have been connected with the Stone of Destiny, beneath the Coronation Chair in Westminster Abbey. Whether or not you are fascinated by legends of this type, you will enjoy the walk around the hill from Garnfadryn village. Enquire at Garnfadryn if it is in order to walk to the top, on the path that starts near the telephone box (turn left at Point H, and in .6 turn right at T-junction). There are fine views to be had from this summit.

Capel Newydd
Located at the end of a long farm track between Points N and O (right of way for walkers,) it is believed to be the earliest surviving nonconformist chapel in North Wales. Dating from 1769, it is a simple barn-like structure with earth floor and box pews. When we last called here the key was available from the house on the road where the track starts.

Mynytho
This scattered parish occupies much of the high ground inland from Llanbedrog and Abersoch. Most of it is common land, on which there are several springs and ancient wells.

Llandbedrog (See also page 104)
Apart from one or two 17th century cottages nestling at the foot of the tree-covered headland of Mynydd Tirycwmwd, and the much restored little church with its tiny lych gate, the seaward portion of Llandbedrog, almost hidden in the trees between the main road and the sea, is entirely modern. The wide sandy beach is sheltered by the headland from the south-west, and the sands extend eastwards almost unbroken to Pwllheli. The old village straggles up the hill above the village along B4413 towards Mynytho.

1. Carn Fadryn

2. View from Carn Fadryn

3. Cottages at Llaniestyn

4. Springtime near Inkerman Bridge

Map 59

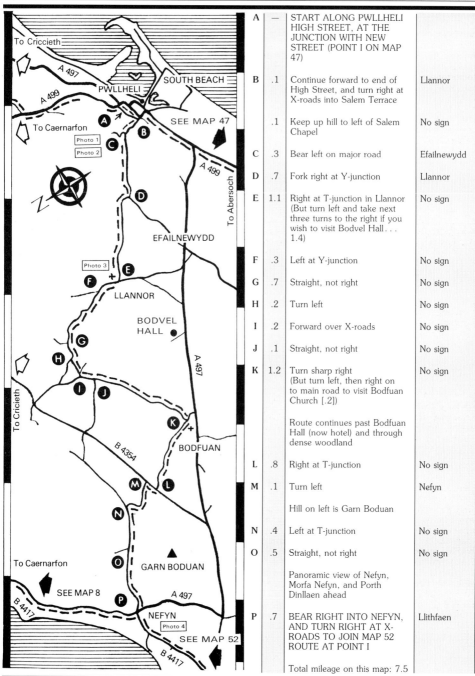

	kms Ref. Miles	Directions	Sign-posted
A	—	START ALONG PWLLHELI HIGH STREET, AT THE JUNCTION WITH NEW STREET (POINT I ON MAP 47)	
B	.1	Continue forward to end of High Street, and turn right at X-roads into Salem Terrace	Llannor
	.1	Keep up hill to left of Salem Chapel	No sign
C	.3	Bear left on major road	Efailnewydd
D	.7	Fork right at Y-junction	Llannor
E	1.1	Right at T-junction in Llannor (But turn left and take next three turns to the right if you wish to visit Bodvel Hall... 1.4)	No sign
F	.3	Left at Y-junction	No sign
G	.7	Straight, not right	No sign
H	.2	Turn left	No sign
I	.2	Forward over X-roads	No sign
J	.1	Straight, not right	No sign
K	1.2	Turn sharp right (But turn left, then right on to main road to visit Bodfuan Church [.2])	No sign
		Route continues past Bodfuan Hall (now hotel) and through dense woodland	
L	.8	Right at T-junction	No sign
M	.1	Turn left	Nefyn
		Hill on left is Garn Boduan	
N	.4	Left at T-junction	No sign
O	.5	Straight, not right	No sign
		Panoramic view of Nefyn, Morfa Nefyn, and Porth Dinllaen ahead	
P	.7	BEAR RIGHT INTO NEFYN, AND TURN RIGHT AT X-ROADS TO JOIN MAP 52 ROUTE AT POINT I	Llithfaen
		Total mileage on this map: 7.5	

CROWN COPYRIGHT RESERVED

On Route

Pwllheli (See page 103)

Llannor

In a rather dull village with some ugly council houses, the church has a bold outline, with stepped gables above a plain tower; there is a late Roman tombstone in the porch. Well to the west, and just off the A497, is Bodvel Hall, the house where Dr Johnson's friend, the beautiful Mrs Hester Thrale, was born in 1741. A range of farm buildings now contains a crafts and country pursuits centre, complete with coffee shop and other attractions — ☏ (0758) 613386.

Bodfuan

The neo-Norman sandstone church (1894) beside the main road has a **X**-shaped interior and some good monuments of the Wynn family of Bodvean. The Hall, early 18th century with Victorian additions, almost hidden in dense woods of beeches and rhododendrons, is now an hotel. The prominent hill just south of Nefyn is Garn Boduan, 280 m (918 ft), and has remains of an Iron Age fort near its summit. (Bodfuan, Bodvean, and Boduan are all variations of the same name.)

Nefyn (See Map 52)

Although there is little to show for it now, this place has a long history. In 1224 King Edward I of England celebrated his victory over Llywelyn the Last by holding a tournament here, and in 1355 it was designated one of the ten Royal Boroughs of Wales. No buildings remain from that period, and most of the town is comparatively modern. Even the old church of St. Mary, rebuilt in 1820 with a rather narrow tower which has an over-large ship as a weather-vane, is now derelict. However do not miss a visit to the interesting Lleyn Historical and Maritime Museum. It should also be possible to take a boat trip to Carreg y Llam, near Penrhyn Glas, a massive sea cliff to the north-east, where a wide variety of sea birds can be spotted.

Portmeirion (See map 57)

Situated on a rocky peninsula between the estuaries of the Afon Glaslyn and the Afon Dwyryd, Portmeirion is the creation of the famous architect, Sir Clough Williams Ellis. Here on a densely wooded south-facing slope amidst a wild garden of rhododendrons and azaleas, he created for us a magnificent 'folly', an Italianate village that has become one of the great showplaces of North Wales. He always intended that it should be an 'eye-opener' to awaken the visitors' sense of pleasure in architecture, and to provide an object lesson in how a very beautiful site could be developed without spoiling it. There can be very little doubt that he achieved this aim.

His village contains an astonishing variety of romantic fantasies and detailed architectural features, some of which Williams Ellis himself rescued from buildings in course of demolition. Amongst the

Continued on Page 129

1. Street in Old Pwllheli

2. Pwllheli Harbour

3. Llannor Church

4. Three Herrings Inn, Nefyn

Map 60

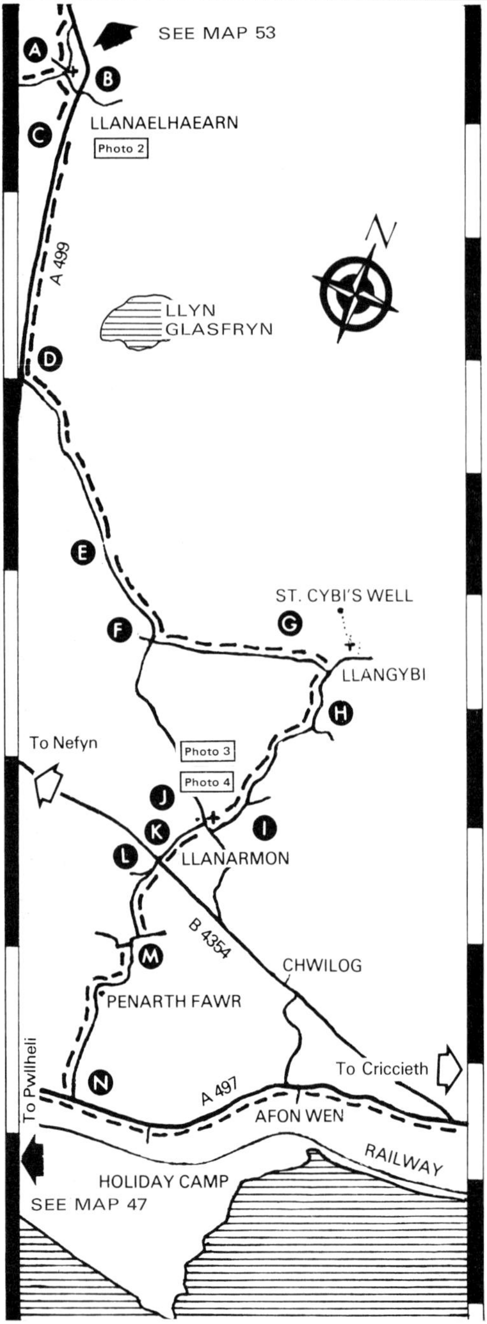

Ref	kms/Miles	Directions	Sign-posted
A	—	START IN VILLAGE OF LLANAELHAEARN, TURNING RIGHT AT X-ROADS (POINT C ON MAP 53 ROUTE) Parish Church on left	No sign
B	.1	Right at X-roads on to A499	No sign
C	.2	Straight, not left	No sign
D	1.4	Turn left from A499	Pencaenewydd
E	1.2	Straight over X-roads	Llanarmon
F	.6	Left at X-roads	Llangybi
G	1.0	Right at Y-junction in Llangybi (But turn left to visit Llangybi Church and St. Cybi's Well [see facing page])	Llanarmon
H	.4	Turn right	Llanarmon
I	.6	Right at T-junction	No sign
J	.3	Right at T-junction, then fork left, keeping Llanarmon Church and school on your right	Y Ffor
K	.3	Forward at X-roads over B4354	No sign
L	.1	Straight, not right	No sign
M	.4	Right at T-junction	No sign
	.1	Straight, not right	No sign
	.4	Bear left round farm — on left just after corner is Penarth Fawr (medieval hall)	
N	.6	RIGHT AT T-JUNCTION ON TO A497 TO JOIN MAP 47 ROUTE AT POINT D — OR TURN LEFT FOR BUTLINS' HOLIDAY WORLD (.5), CRICCIETH, PORTHMADOG, ETC.	

Total mileage on this map: 7.7

CROWN COPYRIGHT RESERVED

On Route

Portmeirion *Continued from Page 127*
village's many pastel-coloured buildings, there will be found a number of shops, including the Portmeirion Pottery Seconds Shop, and a restaurant. Below it and within yards of the sandy shore, is the Portmeirion Hotel, converted from a handsome early 19th century house. This has its own 'folly', a trim little sailing ship made of concrete, safely 'moored' to the quayside outside the hotel windows. There is ample parking above the village, and day visitors are welcome on payment of a fee — ☏ (0766) 770457.

Llanaelhaearn (See also Map 53)

The cruciform Parish Church of this village in the shadow of Yr Eifl dates back to the 12th century, but was very much restored and enlarged at the end of the 19th century. It has a fine 15th or 16th century rood screen and attractive box pews. Several inscribed stones, probably 6th century, were found during restoration, and link the church with the period of the pilgrimages to Bardsey.

Llangybi

Small village below a wooded hill topped by the fragmentary remains of a hill fort — Carn Bentyrch. The simple church of St Cybi occupies the site of one founded by this 6th century Cornish saint and healer of the sick. A path leads through the churchyard and over the field beyond to Fynnon Gybi (St Cybi's Well), well-known for its curative powers over the course of many centuries. Now a roofless stone structure attached to the ruins of a later cottage, this well was turned into an 18th century spa by local squire, William Price of Rhiwlas, and this appears to be the reason for the ruined buildings that remain today. The nearby almshouses were also built by Price, in 1760. There are pleasant walks around here, notably northwards to the coast and westwards to Llyn Glasfryn, but be sure to keep to the rights of way shown on the Ordnance Survey's Landranger Map 123.

Llanarmon

The adjacent church and school were both built in the 15th century; the church has a graceful arcade between its two aisles and a primitive contemporary rood screen.

Penarth Fawr (CADW)

This well-preserved stone building was the hall of a Welsh gentleman's house of the early 15th century, and contains some fine timber work and an impressive stone fireplace. The roof and windows are however comparatively modern. It is open at all reasonable times, but be careful not to obstruct the roadway or damage the grass verges when parking.

1. Portmeirion

2. Llanaelhaearn Church

3. View from Llanarmon Porch

4. Llanarmon Church

Other Places of Special Interest

A description of the interesting features in Snowdonia, Anglesey and the Lleyn Peninsula not included in our planned routes on pages 4–129, and continuations of those not described in full on those pages.

Aberangell *(14 mi. SE Dolgellau) (Approach from Map 26)* Small village in the delightfully wooded valley of the River Dovey (Afon Dyfi), and on the eastern fringes of the great Dyfi Forest. There is an interesting and beautiful forest road leading west from here to the little village of Aberllefenni.

Aberdyfi (Aberdovey) *(10 mi. W Machynlleth) (Approach from Map 16)* Cheerful holiday village situated on a narrow strip of land between the mountains and the beautiful sweeping sands of the Dovey (Dyfi) Estuary. Like many other holiday resorts, its architecture is largely Victorian, but here it is much cosier in feeling than most, and it is further flavoured by a wharf and jetty with many colourful boats at their moorings close by. There is a small Maritime Museum on the seafront. Sea fishing trips are available, and it should also be possible to hire motor boats or sailing dinghies or to take the passenger ferry across the estuary to the Ynyslas shore.

Abergynolwyn *(7 mi. NE Tywyn) (Approach from Map 27)* This small village in the Dysynni Valley was once an important slate quarrying centre, and vast quarries lie at the head of the attractive valley to its south-east. Here is Nant Gwernol Station, the north-eastern terminus of the highly popular Talyllyn Railway (see page 139). There are an attractive series of forest walks starting from the Nant Gwernol Station where there is a useful car park and picnic site.

Aberllefenni *(2 mi. NE Corris) (Approach from Map 27)* There is an attractive forest road some five miles in length, leading east from this minute slate-mining village on the western fringes of Aberdyfi Forest to the small village of Aberangell. There is also a pleasant two-mile-long forest trail starting across a footbridge from the Forestry Commission's picnic site at Foel Friog on the small road into Aberllefenni from Corris.

Abermenai Point *(3 mi. SE Newborough) (Approach from Map 32, Point G)* Standing at the southern entrance to the Menai Strait, this is the southernmost

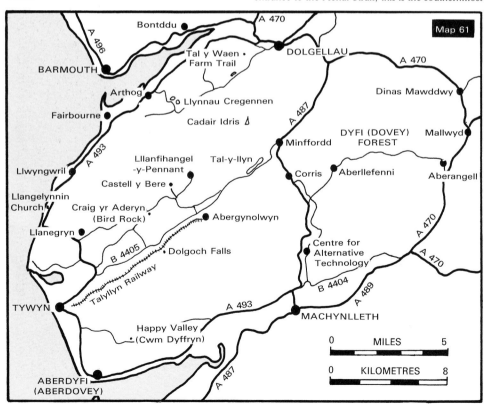

tip of Anglesey. Until the early 19th century one of the main routes into Anglesey used a ferry across the Strait here. The remains of an old breakwater may still be seen, and there is a safe anchorage for day picnickers from sailing dinghies, with good views across the Strait to Fort Belan (see page 134). It is also possible to walk here from Newborough, across Newborough Warren, but ask locally for advice before setting out (see also Newborough, page 71).

Arthog *(6 mi. SW Dolgellau) (Approach from Map 16)* Small village beneath steep wooded hillsides, with a plain little 19th century church. Climb up from here past the Arthog waterfalls, to obtain fine views out over the Mawddach estuary and to visit the lakes of Cregennen.

1. *Aberdyfi (Aberdovey)*

Blaenau Ffestiniog (See Page 11) (Go straight ahead at Point G) Small town situated at the head of the Vale of Ffestiniog, about four miles north of our route. Its prosperity was due almost entirely to the great slate caverns and quarries nearby, and today two of these caverns provide a variety of interesting experiences for visitors (see below). The town is on British Rail's Conwy Valley Line, and is also served by the Ffestiniog Narrow Gauge Railway coming up from Porthmadog. There is a Snowdonia National Park and Ffestiniog Railway Travel and Information Centre at Isallt in the centre of the town — ☏ (0766) 830360), and from here a leaflet can be purchased describing the interesting Blaenau Ffestiniog Town Trail. The Ffestiniog Hydro-Electric Scheme is at Tanygrisiau, a mile to the west of the town. Opened by the Queen in 1963, this is Wales' first hydro-electric pumped storage power station. There is an Energy Information Centre, a tour of the power station itself, and a dramatic 1,000 foot climb by bus, up to the Stwlan Storage Dam, from which there are panoramic views out over the National Park. The power station is accessible by road, and is also on the doorstep of the Ffestiniog Railway's Tanygrisiau request halt. Souvenir Shop, cafe, walks — ☏ (0766) 830310.

The Gloddfa Ganol Slate Mine, a mile to the north of the town is claimed to be 'the world's largest slate mine', and there is over ½ mile of awe-inspiring chambers and galleries on show. There is a museum illustrating the history of the slate industry, and three miners' cottages depict three periods during the last 100 years. In the mill slate blocks are processed into roofing slates, hearths and building stone, and slate goods for the adjoining shop. Panoramic walks. Landrover tours. Refreshments. Souvenir Shop — ☏ (0766) 830664.

2. *At the Gloddfa Ganol Slate Mine*

The Llechwedd Slate Caverns, also about a mile to the north of Blaenau Ffestiniog, to E of A470, are described as the biggest working slate mine in Wales and much of it is open to the public. The Miner's Tramway (the first ride) runs underground into 19th century slate mine workings, and there is a second ride, which offers further underground vistas and tableaux. The circular tour leads down even further until the Incline Railway is eventually joined for the return to the surface. There is also a Slate Heritage Theatre giving an audio-visual presentation, a Tramway Exhibition, a 'Harpist's Cottage', a Victorian-style pub, the Miners' Arms, and craft and gift shops. Sturdy shoes and moderately warm clothing are recommended — ☏ (0766) 830306.

3. *In the Llechwedd Slate Caverns*

1. The Mawddach Estuary, near Bontddu

2. Castell y Bere

3. At the Centre for Alternative Technology

4. Colwyn Bay

Bontddu *(On our route — see page 37)* Small village on the northern shore of the Mawddach estuary. Turn right just beyond the Bontddu Hall Hotel (Point G) for a car park beside a small road into the hills. Near this road up Cwm-Hirgwm is at least one gold mine, the Clogau St David's, which was still working when we called here last, and which has been the traditional source of Royal wedding rings since the turn of the century. There is a Gold Interpretative Centre in Bontddu village, from where it is possible to visit the workings. These are situated about 200 yards downstream of a bridge over the Hirgwm stream, on the west side of the road up from Bontddu.

Cadair Idris *(3 mi. S Dolgellau) (Approach from Map 16)* This rugged mountain range is made up of volcanic rocks eroded by glacial action over millions of years, and takes its name from one of the great hollows created thus, the legendary 'Chair of Idris', which shelters the waters of Llyn y Gadair. The Pony Path is the easiest route, the Fox's Path is dangerous and is not recommended, but there are leaflets available from the National Park Information Centres describing the Minffordd Path, up from the A487 in the south, the Pony Path from Ty Nant and the Pony Path from Llanfihangel-y-pennant in the south-west.

Castell y Bere *(11 mi. NE Tywyn) (Approach from Map 27)* Dramatically sited on a great rocky outcrop above the Dysynni valley, the ruined Castell y Bere was begun by Llywelyn the Great soon after 1221, but was regrettably captured by the English in 1283. However Edward I failed to hold it for long and after its fall in the uprising of 1294 it was finally abandoned. It is a romantic place with breathtaking views down the valley to Craig yr Aderyn, (The Bird Rock).

Centre for Alternative Technology *(4 mi. N Machynlleth) (Approach from Map 27)* Situated in an old slate quarry just to the east of the A487, the Centre is a public demonstration of energy conservation, solar power, water power and wind power. There is also an organic garden, an energy conserving house, blacksmith's forge, smallholding, restaurant and large bookshop. Do not miss a visit to this most interesting and thought-provoking place.

Colwyn Bay *(5 mi. E Conwy) (Approach from Map 1)* This major seaside resort runs along a 3 mile promenade westward from Penmaen Head to Rhos-on-Sea, and grew out of the villages of Old Colwyn and Llandrillo-yn-Rhos after very rapid development starting in the late 1860s. It is a lively place with a wide range of accommodation and a host of leisure activities for visitors of all ages. See especially the 50-acre Eirias Park, with its Leisure Centre, the Welsh Mountain Zoo, the Pier, two cinemas, a puppet theatre and a theatre. Beach and promenade attractions include a miniature railway, paddling pool and donkey rides. There is a Scenic Trail up to Bryneuryn, to the south of Llandrillo.

Conwy Continued from Page 23
Street, close to the Water Gate, is Aberconwy (NT), dating from 1300 and reputed to be the oldest house in Wales. This now houses the Conwy Exhibition,

depicting the life of the borough from Roman times to the present day. There is also a pleasant National Trust shop — ☏ (0492) 592246.

The Conwy Visitor Centre will be found in Rose Hill Street. This also tells the story of Conwy's past, with exhibitions, films shows and a craft shop. There is another Visitor Centre in Castle Street — ☏ (0492) 592248, and in the Bodlondeb Gardens to the north of the Town Wall, will be found the Conwy Butterfly Centre — ☏ (0492) 593149.

Corris *(10 mi. S Dolgellau) (Approach from Map 27)* Small slate mining and quarrying village in a valley now devoted more to forestry. The village's little sloping streets have considerable character and there is also an interesting Railway Museum here, which relates to the Corris Railway, a narrow-gauge line which once carried slate from the great quarries. There are also a number of interesting craft workshops within the Corris Craft Centre — ☏ (064) 73244 devoted to pottery, weaving, and wooden toys, and there is a restaurant and children's playground.

Craig yr Aderyn (Bird Rock) *(7 mi. NE Tywyn) (Approach from Map 27)* Stark rocky hill rising 762 feet from the floor of the attractive Dysynni Valley. Its unique shape is the oustanding feature of this valley, and it is the only place in inland Britain where cormorants nest.

Dolgoch Falls *(5 mi. NE Tywyn) (Approach from Map 27)* These delightful waterfalls may be reached by a 5-minute walk up a wooded valley from the B4405, or by an even shorter walk from the Dolgoch Falls Station on the Tallyllyn Railway. The two higher falls may be reached by further steep paths up through the woods.

Dyfi (Dovey) Forest *(Approach from Maps 26 or 27)* Large forest area situated in mountain country between Dolgellau and Machynlleth. The best bases from which to explore this are at Tan-y-Coed, just off the A487, 4 miles north of Machynlleth, and Foel Friog, which is on a minor road running north-east from the A487 at Corris. There is also a Forest Walk from Nant Gwernol, at the head of the Talyllyn Railway, near Abergynolwyn. It is also possible to drive on the forest road from Aberllefenni (see page 130) eastwards to Aberangell (see page 130).

Fairbourne *(7 mi. SE Dolgellau) (Approach from Map 16)* Bungalows are the predominant feature of this largely 20th century village, but there is a fascinating 2-mile long, 15″ gauge miniature railway (a horse-drawn tramway until 1916) running to the sand spit of Penrhyn Point, from whence there is a small passenger ferry across the mouth of the Mawddach estuary to Barmouth. It is also possible to drive almost as far as this, into an area of rough dunes. In summer this is a holiday place with many pleasure boats brought here for the day, and glorious

1. Craig yr Aderyn (The Bird Rock)

2. The Dolgoch Falls

3. In the Dyfi (Dovey) Forest

4. The Miniature Railway at Fairbourne

1. Barmouth—across the estuary from Fairbourne

2. The Happy Valley

3. Railway beside Llyn Padarn (see page 29)

views up and across the broad estuary to the wooded slopes of the mountains on either side. But in winter time the mood changes, and the boats are gone, the railway ceases to run, and this becomes a wild, deserted place from which to observe a wide variety of waterfowl.

Fort Belan (See Page 117)

This was built opposite Abermenai Point towards the end of the 18th century by the first Lord Newborough, as a 'sister' to Fort Williamsburg (see Glynllifon, page 117 and below). It was built here to defend the southern entry to the Menai Strait against the French and still has cannons upon its battlements. The peninsula on which it stands is not open at the time of writing, but this situation may change — ☏ (0286) 830220.

Glynllifon *Continued from Page 117*

Newborough Craft Workshops are open from Easter to October. There is an arboretum, a dingle and fountain, and a charming little stone building known as the Hermitage, which is situated above the delightfully wooded valley of the Afon Llifon. The little Fort Williamsburg was built in about 1761, at the same time as its sister, Fort Belan (see above), which commanded the south-western entrance to the Menai Strait. Fort Belan had serious military significance, but Williamsburg was never intended to be more than a place for military practice and social gatherings — in fact its purpose was probably not far removed from that of a folly — always a popular conceit in 18th century society.

Happy Valley (Cwm Dyffryn) *(4 mi. E Tywyn) (Approach from Map 27)* Cwm Dyffryn once sheltered the old coach road between Tywyn and Machynlleth, but Victorian visitors to Aberdyfi were soon being introduced to it as 'Happy Valley', and both this and Llyn Barfog (the 'Bearded Lake') became an almost obligatory visitors' jaunt. It is possible to walk up into the Happy Valley from Aberdyfi.

Llanberis *Continued from Page 29*

the Country Park. There are two other trails starting from the car park at Gilfach Ddu — The Vivian Trails which take their name from the great Vivian Quarry just to the north. This was one of several quarries belonging to the Dinorwic Quarry Company, and was itself named after W.W. Vivian, the company's manager in the closing years of the 19th century, and whose office now forms part of the craft workshops to which we refer below. Further information will be obtained by visiting the Welsh Slate Museum which is housed in the old workshops of the Quarry Company, and which contains much of the original workshop machinery, including a foundry and the well known Dinorwic water-wheel. These quarries were, until their closure in 1969, one of the largest in Britain, employing over three thousand men in their heyday. There is an interpretative gallery, and films depicting life and work here are shown at regular intervals. It is also possible to take a ride into the main quarry by Landrover. Not far from the Slate Museum there is a group of Craft Workshops and a Woodcraft Centre, and it is possible to watch craftspeople at work here, and to buy their products. Between the A4086 and the shore of Llyn Padarn will be found the Power of Wales Museum, which provides an interpretation of the environment with a special emphasis on the countryside of Snowdonia. Tourist Information is available here — ☏ (0286) 870765. Conducted minibus tours of the great Dinorwic Power Scheme are available from here (see below).

Beneath the mountainside between Llanberis and the little village of Dinorwic, is the vast cavern and tunnel system comprising Europe's largest pumped storage power scheme. This pumps water up from Llyn Peris to the high Marchlyn Mawr Reservoir at times when demand on the National Grid is low, and then releases the stored water to generate massive amounts of power in the cheapest possible way at times of high demand. The main machine hall is some 587 feet long, 80 feet wide and no less than 200 feet deep, and is believed to be the largest man-made civil engineering excavation in Europe.

1. *At the Welsh Slate Museum, Llanberis*

2. *Llandudno from the Great Orme*

Llandudno *(4 mi. NE Conwy) (Approach from Map 1)* Situated on a sweeping bay between the two limestone headlands of the Great and Little Ormes, this is the outstanding holiday resort of North Wales, having accommodation for at least 25,000 visitors. It not only has the large and lively North Shore but also the quieter 'West Shore' facing the Conwy Estuary. Development started here in the 1840s and within two decades Llandudno had already achieved the status of a major holiday town. Its fine terraces and stylish shops have survived long enough for it now to be regarded as one of Britain's most distinguished Victorian towns.

There are splendid views of the North Wales coast from the summit of the Great Orme, which can be reached by one of the well-known trams which have been climbing up here from the Tram Station since 1902, or by the equally popular Cabin Lift. The nearby slopes are the site of a dry-ski complex known as 'Ski Llandudno' — ☏ (0492) 74707. There are all the usual seaside features for children on the North shore, together with the lively Pier (departures by 'steamer' for the Isle of Man on certain days each week during the summer season), and the extensive Happy Valley Gardens close by. There is a Marine Drive enabling visitors to drive around the Great Orme in an anti-clockwise direction, starting from the vicinity of the Pier and the Happy Valley, and this provides impressive sea and mountain views. The White Rabbit Memorial, on the West Shore reminds visitors of Lewis Carroll, who met the young Alice Liddell and her family while staying in Llandudno, and whose visits with her to the sand dunes nearby, helped to inspire his famous story, *Alice in Wonderland*.

The Mostyn Art Gallery at 12, Vaughan Street holds a variety of exhibitions throughout the year, the Canolfan Aberconwy, is a conference and leisure centre with a wealth of facilities, and there are no fewer than three 18-hole golf courses, one at Penrhyn Bay and two on the West Shore. There is also a

3. *Cabin Lift at Llandudno*

4. *On the Talyllyn Railway, near Dolgoch Falls (see page 139)*

1. Llanegryn Church

2. At the Old Llanfair Quarry Slate Caverns

3. Llanfihangel-y-pennant — a distant view

heated indoor swimming pool, bowling greens, tennis courts and putting courses. British Rail run a service south through the lovely Conwy Valley and up to Blaenau Ffestiniog, where there is a connection with the privately run Ffestiniog Railway (see page 13).

Llanegryn *(4 mi. N Tywyn) (Approach from Map 27)* Small village overlooking the broad Dysynni valley with an interesting little bell-coted church on high ground to its north. Its interior was restored in 1878, but by a small miracle its atmosphere has survived intact. There are elegant memorials to the Owens and the Wynnes of nearby Peniarth, but inevitably the eye is drawn upwards to the exquisite rood screen — a delicately carved piece of 16th century craftsmanship, with complex carvings of vines, berries, leaves and flowers. This was possibly executed by the same group of craftsmen who created the screens at Llanbedrog (see page 125) and Llanengan (see page 105), although this is by far the finest specimen of the three and may have been moved here from Cymmer Abbey (see page 37). Just over a mile to the south, on the north banks of the Afon Dysynni, there is a small mound, Domen Dreiniog, all that remains of a 13th century wooden castle that once dominated this lowest crossing of the river.

Llanfair *(1 mi. S Harlech) (Approach from Map 18)* Small village situated just above the busy A496, with a church largely rebuilt in the mid-19th century and not of great interest to visitors. The Old Llanfair Quarry Slate Caverns, a series of caves and tunnels blasted from the hillside in the quest for slate, are open to the public. Visitors, wearing authentic safety helmets, are taken on a guided tour, and when they emerge once more into the daylight, there are fine views out over Cardigan Bay. On a hot summer day the contrast in temperature once inside the caverns is considerable and visitors are advised to wear something reasonably warm. There is a cafe and souvenir shop — ☏ (0766) 780247.

Pensarn, less than a mile south on the A496, once had a small harbour on the estuary of the Afon Artro, where sailing coasters were loaded with slate from the nearby caverns, but this has long since silted up.

Llanfihangel-y-pennant *(9 mi. NE Tywyn) (Approach from Map 27)* Here in the valley not far above Castlell y Bere, are a few farms and cottages and a delightful little church. This is a long low building with a pleasant old roof and an odd little medieval font. However most visitors will go just to the north of the village to look at the ruined cottage at Tyn-y-ddol, where Mary Jones once lived. A plaque recalls that in 1800, when Mary was only sixteen, she walked barefoot over the mountains to Bala, a distance of thirty miles, in order to obtain a bible from Methodist minister, Thomas Charles. He was so inspired by her enthusiasm for the scriptures that he started a campaign that was to lead eventually to the foundation of the British and Foreign Bible Society. The village is beautifully situated beneath the south-western flanks of Cadair Idris, and marks the southern end of the Pony Path, which runs north-eastwards up Cadair Idris (see page 132).

Llangelynnin Church, nr Tywyn *(7 mi. N Tywyn) (Approach from Map 27)* Attractive little stone building lying just below the A493 road, and not far from the shingly sea shore. It has a small porch complete with a minute bell-cote, and a delightfully unspoilt interior with a medieval roof and early 19th century benches with the names of their original occupants still painted upon them. Some of these are labelled 'Gent', some 'Esquire' and some neither — indicating thereby the strict divisions of class that existed in the 19th century, even in a place as remote as this. There is also a Jacobean pulpit and an unusual wheel-less horse-bier with shafts at both ends, once used on the mountainous tracks in the neighbourhood.

Llwyngwril *(3 mi. SW Fairbourne) (Approach from Map 16)* Tidy village astride the A493, with a small bridge over the Afon Gwril, emerging here from the mountains on its short journey to the sea. Access to the beach where there is sand at low tide is by a path beside an old Quaker burial ground to the north of the village. The church was built in 1843 — a pleasant little building — but not of great interest to visitors. There are the earthworks of a small Iron Age settlement, Castell y Gaer, on a hill to the south of the village, and standing stones in the hills to the north-east.

Llynnau Cregennen *(6 i.m SW Dolgellau) (Approach from Map 16)* These two lakes (hence 'Llynnau' rather than 'Llyn') together with a large area of mountain plateau between Arthog and Cadair Idris, were given to the National Trust by Major C. L. Wynne-Jones in memory of his two sons, sadly both killed in the 39–45 War. The Trust has provided a good car park overlooking the lakes, and it makes an excellent base for exploring this delightful area, with its fine views of the northern flanks of Cadair Idris.

Llyn Gwernan *(2 mi. SW Dolgellau) (Approach from Map1)* Small mountain lake partly hidden from the road by trees, and overlooked by the pleasant Gwernan Lake Hotel. The Fox's Path up Cadair Idris starts from here, but it is dangerous, and not recommended.

Machynlleth *(16 mi. S Dolgellau) (Approach from Map 27)* Attractive market town in the Dyfi valley, with its main streets meeting T-fashion at a splendidly ornate Victorian Clock Tower. This was built in 1873 to commemorate the family of the Marquess of Londonderry, who then owned Plas Machynlleth (see below). Close by the clock tower is the hospitable Wynnstay Hotel, one of a series of unusually pleasant 18th and early 19th century buildings in the wide street called Maen Gwyn, which runs eastwards from the clock tower. George Borrow stayed at the Wynnstay Hotel during the great journey of 1854 recorded in his classic travel book *Wild Wales*, although it was then known as the Wynstay Arms. He was waited on by a 'brisk, buxom maid who told me that her name was Mary Evans', and on being asked if there were any books in the house, she lent him her own volume of Welsh poetry. During his stay he

1. Llynnau Cregennen and Cadair Idris

2. Llyn Gwernan

3. Machynlleth

4. Tal-y-llyn (see page 139)

attended the trial of a poacher in the court being held in the town hall, or market cross, a building later to be swept away to make room for the clock tower. Borrow does tend to ramble on at times, but the account of his journeys in *Wild Wales*, is well worth reading by visitors to towns and villages like Machynlleth.

Further along the Maen Gwyn stands the Owain Glyndwr Centre, which incorporates the remains of a building that housed Wales' first and only Parliament, established here in 1404 by the Welsh hero Glyndwr in the first heady months after his victories over the English, a triumph that was to prove to be short-lived. Opposite the Centre are the handsome wrought-iron gates of Plas Machynlleth, a fine 17th century house in an extensive park, given to the town by the Marquess of Londonderry just before the Second World War. The Plas houses the town's offices and the nearby grounds provide a Public Park with tennis courts and a children's playground.

Mallwyd *(12 mi. E Dolgellau) (Approach from Map 26)* George Borrow spent a pleasant evening at the Brigand's Inn in 1854 after his depressing afternoon at Dinas Mawddwy (see page 57), and the inn and its tradition of hospitality has survived to this day. Borrow described the village as 'small but pretty' and also remarked upon the size of the yew tree in the churchyard. This still stands beside the long low church 'standing on a slight elevation' above the road, with its small weather-boarded tower and its wooden framed porch dated 1641.

In the time of Queen Mary the red headed 'banditti' of Dinas and Mallwyd had become such a menace that a certain Baron Owen was appointed judge and specially commissioned to put them down. However, despite his initial success in having no less than eight of them hanged, he was himself subsequently ambushed and murdered on his way home from Montgomery Assizes, at a bridge on the road east of Mallwyd, which is still known as Llidiart y Barwyn — the Baron's Gate.

Head due west from Mallwyd for a short distance to reach a pleasant minor road running down the Dyfi (Dovey) valley, to Aberangell, and beyond to Machynlleth. It is also possible to drive across the Dyfi Forest from Aberangell (see page 130).

Minffordd *(7 mi. S Dolgellau) (Approach from Map 27)* This is little more than a road junction, where the B4405 heads south-westwards from the A487 Dolgellau-Machynlleth road, to Tal-y-llyn Lake and Abergynolwyn. However, to the right of the B4405, about a quarter of a mile beyond this junction, there is a path starting through gates, which leads to Cadair Idris — known as the Minffordd Path (see Cadair Idris, page 132).

Penmynydd *See Page 91*
The Tudors became prominent in the 14th century and traditionally lived at Plas Penmynydd for 300 years — among them was the great-grandfather of King Henry VII. The present farmhouse, which dates from the 16th century, is not open to the public. Penmynydd Church, dedicated to St. Gredifael, dates from the 14th and 15th centuries, and was restored in 1848. It has many connections with the Tudor family. There is a magnificent alabaster altar tomb, believed to have been brought from Llanfaes Priory at the Dissolution, which commemorates an early Tudor, Gronwy Fychan, and his wife; he died in 1385 and had been a friend of the Black Prince.

Plas Newydd (NT) *Continued from Page 69*
Standing on the shore of the Menai Strait, with splendid views across the water to Snowdonia, this late 18th and early 19th century house in Gothic and neo-Classical styles was the work of James Wyatt and the less well-known Joseph Potter, a Lichfield architect. It has a Gothic Hall complete with a gallery and sumptuous plasterwork fan vaulting. The long dining room contains Plas Newydd's outstanding treasure, the magically beautiful *trompe l'oeil* mural painting by Rex Whistler, featuring a wealth of architectural fantasies worked into a highly romanticised landscape derived at least in part from the views of the Menai Strait and Snowdonia from Plas Newydd.

There is also a military museum housing relics of the Battle of Waterloo, where the first Marquess of Anglesey lost his leg (see also the Marquess of Anglesey's Column, Page 69). These relics include the mutilated trousers worn on the fatal day and the wooden leg used by the first Marquess in the years that followed. The conversation with the Duke of Wellington following this unfortunate wounding is supposed to have run something like this: 'By God, sir, I've lost my leg' — 'By God, so you have', replied the Duke somewhat casually.

The gardens here are especially fine in spring, with azaleas, camellias and rhododendrons, but for the rest of the year shrubs and trees, and the terrace garden with its cypresses, are a delightful complement to the house and it setting on the shore of the Strait. In front of the house, on the edge of the lawn, there is, surprisingly, a large prehistoric burial chamber. Teas. Shop — ☎ (0248) 714795.

Porthmadog *Continued from page 123*
Narrow Gauge Railway, the terminus of which is close to the quays. (For details see page 13.) The revived Welsh Highland Railway is based at Madoc Street West, at the north-western end of the town. As yet it only runs a short distance from the town, but it is hoped that it will eventually be re-opened as far as Beddgelert — ☎ (0766) 513402.

With its symmetrical street plan and wide tree-lined streets, Porthmadog is a tribute to Madocks' skills as a town planner, for he not only created The Cob and drained the marshy estuary, but he also created the town itself. It was named Porthmadog, after both Madocks, and the legendary Madog, a Welsh folk hero who was supposed to have set out for the New World from here.

There is a Tourist Information Centre in the High Street — ☎ 0766 2981, and also the office where David Lloyd George (see Llanystumdwy, page 103) and his brother Dr William Lloyd George practised as solicitors. Dr William was still in practice here when he reached the age of 100, and he died two years later, in 1967. Do not miss a visit to the Porthmadog Pottery, nor the Motor Museum, both of which are at the northern end of Snowdon Street. For what is perhaps the finest distant view of Snowdon, walk westwards along The Cob. Despite road and narrow

gauge rail traffic there is ample room for pedestrians.
 The Park in the centre of the town offers tennis, putting and a children's playground. There is river and sea fishing, with boats that can be taken out to sea, and there is an 18-hole golf course at Morfa Bychan, less than two miles to the south-west.

Tal-y-llyn *(10 mi. S Dolgellau) (Approach from Map 27)* A beautiful lake set in a deep valley below Cadair Idris, with great sweeping mountain sides dropping down to its shores. In winter swans and ducks will be found here and trout are plentiful in the clear waters beneath. Overlooking the south-western end of the lake, not far from the attractive Tyn-y-Cornel Hotel, is an interesting little church, with a pleasantly unspoilt interior which includes early 17th century carved panels in its chancel ceiling.

Talyllyn Railway *(13 mi. S Dolgellau) (Approach from Map 27)* The oldest 2 foot gauge railway in the world, the Talyllyn has been in continuous service since 1867, and it was the first railway in Britain to be saved by volunteers. It runs 7¼ miles inland from Tywyn through magnificent scenery including the Dolgoch Falls (see page 133), to its upper terminus at Nant Gwernol where there are extensive forest walks (see Abergynolwyn, page 130). The original purpose of the railway was for the transport of slate to the main line at Tywyn, but from its inception passengers were also carried. Two of its locomotives are over a hundred years old, and there is a Narrow Gauge Museum and Railway Shop at Wharf Station, Tywyn. Duration of the full journey from Tywyn to Nant Gwernol is 55 minutes. For details of services ☏ (0654) 710472.

Tal y Waen Farm Trail *(2 mi. W Dolgellau) (Approach from Map 16)* Here beneath the crags of Craig y Castell is an interesting 2-mile walk around a working hill farm, with spectacular views out over the Mawddach estuary to the peaks of Diffwys and the Rhinogs. There is also a covered licensed barbecue, a Welsh tea and craft shop, a video depicting the farm trail story, and various attractions for children — ☏ (0341) 422580.

Tywyn *(4 mi. N Aberdyfi) (Approach from Map 16)* The rugged arcading of St Cadfan's church reveals that its history dates back as least to early medieval times. In the church will also be found a 7th century inscribed stone, which was subsequently used as a gatepost until rescued. This has for many years been known as St Cadfan's Stone, but its connections with that saint appear to be somewhat tenuous. There is no doubt, however, that St Cadfan founded a teaching cell here in the 6th century, and it appears to have remained a centre of learning until the time of Henry VIII.
 Tywyn's early popularity as a seaside resort was due to the activity of a wealthy Droitwich salt baron, John Corbett. He was responsible for the Marine Terrace, the Market Hall, and the quaint and colourful Assembly Rooms beside the church. The handsome Corbett Arms Hotel was built in the early 19th century, and was originally called the Corbet Arms, following the purchase by John Corbett of the local estate from a family with almost the same name as his own.
 See also the excellent modern design of the Roman Catholic church with its attendant sculpture in green slate; the fascinating Narrow Gauge Museum, which is part of the Wharf Station Terminus of the Talyllyn Railway; and of course, the line of beautiful sands along the front. There is tennis and putting near the promenade, paddling pools, cafes, plenty of shops, and an indoor heated swimming pool.

Tourist Information Centres in Snowdonia, Anglesey and the Lleyn Peninsula

* = *not open in winter months*

Aberdyfi (Aberdovey)* The Wharf ☏ *(0654) 72321*
Bala* High St ☏ *(0678) 520367*
Bangor* Theatr Gwynedd ☏ *(0248) 352786*
Barmouth (Abermaw)* Station Road ☏ *(0341) 280787*
Beddgelert Llywelyn Cottage (NT) ☏ *(0766) 86293*
Betws-y-Coed* Y Stablau ☏ *(06902) 426 or 665*
Blaenau Ffestiniog* Isalt ☏ *(0766) 830360*
Caernarfon Oriel Pendeitch ☏ *(0286) 672232*
Colwyn Bay Station Road ☏ *(0492) 530478*
Conwy Castle* St ☏ *(0492) 592248*
Corris* The Craft Centre ☏ *(0654) 73244*
Criccieth* The Sweet Stop, 47, High Street ☏ *(0766) 523303*
Dolgellau* The Bridge ☏ *(0341) 422888*
Harlech* In centre ☏ *(0766) 780658*
Holyhead Marine Square, Salt Island ☏ *(0407) 2622*

Llanberis* Power of Wales Museum ☏ *(0286) 870765*
Llandudno Chapel St. ☏ *(0492) 76413*
Llanfair P.G. Station Site ☏ *(0248) 713177*
Machynlleth. Owain Glyndwr Centre ☏ *(0654) 2401/702401*
Porthmadog High St. ☏ *(0766) 512981*
Pwllheli* Y Maes ☏ *(075861) 3000*
Tywyn* High St. ☏ *(0654) 710070*

Other Useful Addresses and/or Telephone Numbers
Forestry Commission Gwydyr Uchaf, Llanrwst, LL26 0PN ☏ *(0492) 640578)*
National Trust Trinity Square, Llandudno, LL30 2DE ☏ *(0492) 74421*
National Park Daily Weather Forecast
 ☏ *Llanberis (0286) 870120*
Snowdonia National Park Penrhyndeudraeth, LL48 6LS ☏ *(0766) 770274/770701*

A Few Welsh Place-Names

Aber — *estuary, or confluence*
Afon — *river*
Allt — *hill, slope*
Bach — *little*
Bedd — *grave*
Betws — *chapel of ease*
Bod — *dwelling place*
Bont — *bridge*
Bryn — *mound*
Bwlch — *pass or gap*
Bychan — *small, the lesser*
Caer — *camp or fort*
Capel — *chapel*
Carn — *cairn, rock, mountain*
Carnedd — *cairn, tumulus, mountain*
Carreg — *stone or rock*
Castell — *castle*
Cefn — *ridge*
Celli — *grove or copse*
Ceunant — *ravine or gorge*
Coch — *red*
Coed — *forest, wood, tree*
Cors — *bog*
Craig — *crag*
Croes — *cross, cross-roads*
Cwm — *valley*
Cymmer — *junction or confluence*
Din — *town or hill fort*
Drws — *gap or narrow pass*
Du (or Ddu) — *black*
Dyffryn — *valley*
Fach — *little*
Fawr — *great, large*
Felin — *mill*
Fford — *way or road*
Ffynnon — *spring*
Foel — *bare hill*
Fynydd — *mountain*
Gaer — *camp or fort*
Garn — *a prominence*
Garth — *hill or headland*
Glas — *green or blue*
Glyn — *glen*
Goch — *red*
Graig — *crag*
Groes — *cross, cross-roads*
Gwaun — *common or moor*
Gwyn — *white*
Hafod — *summer dwelling*
Hendre — *winter dwelling*
Hen — *old*
Isaf — *lower, lowest*
Llan — *enclosure, sacred enclosure, hence a church*
Llech — *flat stone*
Llyn — *lake*
Maen — *stone*
Maes — *open field, or open place*
Mawr — *great, large*
Mign — *bog*
Moel — *bare hill*
Mynach — *monk*
Mynydd — *mountain*
Nant — *brook or dingle*
Newydd — *new*
Ogof — *cave*
Pant — *hollow, or valley*
Pen — *head, or top*
Pistyll — *spouting waterfall*
Plas — *hall or mansion*
Pont — *bridge*
Porth — *gateway or harbour*
Pwll — *pool or hollow*
Rhaeadr — *waterfall*
Rhiw — *slope*
Rhyd — *ford*
Sarn — *causeway*
Tal — *brow of hill, or headland*
Tomen — *mound*
Traeth — *strand, beach o shore*
Tre — *dwelling or village*
Twyn — *small hill, or knc*
Ty — *house*
Uchaf — *higher, highest*
Waun — *common or moo*
Wyn — *white*
Y, Yr — *the, of the*
Yn, Ym — *in*
Ynys — *island*
Ysbyty — *hospital or hospice*

Advice on Mountain Safety for Climbers and Walkers

1. Wear **boots** (**not** shoes) fitted with rubber mountaineering soles (Commando, Vibram etc.).
2. Have plenty of warm clothing, especially wind and rainproof outer garments (jacket or anorak **with hood** and over-trousers). Never wear jeans: when wet and subjected to a cold wind, they are liable to cause 'exposure' (hypothermia) — a dangerous and often fatal condition which can occur **at any time of the year, even in summer**.
3. Carry map and compass, **and know how to use them**. Also take watch, whistle, torch, small first-aid kit and one or two spare long-sleeved pullovers.
4. Have a reserve supply of food in case of emergency (chocolate, mint cake, biscuits, glucose tablets). A hot drink in a vacuum flask is strongly recommended.
5. Plan walks carefully. Do not overestimate your physical ability. Study routes and allow enough time to be back well before dark. This is especially important when daylight hours are limited. **(There is a 24 hour pre-recorded Weather Forecast Service for the whole National Park on Llanberis ☎ 870120.)**
6. Check weather forecasts. Keep a constant lookout for changes. On high ground, mist and rain can close in with alarming speed.
7. Do not hesitate to turn back or cut a walk short if the weather deteriorates, or if the route is too much for you or for one of your companions. 'Pressing on' is folly, not pluck, and it can have disastrous results. **Stay together as a group and accept all decisions by the group leader.**
8. **Always leave word where you are going, and when you expect to be back.** Tell someone at the place where you are staying, or leave a note on the seat of your car. A search party has little hope of finding you if no-one knows where you went. Remember to report your return.
9. Keep to your planned route as far as possible. If for some reason you cannot return to base and have to spend the night in other accommodation, **telephone either the police, or some place where you are staying and explain what has happened.** Failure to do this **promptly** may result in search parties spending many wasted hours (and risking their lives) looking for you.
10. **Know what to do in an emergency** (eg accident, illness, or being overtaken by bad weather or darkness). Find out by reading the booklet *Safety on Mountains*, published by the Central Council of Physical Recreation and the *Mountain Rescue Handbook*, published by the Mountain Rescue Committee. Both are obtainable from most climbers' shops.

Index

Entry	Page
Aber	21
Aber Cywarch	57
Aber Falls	21
Aber Geirw	60
Aberangell	130
Aberconwy (house)	132
Aberconwy Abbey	5,7
Aberdaron	109
Aberdesach	116
Aberdyfi (Aberdovey)	130
Abererch	103
Aberffraw	72,73,88,89
Aberglaslyn Pass	13
Abergynolwyn	130
Aberllefenni	130
Abermenai Point	130-131
Abersoch	105,125
Afon Alaw	95
Afon Cadnant	17
Afon Cedig	52
Afon Cefni	73,91
Afon Clywedog	59
Afon Colwyn	14
Afon Cwm Nantcol	38
Afon Cwmystradlyn	123
Afon Cynfal	11,42,45,63
Afon Disgynfa	51
Afon Du	6
Afon Dwyfach	100,120
Afon Dwyfor	100,103,123
Afon Dyfi	55
Afon Dyfrdwy	49
Afon Erch	103
Afon Eunant Fawr	54
Afon Gain	63
Afon Gamlan	61
Afon Glaslyn	14,32,33
Afon Goch	21
Afon Gwyrfai	17
Afon Lledr	9
Afon Llifor	116
Afon Lliw	63,65
Afon Llugwy	6,7,9,24,25
Afon Llyfni	117,120
Afon Mawddach	63
Afon Nant Peris	30
Afon Ogwen	27
Afon Rhiwlech	55
Afon Seiont	17,119
Afon Soch	105
Afon Wen	102,128
Afon Wnion	59
Afon Ysgethin	38
Air Museum, Dinas Dinlle	117
Alaw Reservoir	95
Amlwch	79,81
Anglesey	16,18,21,26
Anglesey Column	69,90
Anglesey Heritage Centre	91
Anglesey, Marquess of	69,138
Anglesey Sea Zoo	71
Aran Benllyn	56,65
Aran Fawddwy	55
Arans, The	39,57,63
Arenig Fach	11,45
Arenig Fawr	11,45
Arenigs, The	45,55
Arfon Leisure Centre	19
Arthog	131
Arthur's Quoit	107,111
Arthur's Table	125
Axe Factory, Penmaenmawr	23
Bala	47,65
Bala Lake Railway	48,65
Bala, Lake	43,47,49
Bangor	21,25,26,86,91
Bangor-is-Coed	111
Barclodiad-y-gawres Burial Chamber	73
Bardsey Island	105,109,111,129
Barmouth	39
Barwyn Mountains	49,63
Beaumaris	21,85,87,89
Beddgelert	15,17,33
Beddgelert Forest Park	15
Bedivere, Sir	25
Belgian Promenade	68,91
Benllech	83
Benllech Bay	83
Bethania Bridge	33
Bethesda	27
Betws Garmon	17
Betws-y-Coed	6,9
Black Point	85
Black Prince, The	138
Black Rock Sands	101
Blaen Pennant	21
Blaenau Ffestiniog	10,13,131
Blythe Farm	119
Bod Deiniol	95
Bodedern	75
Bodewryd	95
Bodfuan (Boduan, Bodvean)	127
Bodnant Garden	5
Bodorgan	72,89
Bodowen	72,89
Bodowyr Burial Chamber	68,71
Bodvel Hall	127
Bodwrdda	108
Bont Fechan	100
Bontddu	36,132
Bontddu Gold Mine	44,132
Bontnewydd (nr Aber)	21
Bontnewydd (nr Caernarfon)	118
Borrow, George	27,57,65,137-138
Borth Wen	112
Borth-y-Gest	101,122
Borthwen	76
Botwnnog	106
Braich-y-Pwll	109
Britannia Bridge	69,91
Brygwran	74
Bryn Bras Castle	29
Bryn-celli-ddu Burial Chamber	68,71
Brynawelon	103
Brynkir Woollen Mills	121
Brynsiencyn	68,71
Brynteg	82,92
Buckley Arms	57
Bulkeley, Sir Richard	85
Bull Bay	78,81
Butlin's Holiday World	102,128
Bwlch Drws	41,53
Bwlch Oerddrws	59
Bwlch Sirddyn	55
Bwlch Tocyn	105
Bwlch-y-Groes	55,65
Cable Bay	73
Cadair Berwyn	49
Cadair Idris	37,39,59,109,132,136,137
Cadfan	89
Cadwaladr	89
Cae Ddu Farm Park	15
Caeathro	28
Caer Engan	121
Caer Gai	43,47
Caer Gybi (Holyhead)	97
Caer Leb	68,71
Caer Llugwy Fort	25
Caer-y-Twr	97
Caerhun (Canovium)	25
Caernarfon	17,19,28,71,75,91
Caernywch Estate	59
Canolfan Aberconwy	135
Capel Carmel	110
Capel Celyn	25,30
Capel Curig	25,30
Capel Hermon	60,63
Capel Lligwy	83
Capel Newydd	125
Carmel Head	77
Carn Fadryn	125
Carn Pentyrch	121
Carnedd Dafydd	25,27
Carnedd Filiast	27
Carneddau Hengwm	39
Carreg Fawr	23
Carreg y Llam	127
Carreglwd	77
Carroll, Lewis	135
Castell Aberlleiniog	87
Castell Bryn Gwyn	71
Castellmarch	105
Castell Odo	109
Castell y Bere	132
Castell y Gaer	137
Cefn-Isa Farm Trail	41
Cefnamwlch Burial Chamber	107,111
Cefni Estuary	73,75,89
Cefni Reservoir	91
Cemaes	78
Cemaes Bay	79
Cemlyn Bay	79
Centre for Alternative Technology	132
Cerrigceinwen	89
Charles, Thomas	47,65,136
Chester, Earl of	87
Church Bay	77
Church Island	68,91
Chwilog	102,128
Cist Cerrig	101
Clynnog Fawr	117
Cnicht	13
Clogau St David's Gold Mine	132
Coastal Heritage Centre	73
Cob, The (Malltraeth)	73
Cob, The (Porthmadog)	123
Coed Cyrnol	91
Coed-y-Brenin Forest	61
Coedydd Aber Trail	21
Colwyn Bay	132
Constantine the Great	19
Conway, H.M.S.	69
Conwy	5,23,132
Conwy Falls	9
Conwy River	7,9,11
Conwy Valley	5,25
Corbett, John	139
Corris	133
Corris Railway Museum	133
Cors-y-Gedol	38,45
Corwen	49
Cox, David	9
Craig Cwmdulyn	121
Craig Cywarch	57
Craig Ddu	115
Craig Llugwy	25
Craig Wen	51
Craig-y-Garn	120
Craig-y-Ogof	65
Craig-y-Pant	55
Craig-y-dinas	69
Craig yr Aderyn	133
Creiglyn Dyfi	55
Crib Goch	31,33
Crib-y-Ddysgl	31
Criccieth	101,122
Croesor	13
Cromwell, Oliver	53
Cross Foxes Hotel	58
Cwm Bychan	41
Cwm Croes	55
Cwm Cynllwyd	55,57
Cwm Cywarch	57
Cwm Dyffryn (Happy Valley)	134
Cwm Hirnant (nr Penybont)	49
Cwm Hirnant (nr Rhos-y-Gwalias)	49,55
Cwm Mynach	37,61
Cwm Nantcol	38,53
Cwm Nantcol Nature Trail	41
Cwm Pennant (nr Llangynog)	51
Cwm Pennant (nr Porthmadog)	121
Cwm Rhiwarth	51
Cwm-y-Glo	28
Cyffdy Farm Park	65
Cyfty Lead Mine	6
Cymmer Abbey	37,61
Cymmrodorion Society	81
Cynfal Falls	11
Dafarn Faig Farm	120

	Page
Danes, The	85
Dduallt	125
Dee, River	47,49
Derlwyn	30
Devil's Kitchen	25
Din Dryfol Burial Chamber	89
Din Lligwy	80,83
Dinas	124
Dinas Dinlle	116,119
Dinas Emrys	33
Dinas Gynfor	79
Dinas Mawddwy	55,57
Dinas Oleu	39
Dingle, The	91
Dinorwic	135
Dinorwic Quarries	29,134
Dinsylwy Hill Fort	85
Diphwys	37
Dolbadarn Castle	29,31
Dolbenmaen	121
Dolgarrog	5
Dolgefeiliau Forest Trail	61
Dolgellau	11,36,49,59
Dolgoch Falls	133,139
Dolmelynllyn	60
Dolwyddelan	9
Domen Ddreiniog	136
Dovey Valley	55,57
Drofa Point	000
Druids, The	71
Dwygyfylchi	23
Dwyran	70
Dyfi (Dovey) Forest	133
Dyffryn Ardudwy	38,49
Dysynni Valley	132,133
Edern	112
Edwards, Sir O.M.	65
Efailenewydd	102,126
Eiras Park	132
Elidir Fawr	31
Ellis, Thomas	47
Eryri	31
Eunant	55
Fairbourne	133-134
Fairbourne Miniature Railway	133
Fairy Glen, Betws-y-Coed	9
Fairy Glen, Penmaenmawr	23
Farchynys Woodlands Walk	36,45
Felin Faesog Museum	117
Felinheli (Portdinorwic)	19,71
Fferram Rhosydd	88
Ffestiniog	11,43
Ffestiniog Hydro-Electric Scheme	10,131
Ffestiniog Railway	13,123,125,131
Ffestiniog, Vale of	10,13
Ffynnon Fair (St Mary's Well)	109
Foel	71
Foel Cynwch	37
Foel Faner	37
Foel Friog	133
Foel Goch	27
Foel Lus	23
Fort Belan	131,134
Fort Williamsbourg	134
Foryd Bay	116,118
Four Mile Bridge	96
Fox's Path, The	132,137
Gallows Point	86
Gallt-yr-Ogof	25
Ganyllwyd	61
Garn	125
Garn Boduan	127
Garn Dolbenmaen	121
Garnedd Goch	121
Garth Coch	49
Gelert's Grave	15
Gellilydan	11
Gibberd, Sir F.	47
Gilfach Ddu	29,134
Gimblet Rock	103
Gladstone Rock	33
Glan Faenol	19
Glaslyn Estuary	123,127
Gloddfa Ganol Slate Mine	131
Glyders	25,33
Glyndwr, Owain	17,21
Glyn Farm	83
Glynllifon	117
Goat Hotel	15

	Page
Gold Interpretative Centre	132
Gold Mines	45,61,132
Great Orme	83,84,135
Groeslon	119
Gronwy Fychan	138
Gruffydd, Robert	43
Gurn Ddu	114,117
Gurn Goch	114
Gwredog	95
Gwydir Castle	7
Gwydir Chapel, Llanrwst	7
Gwydir Forest	9
Gwydir Uchaf	7
Gwyniad	49
Hafod Fadog	47
Happy Valley (Cwm Dyffryn)	134
Harlech	41,55,101
Helen, Empress	19
Hell's Mouth (nr Porth Wen)	79
Hell's Mouth (Porth Neigwl)	105,107,109
Hen Borth (Anglesey)	77
Hen Borth (Lleyn Peninsula)	109
Hen Capel	80,83
Hengwm Valley	57
Hirnant	53
Holyhead (Caer Gybi)	21,69,75,88,93,97
Holyhead Mountain	76,97
Hut Circles	97
Indefatigable, The	68
Inigo Jones Tudor Slate Works	119
Inkerman Bridge	127
Ireland	73,79
Isallt	11
Isle of Man	115
James Pringle Woollen Mill	69
Joan, Princess	87
Jones, Inigo	7
Jones, John	7
Jones, Mary	47,136
Jubilee Path, Betws-y-Coed	9
Keating Family	109
King Arthur	25,31
King Edward I	5,27,41,71,87,132
King George IV	97
King Henry VII	138
King John	87
King William Rufus	11
Lady Mary's Walk	7
Lawrence, T.E.	123
Lladdyfnan	83
Llanaber Church	39
Llanaelhaearn	115,129
Llanallgo	80,83
Llanarmon	127,129
Llanbabo	95
Llanbadrig	79
Llanbeblig Church	29
Llanbedr	41
Llanbedr-y-Cennin	5
Llanbedrgoch	82
Llanbedrog	104,125
Llanberis	29,134-135
Llanberis Lake Railway	19,29
Llanberis Pass	29,31,33
Llanddeiniolen	19
Llanddeusant	95
Llanddona	85
Llanddwyn Island	70,75
Llanddwywe Church	39
Llandecwyn	43
Llandegai	27
Llandegfan	86,91
Llandegwning	107
Llandudno	135-136
Llandudwen	125
Llandwrog	116,119
Llandyfrydog	93
Llandysilio	69,91
Llanedwyn	19,71
Llanegryn	136
Llaneilian	81
Llanelltyd	61
Llanengan	105,107
Llanerchymedd	93
Llanfachraeth	76
Llanfaelog	74
Llanfaelrhys	108
Llanfaes	87,138

	Page
Llanfaethlu	77
Llanfaglan Church	17,119
Llanfair Mathafarn Eithaf	82
Llanfairfechan	23
Llanfair	136
Llanfairpwll	69,90
Llanfairynghornwy	77
Llanfigael	75,94
Llanfihangel Dinsylwy	85
Llanfihangel-y-pennant	136
Llanfwrog	76
Llangadwaladr	72,89
Llangaffo	89
Llangefni	91
Llangeinwen	71
Llangelynnin Church	137
Llangian	107,109
Llangoed	85,86
Llangollen	49
Llangristiolus	89
Llangwnnadl	107,110
Llangwyfan	73
Llangybi	129
Llangynog	51
Llanidan	68,71
Llaniestyn (nr Beaumaris)	85
Llaniestyn (nr Abersoch)	125
Llanllyfni	121
Llannor	127
Llanrhaeadr-ym-Mochnant	50
Llanrhuddlad	77
Llanrhwydrys	77,79
Llanrhychwyn	7
Llanrug	29
Llanelltyd Bridge	37
Llantrisant	95
Llanuwchllyn	49,65
Llanwenllwyfo	81
Llanwnda	119
Llanwrst	7
Llanwyddyn	53
Llanymawddwy	57
Llanystumdwy	101,103
Llech Idris	63
Llechwedd Slate Caverns	131
Lledr Valley	9
Lleyn Museum	127
Lligwy Burial Chamber	80,83
Llithfaen	115
Lloyd George, David	17,101,103,138
Llwyngwril	137
Llyn Alaw (Alaw Reservoir)	92,95
Llyn Barfog	134
Llyn Bodlyn	39,45
Llyn Bychan	41
Llyn Celyn	47
Llyn Celyn Dam	47
Llyn Conwy	11
Llyn Coron	72,88
Llyn Cowlyd	5
Llyn Crafnant	6,7
Llyn Cwellyn	15
Llyn Cwmdulyn	121
Llyn Cwmystradlyn	121
Llyn Cynwch	37
Llyn Dinas	33
Llyn Eigiau	5
Llyn Geirionydd	6,7
Llyn Glasfryn	129
Llyn Gwernan	137
Llyn Gwynant	33
Llyn Hywel	37
Llyn Idwal	25
Llyn Irddyn	39,45
Llyn Llydaw	31,33
Llyn Llywenan	75,94
Llyn Maelog	75
Llyn Morynion	10,11
Llyn Mynach	37
Llyn Nantlle	119
Llyn Ogwen	25
Llyn Padarn	29,135
Llyn Peris	29,135
Llyn Tecwyn Isaf	43
Llyn Tecwyn Uchaf	43
Llyn Tegid	47,49
Llyn-y-Bi	37
Llyn-y-Gadair	15,132
Llynnau Cregennen	137

	Page
Llynnau Mymbyr	25
Llys-Helig	19,21
Llysdulas	81
Llythwyrdy Post Office	84
Llywelyn's Cottage	15
Llywelyn's Old Church	7
Llywelyn the Great	7,9,15,21,85,87,132
Lynon Hall	94
Lynon Windmill	95
Machno Falls	8,9
Machynlleth	137-138
Madocks, William, M.P.	13,113,138
Maenaddwyn Post Office	92
Maenan Abbey	7,23
Maentwrog	13,43
Maes-y-Garnedd	53
Malltraeth	73,75
Malltraeth Marsh	89
Malltraeth Sands	72
Mallwyd	138
Manod Mawr	45
Marchlyn Mawr	135
Marchros	105
Marianglas	82
Maritime Museum, Caernarfon	17
Maritime Museum, Holyhead	97
Maritime Museum, Porthmadog	123
Marquess of Anglesey's Column	69
Mawddach Estuary	39,45
Mawddach Falls	61
Mawddach, River	37
Maximus, Emperor	19
Meirion Mill	57
Menai Bridge	21
Menai Bridge Town	68,86,91
Menai Strait	17,18,21,69,71,86,91,119
Menai Suspension Bridge	69,87,90
Mermaid Inn	71
Meyrick Family	89
Migneint, The	11
Millionaires' Mile	91
Miners' Bridge	7
Miners' Path	3,31
Minffordd	138
Minffordd Path	132,138
Mochras Peninsula	41
Moel Bach	13
Moel Eilio	15,17
Moel Gwynnus	114
Moel Hebog	15,33,121
Moel Lefn	15
Moel Penllechog	114
Moel Siabod	8,25
Moel Sych	49
Moel-y-don	19,68,71
Moelfre	80,83
Moelwyn Bach	13
Moelwyn Mawr	13
Monk's Grave	63
Morfa Abererch	103
Morfa Bychan	139
Morfa Dinlle	116
Morfa Nefyn	113,126
Morgan, Bishop	9
Morris Memorial	81
Morton, John	15
Museum of Childhood, Beaumaris	87,89
Museum of Welsh Antiquities	21
Museum of Welsh Fusiliers	17
Mynydd Bodafon	93
Mynydd Cilan	105
Mynydd Craig Goch	121
Mynydd Drws-y-Coed	15
Mynydd Ednyfed	101
Mynydd Eilian	81
Mynydd Mawr (Snowdonia)	15
Mynydd Mawr (Lleyn Peninsula)	109
Mynydd Perfedd	27
Mynydd Rhiw	109
Mynydd Tircwmwd	105
Mynydd Ystum	109
Mynytho	125
Nanhoron	124
Nannau Estate	37
Nant Ffrancon Valley	25,26
Nant Gwernol	130,133,139
Nant Gwynant Valley	31,33
Nant Mills Waterfall	15
Nant Peris	31
Nant-y-Groes	44
Nant-y-Gwrtheyrn	115
Nantgwryd Valley	30
Nantlle	119,120
Nantmor	33
Nasareth	120
Nature Centre, Penmaenpool	45
Nebo	121
Nefyn	113,127
Nelson, Lord	69
Newborough	71,72,75,131
Newborough Forest	71,75
Newborough Warren	71,75,131
North Stack	96
Oakley, William	43
Ogof Ddu	55
Ogwen Bank	27
Ogwen Cottage	24
Old Country Life Museum	39
Old Llanfair Quarry Slate Caverns	136
Oriel Pendeitch	19
Owain Glyndwr Centre	138
Owen, Goronwy	83
Owen, Sir John	123
Owens of Bodowen	89
Padarn Country Park	29
Panorama Walk	39
Parys Mountain	81
Peel, Robert	87
Pemmaenmawr	23
Pen Llithrig-y-Wrach	25
Pen-y-Gaer	5
Pen-y-Gwryd Hotel	30,33
Pen-y-Pas	33
Pen-yr-Helgi-du	25
Pen-yr-Ole-Wen	27
Penarth Fawr	103,129
Pengorffwysfa	80
Penllech Church	107,111
Penmachno	9
Penmachno Woollen Mill	9
Penmaenmawr	27
Penmaenpool	36,45
Penmaenpool - Morfa Mawddach Walk	45
Penmon Cross	85
Penmon Dovecot	85
Penmon Priory	85
Penmorfa	123
Penmynydd	87,90,138
Pennant Melangell	51
Pennant, Richard	27
Pennant, Thomas	27
Penrhos Feilw Standing Stones	97
Penrhos Nature Reserve	93,96
Penrhyn Castle	21,27
Penrhyn Farm	81
Penrhyn Nefyn	113
Penrhyn Quarries	27
Penrhyn, Porth	21
Pensarn	136
Pentir	18
Pentraeth	83
Pentre Eirianell	81
Pentre-Du	7
Pentrefelin	101
Pentrellwyn	85
Penybont	65
Penybont Fawr	51
Penygroes	114,119,120
Penysarn	80
Pig Track	15,31
Pili Palas	91
Pistyll	115
Pistyll Dyfi	55
Pistyll Gain	61
Pistyll Gwyn	57
Pistyll Rhaeadr	51
Pitt's Head Rock	15
Plas Coch	68,71
Plas Gwyn	83
Plas Llanfair	68
Plas Llanfigael	97
Plas Mawr, Conwy	5,23
Plas Menai	19
Plas Newydd	69,138
Plas-yn-Rhiw	109
Point Lynas	81
Pont Blaen-Lliw	62
Pont Cyfyng	25
Pont Fadog	45
Pont Gyfyng	123
Pont Minllyn	57
Pont Pen-y-Benglog	25,27
Pont-y-Cim	117
Pont-y-Gromlech	33
Pont-y-Pair	6,9
Pont-y-Pennant	54
Pontlyfni	117
Pony Path	132,136
Pool Quay	51
Portdinorwic (Felinheli)	19,71
Porth Ceiriad	105
Porth Colmon	111
Porth Cwyfan	73
Porth Darfach	97
Porth Diana	97
Porth Dinllaen	113,123,126
Porth Eilian	81
Porth Iago	111
Porth Llanlleiana	79
Porth Meudwy	109
Porth Nefyn	113
Porth Neigwl (Hell's Mouth)	105
Porth Nobla	73
Porth Oer (Porthor)	111
Porth Penrhyn Mawr	77
Porth Swtan	77
Porth Towyn	113
Porth Trecastell	73
Porth Trefadog	77
Porth Trwyn	77
Porth Tywyn Mawr	77
Porth Uechog	78,81
Porth Wen	79
Porth Ychen	111
Porth Ysgaden	113
Porth Ysglaig	113
Porth Ysgo	108
Porth-y-Nant	115
Porth-y-Pistyll	109
Porth-y-Post	96
Porthaethwy	86,91
Porthmadog	13,101,123,138
Portmeirion	43,63,101,123,127,129
Poucher, W.A.	15,25,31
Power of Wales Museum	135
Precipice Walk	37
Presaddfed Burial Chamber	75
Priestholm	85
Pritchard, David	15
Publicius	19
Puffin Island	83,85
Pwllheli	103,105,124,127
Quaker Memorial	47
Queen Eleanor	17
Queen Elizabeth I	27
Raven Falls	11
Red Wharf Bay	83,85
Rhaeadr Buarth Meini	61
Rhaeadr Du (nr Ganyllwyd)	61
Rhaeadr Du (nr Maentwrog)	11,43
Rhaeadr-y-Cwm	11,45
Rhaeadr-y-Cynfal	11
Rhinog Fach	37,53
Rhinog Fawr	38,53
Rhinogs, The	37,53
Rhiw	109
Rhos-y-Gwaliau	49,55
Rhosbeirio	95
Rhoscolyn	97
Rhosgoch	92,94
Rhosneigr	75
Rhostryfan	17
Rhosybol	92
Rhyd-Ddu	15
Rhydd-ddu	119
Rivals, The (Yr Eifl)	113,114
Roewen	4,5
Roman Bridge (Machno)	9
Roman Bridge (Ogwen)	25
Roman Steps, The	41,53
Romans, The	71,81
Royal Charter, The	83
Ruskin, John	37
St Beuno	73
St Beuno's Well	117
St Cadfan	111,139
St Cadwaladr	89

	Page
St Curig	25
St Cybi	93,96
St Cybi's Well	129
St Cyngar	91
St David's Gold Mine	45
St Deinwen	75
St Eilian	81
St Garmon's Church	17
St George's Pier	91
St Gredifael	91
St Gwenfaen's Well	97
St Iestyn	85
St Kelert	15
St Maethlu	77
St Mary & St Nicholas	87
St Melangell	51
St Michael	85
St Nidan	71
St Patrick	79
St Peblig	19
St Seiriol	85
St Tudwal's Roads	104
St Tysilio	91
Salem Chapel	41
Salt Island	97
Sarn Bach	105
Sarn Helen	11,43
Sarn Meyllteryn	107
Scott, Sir Gilbert	21,93,125
Segontium Roman Fort	29,63,117,121
Shell Island	41
Shelley, Percy Bysshe	123
Siloam Chapel, Bethesda	27
Skerries, The	77
Ski Llandudno	135
Snowdon	15,25,31,33,37,43,55,115,119,123,129
Snowdon Pleasure Flights	119
Snowdon Railway	29,30
Snowdon Ranger	15
Snowdon Sherpa Bus Service	31
Soldiers' Point	96
South Stack	97
Spence, Sir Basil	11
Stanley Embankment	95
Stanley of Alderley, Lord	75,79,93
Stephenson, Robert	5,69
Stwlan Storage Dam	11
Swallow Falls	6,7
Sychnant Pass	23
Sygun Copper Mine	15
Tallyllyn Railway	133,139
Tal-y-Bont	39
Tal-y-foel	70
Tal-y-llyn	139
Tal-y-Waen Farm Trail	139

	Page
Talysarn	119,121
Tan-y-Bwlch	43
Tan-y-Bwlch Station	10,11,13
Tan-y-Grisiau	131
Tan-y-Coed	133
Tan-yr-Allt	123
Tanat Valley	51
Tanat Valley Railway	51
Tegfryn Gallery	86
Telford, Thomas	5,9,69,91
Thrale, Mrs Hester	127
Timelock, The	89
Tomen-y-Bala	65
Tomen-y-Mur Roman Fort	11,25,42
Torrent Walk	59
Traeth Bach	57,63
Traeth Bychan	83
Traeth Cemlyn	79
Traeth Coch	83,84
Traeth Dulas	81
Traeth Lafan	21
Traeth Mawr	13
Traeth Penllech	111
Traeth Lligwy	81
Traeth yr Ora	81
Trains - Railway Museum	9
Trawsfynydd Lake	43,63
Trawsfynydd Power Station	11,43
Tre'r Ceiri Hill Fort	115
Trefdraeth	73
Trefignath Burial Chamber	85
Trefor	115,117
Trefriw	7
Trefriw Wells Roman Spa	7
Trefriw Woollen Mills	7
Tregele	78
Treghwhelyd Standing Stone	74
Tregwhelyd Farm	74
Tremadog	13,123
Tremadog Bay	41,43,55
Trinity House	97
Trwyn Cemlyn	79
Trwyn Cilan	105
Trwyn Llanbedrog	105
Trwyn Llech-y-doll	105
Trwyn-y-Gorlech	115
Tryfan	25
Tryweryn, River	47
Tu Hwnt i'r Bont	7
Tudor Family	138
Tudor Rose, Beaumaris	87
Tudweiliog	113,122,125
Tunnicliffe, Charles	91
Twrog	13,43
Ty Hyll (The Ugly House)	6,7,24,25
Ty Mawr	9

	Page
Ty Mawr Standing Stone	93,96
Ty Nant	65
Ty Newydd Burial Chamber	75
Tyn Llan Farm	123
Tyn-y-Groes Forest Trail	61
Tyn-y-Maes	27
Tynygongl	83
Twyn	139
Twyn Aberffraw	73,88
Twyn Fferram	72
Valley	75,96
Vaughan Family	39,45,61
Vaynol Chapel	19
Vaynol Hall	19
Vivian Trails	134
Vortigern	33
Vortigern's Valley	115
Vosper, S.C.	41
Vyrnwy, Lake	49,53
Vyrnwy Visitor Centre	53
Warren, The	105
Waterloo Bridge	9
Waterloo, Battle of	69,138
Watkin Path	33
Watling Street	117
Waun-y-Gadfa	55
Wellington, Duke of	69,138
Welshpool	51
Welsh Highland Railway	138
Welsh Language Centre	115
Welsh Mountain Zoo	132
Welsh Slate Museum	29,134
West Mouse Lighthouse	76
Wheeler, Sir Mortimer	19,121
Whistler, Rex	69,138
Williams, Ken	93
Williams-Ellis, Sir Clough	101,103,109,127
Wyatt, James	138
Wyatt, Samuel	27
Wylfa Head	79
Wylfa Power Station	79
Wynne Family	7
Wynne, Robert, of Gwydir	23
Y Garn	27,31
Y Lliwedd	31
Y Myd	21
Y Stabliau Information Centre	7
Y Wyddfa	31,33
Ynys	40,63
Ynys Enlli (Bardsey Island)	109,111
Ynys Seiriol	85
Ynys-y-fydlyn	77
Ynyspandy Slate Mill	121
Ynyscynhaearn	101
Yr Eifl (The Rivals)	113,114

The Upper Dovey Valley beyond Bwlch-y-Groes